CUSTOMER RELATIONSHIP MANAGEMENT

THE BOTTOM LINE TO OPTIMIZING YOUR ROI

Second Edition

Dr. Jon Anton

Purdue University

Dr. Natalie L. Petouhoff

BenchmarkPortal.com

Management Skills
NETEFFECT SERIES

Prentice Hall

Upper Saddle River, New Jersey 07458

Executive Editor: Elizabeth Sugg
Editor-in-Chief: Steve Helba
Editorial Assistant: Anita Rhodes
Managing Editor: Mary Carnis
Production Editor: Brian Hyland
Director of Production and Manufacturing: Bruce Johnson
Manufacturing Buyer: Cathleen Peterson
Design Director: Cheryl Asherman
Cover Design: Wanda España
Cover Illustration/Photo: David Ridley, SIS/Image.com (comedy/tragedy masks)
Net Effect Series Design: Rob Richman, La Fortezza Design Group
Composition: BookMasters, Inc.
Full-Service Production Management: BookMasters, Inc.
Printer/Binder: Phoenix Book Tech.

Pearson Education LTD.
Pearson Education Australia PTY, Limited
Pearson Education Singapore, Pte. Ltd
Pearson Education North Asia Ltd
Pearson Education Canada, Ltd.
Pearson Educación de Mexico, S.A. de C.V.
Pearson Education—Japan
Pearson Education Malaysia, Pte. Ltd
Pearson Education, Upper Saddle River, New Jersey

Prentice Hall

10 9 8 7 6 5 4 3 2 1

ISBN 0-13-099069-8

This book is dedicated to my mom, Donna, the divine mother and all moms who bring us into life.

Contents

Section 2: Analytical CRM – Measuring People, Process, and Technology   125

Foreword

I n 1996, Prentice Hall published Dr. Jon Anton's book entitled *Customer Relationship Management*. This was the first book on customer relationship management (CRM), and it literally launched a new business revolution, and a completely new industry of vendors providing CRM solutions to companies worldwide.

Over the past 5 years, thousands of companies have begun the corporate journey to become more "customer centric" by adding CRM solutions to their internal infrastructure thereby hoping to get better connected to their customers. During these past 5 years, we have learned a great deal about what CRM is, and what it is not.

Now, Dr. Jon Anton (a.k.a. "Dr. Jon") has written another book in these series entitled *Customer Relationship Management: The Bottom Line to Optimizing Your ROI*. In this book, Dr. Jon has joined forces with Dr. Natalie Petouhoff to revisit the CRM implementation scene. What they have found is both good news and bad news. The good news is that many companies are thoroughly evaluating their ability to develop one-to-one, personalized interactions with their high-value customers. Furthermore, CRM vendors have developed very effective solutions to "enable" better interactions with customers through all the popular channels, including telephone, e-mail, and the corporate Web site.

The bad news is that often a CRM initiative is limited, if not stymied, by the need to manage the individual employee's willingness to change and adopt new processes and technologies to better interacting with customers. The authors make it clear that CRM does not come "in a box." Instead, CRM is first and foremost a corporate "culture" change, i.e., a different way of doing business, enabled with powerful technology at every customer touch point. To maximize the return on investment (ROI), successful companies are addressing the change management issues up front in the CRM implementation process.

The authors have also found that a successful CRM implementation begins with performance benchmarking of the current customer-facing processes in a company. Purdue University's Center for Customer-Driven Quality in conjunction with BenchmarkPortal maintains the largest data-mart of CRM best practices, thereby allowing companies to truly measure their "as is" CRM status and better understand the gaps in performance that need to be addressed.

Finally, I feel the book gives the reader very practical suggestions on how to manage corporate culture change before, during, and after a CRM initiative is launched. In this process, a company can maximize its ROI from the implementation of the latest enabling technology solutions. I strongly recommend this book to C-level executives who have customer-facing responsibilities. In particular, information technology managers, customer service managers, and field service managers will benefit greatly from reading this book.

Bruce Belfiore
President and CEO
BenchmarkPortal, Inc.

Acknowledgments

I would like to thank all of the wonderful customers who have provided an enormous amount of support and data over the years to make CRM and Customer Contact Center benchmarking possible. I am especially thankful to Purdue University and to Richard Feinberg for his support as well as the whole staff at Benchmarkportal.com, including Dr. Nat, for their support and tremendous work.

Dr. Jon Anton

I would like to first thank my co-author, Dr. Jon, for believing in me enough to ask me to co-author a book with him. I have so much respect for the thoughtful leadership he has brought to the field of CRM and customer service and I am proud to be a part of his world.

Many thanks to the experts who gave their time to provide us with more insights into our own work:

Lisa M. Schwartz and Lana M. Ruffins, LMR Associates

John Roberston and Tanya Koons, Edcor

Manuela Hensman, Centerforce

Bruce Cryer, HeartMath

Nick Petouhoff, Johnson Controls, Inc.

Jack Phillips and Ron Stone, FranklinCovey

I would also like to thank my sister, Tanya Koons, for support through thick and thin; Paul Oravecz for great weekends and making me laugh; and Lisa M. Schwartz and Lana M. Ruffins, my partners at LMR Associates, who are the most amazing business partners and women I know.

Back at Benchmarkportal.com, I would like to thank Andy, Mandy, Linda, Bruce, Dave, Bob, and everyone there who makes it possible to be part of the best benchmarking group in the world. And lastly, I'd like to thank my teachers, Sondra Ray, Anita Coolidge, Meredith Brooks, Faye Snyder, Stan Oravecz, Breck Costin, Judy Rosener, Deepak Chopra, and Marianne Williamson.

Dr. Natalie "Dr. Nat" Petouhoff

Preface

This book is one in a series of books on customer relationship management (CRM). Since the advent of Dr. Jon Anton's first book *CRM: Making Hard Decisions With Soft Numbers* in 1996, the field of CRM has exploded. With Dr. Anton's first insights about measuring what was thought to be a subjective area of business, customer satisfaction, his customer relationship management book not only made the business world stand up and take notice of the kind of data that could change how they did business, but the book literally coined the acronym CRM. Now everything in the field of customer contact centers and call centers, from software to hardware to processes to consulting firms to Web sites, are donning the CRM acronym.

WHAT'S NEW IN THE SECOND BOOK ON CRM

This next book in the Anton CRM series is about the changes that hapen to a business when they begin to evaluate, and then change the way they provide service. While the aspect of change goes underestimated, it is the single most important factor in determining whether a CRM strategy provides the return on the investment projected by adding new technology, processes, and procedures. Statistics from all the large research firms (Garner Group, Forester, DCI and more) show that all the newfangled processes and technology in the CRM world are falling into the same unsuccessful category as Enterprise Resource Planning (ERP).

> *In a study of 100 large companies, only 52% reported achieving their business goals and only 37% could point to a tangible financial impact for technology solutions.*
>
> Boston Consulting Group

As authors and consultants, Dr. Anton and Dr. Nat Petouhoff asked themselves and their clients, "If the writing is on the wall, then why keep doing the same thing and expecting different results? That is insanity!" The answer was that companies did not have the information they needed to manage change. The groundbreaking, paradigm changing insights the Anton-Petouhoff CRM book bring are threefold:

1. Changing how you provide the service does not make a difference to your bottom line unless the people providing the service use the new technology and processes optimally.

2. Whether employees use it optimally has everything to do with the way employees embrace change.

3. The customers you are serving also need to understand, embrace, and participate in the new way you are providing service.

If these aspects of your business have not been addressed (employees and customers reaction to change) and are not dealt with, then the time, money, and energy spent on CRM is a wasteful exercise in futility.

We now want to coin the term *doing the ostrich* or DTO. As you might imagine, doing the ostrich means sticking your head in the sand and not seeing what is in front of you. As a business professional, it is actually much easier to do the ostrich than to face the fact that you might not understand much about the subject of change or the human dynamics involved with the change reaction that take place when CRM technology and processes are changed. Most business schools do not educate business or MBA learners in the subject of change, yet it is the one thing we know is certain in the world of business. Most companies, while grooming employees to be managers, do not understand change and therefore do not include the "management of change" as a number one skill to be able to be qualified for a management or leadership position. Yet change is constantly all around us, every day, day in and day out, especially in this competitive, global marketplace.

As we know, history repeats itself until we are ready to "pull our head out of the sand" and face things that we have held in paradigms as not important, not necessary, soft skills, soft data, un-measurable, un-calculateable. Those days are over and the companies that will thrive in the next century are those that can think outside the boxes, color outside the lines, and embrace new thoughts about customers, about change, and about optimizing CRM. We can point to many times in history when paradigms in thought came back to bite us:

Ptolemy to Copernicus

We spent 2,000 years believing the earth was the center of the universe. It was not until Bruno, Copernicus, and Galileo challenged the current state of thought, comparing the data they were collecting as astronomers and realized that it did not match. At that time there was much to risk by challenging the current state of thought. Bruno lost his life and his students,

Copernicus and Galileo, were threatened to be banned as scientists, as well as with loss of life. Only they and the monks had started writing their theories down and the word spread throughout Europe on parchment paper—the old theory was not valid. As many others began to "see the light," the old paradigm began its dissolution.

The American Auto Industry

Today the risk is as severe, but the consequences a little different. One example to consider in the not-so-distant past is the American auto industry shift. America did not listen to the "quality Guru," W. Edwards Demming, when he suggested that quality and smaller cars were important to the customer. When Demming could not find an audience for his new thoughts, he went to Japan, where—because they were not resistant to new ideas—took Demming's theories and turned them into a profitable reality. The result: American automakers found themselves taken by surprise when they lost major market shares to foreign markets because they had not listened to the voice of the customer.

You Can Be Part of Shifting the Paradigm

Thomas Kuhn's book, *Scientific Revolutions* (1996, University of Chicago Press), does a great job of examining changes in thought paradigms in the evolution of science, as does Joel Barker in his book for the business world, *The Business of Predicting the Future* (1993, Harperbusiness). The bottom line: Stuck thinking limits the future by staying attached to the old ways of thinking and doing. The cornerstone of this next Anton-Petouhoff CRM book is for you to digest some new thoughts on business and be able to turn them into a profitable reality for yourself. The Anton-Petouhoff CRM book introduces the business world to the ideas of *change* and the *management of change* (now called the field of Change Management) and that CRM *Change* is a new thought paradigm needing embracement in the field of customer contact centers and call centers.

If your goal is to be a successful business, we feel that you need to know and fully comprehend the subject of change as it pertains to technology and processes that provide customer service. We hope to bring you new insights into not only how to understant change, but as important, how to measure change so that you end up with the results you desire as you implement new customer service technologies and processes.

As we all go on this journey of the changing business world together, we invite you to read the other books in the Anton-Petouhoff CRM series:

- *Analytical Customer Relationship Management: How To Measure Customer Satisfaction*, 2002

- *Operational Customer Relationship Management: Implementing Technology That Satisfies Customers*, 2002

As you read these books, we invite you to share your experiences of change in the CRM field. Whether you are a student, a professor, or a business professional, we look forward to hearing your ideas, thoughts, and how you implemented the concepts in the book. We might even publish the results if the response is large enough!

Instructional and Learning Features

Many features of Anton-Petouhoff CRM: *The Bottom Line to Optimizing Your ROI* make it an excellent choice for both the student and the instructor.

Learners

Learners will find an easy-to-read text covering the hottest issues being faced by professionals in the real world and presented in a realistic and factual manner. Rather than being all theory, which can put the best of all learners to sleep, this book helps the student understand the theory by seeing how it is applied with great success by various companies. It is as if the student gets to "shadow" the authors and in their consulting, gaining real-world experiences that will make the learner stand out in their field. Learners will appreciate the candid way the information is presented, allowing them to be truly prepared for making a difference in the world. The book shows the path for success is measurement and then shows specifically how to do CRM measurements to create cost/benefit and return on investment calculations.

Learners who read this book will clearly have an advanced knowledge even above that of most people in the CRM business world. This advanced knowledge will allow learners to interview with confidence and land their dream CRM job. Learners who apply themselves to the learnings and observations in this book will become the new leaders of business, whether they are in CRM, the call center and customer contact center world or not. That is because one of main ideas in the book is that customer service is not just something that the customer service department should be interested in; it is a subject that is important to the CEO, CFO, COO, and the CIO as well as all other departments in a company: marketing, quality, manufacturing, assembly, engineering, and so forth.

Customer service and the value customers bring to the bottom line is an issue that affects every single person in the company, because without customers, there is no company for people to work in. The book redirects the idea that data (which can easily be obtained by benchmarking and measuring in the customer contact center) is information that is pertinent for the customer contact center manager to better run their department. It takes the stand that CRM data is what creates *Forward* Intelligence™ for executives to know what is happening in their company, to measure it and then act on it with the data to back them up. So often executives are left to make decisions based on a limited amount of facts, which oftentimes leads to money, time, and energy spent fixing the wrong problem, with the wrong solution. This is also why employees tend to formulate the attitude that "Management does not know what they are talking about—that they are out of touch."

The fact is that unless executives know that the data is there and how to use it, they *are* out of touch. Current financial forecasting and reporting does not provide executives with the kind of real-time data found in a customer care center. Learners who understand this in the book will quickly win their spot in the executive's eyes as being a key player to business success. For instance, Chapter 11 specifically shows how call center data completely changed an airline's policy on frequent flyer miles and saved millions of dollars and customers because executives understood why their most valued customers were unhappy and then made the right decisions. In comparison, a competitor ignored their customer service data, ended up in a class action lawsuit, and lost thousands of customers.

In addition, intuitively we know people make a difference, but until recently, companies had a very difficult time believing this, much less quantifying it. Learners will also enjoy a never-before-seen, fresh look at human capital management and easy, "back-of-the envelope" calculations that drive home the point that without good people, there is no business. This book essentially takes the guesswork out of return on investment for soft skills and human capital management, which has never been available before.

The Trainer

The trainers and professors will enjoy teaching from this text because it will make them a hero by presenting new thoughts in management. It is a book that trainers and professors can believe in. It is one of the first management books that takes theory and applies it with measurable data-containing examples. These examples allow the instructor to be current with the latest in technology applications and fully represent the state of the art in CRM.

The book includes proven methods in CRM return on investment that have never been presented in management theory before. That in itself allows for superior, out-of-the-box thinking and discussion, stimulating the minds of not only the instructors, but also that of the learners who will become the new leaders in business. Many learners, after being taught from this text, will have gained such real-world insight that they will certainly return to thank their teachers for the invaluable experience their class provided.

Supplements for Trainers and Professors

Trainers and professors will find the Anton-Petouhoff CRM series to be organized texts containing real-world case studies for class analysis and discussion, increasing the class participation and learning. The Leader's Guide for the instructor contains:

- suggested course syllabi

- chapter outlines

- answers to questions for review and exams

- suggestions for additional teaching materials

- transparency masters

- training suggestions

E-learning

With respect to e-learning, there is the new, free-access conpanion Web site for distance learning, computer lab, and self-study at www.prenhall.com/neteffect The materials on the accompanying Web site aid in learning and include

- essay questions

- Web links

- multiple choice and true/false questions

- and more!

Ask the Authors

If you have questions or comments about CRM you can tune into *Call Talk™*, a Web-based webinar at *www.benchmarkportal.com*. *Call Talk™* with Dr. Jon and Dr. Nat is the easiest, fastest, and least expensive way to stay current and get expert advice for improving your CRM performance. You can reach Dr. Nat at *doctorofchange@earthlink.net* and Dr. Jon at *drjonanton@aol.com*.

All of these supplemental materials are especially helpful to adjunct faculty, full-time and part-time professors, as well as for learners.

ABOUT THE AUTHORS

Dr. Jon Anton (also known as "Dr. Jon") is the director of benchmark research at Purdue University's Center for Customer-Driven Quality. He specializes in enhancing customer service strategy through inbound call center, and e-business centers, using the latest in telecommunications (voice), and computer (digital) technology. He also focuses on using the Internet for external customer access, as well as Intranets and middleware.

For the past six years, Dr. Jon has been the principal investigator of the annual Purdue University Call Center Benchmark Research Report. This data is now collected at the BenchmarkPortal.com Web site, where it is placed into a data warehouse that currently contains over ten million data points on call center and e-business center performance. Based on the analysis of this data, Jon authors "The Purdue Page" in Call Center Magazine each month, plus the "Dr. Jon Benchmarks" in Call Center News each month.

Dr. Jon has assisted over 400 companies in improving their customer service strategy/delivery by the design and implementation of inbound and outbound call centers, as well as in the decision-making process of using teleservice providers for maximizing service levels while minimizing costs per call. In August of 1996, Call Center Magazine honored Dr. Jon by selecting him as an Original Pioneer of the emerging call center industry. In October of 2000, Dr. Jon was named to the Call Center Hall of Fame. In January of 2001, Dr. Jon was selected for the industry's "Leaders and Legends" Award by Help Desk 2000.

Dr. Jon has guided corporate executives in strategically re-positioning their call centers as robust customer access centers through a combination of re-engineering, consolidation, outsourcing, and web-enablement. The resulting single point of contact for the customer allows business to be conducted anywhere, anytime, and in any form. By better understanding the customer lifetime value, Dr. Jon has developed techniques for calculating the ROI for customer service initiatives.

Dr. Jon has published 75 papers on customer service and call center methods in industry journals. In 1997, one of his papers on self-service was awarded the best article of the year by Customer Relationship Management magazine. Dr. Jon has published seven professional books:

Inbound Customer Call Center Design, Dame Publishers, Inc., 1994

Customer Relationship Management, Prentice-Hall, Inc., 1996

Computer-Assisted Learning, Hafner Publishing, Inc., 1985

Call Center Management by the Numbers, Purdue University Press, 1997
The Voice of the Customer, Alexander Research & Communications, Inc., 1997
Call Center Benchmarking, Purdue University Press, 1999
Call Center Performance Simulation, Purdue University Press, 2000

He is also the editor for a series of professional books entitled Customer Access Management, published by the Purdue University Press.

Dr. Jon's formal education was in technology, including a Doctorate of Science and a Master of Science from Harvard University, a Masters of Science from the University of Connecticut, and a Bachelor of Science from the University of Notre Dame. He also completed a three-summer intensive Executive Education program in Business at the Graduate School of Business of Stanford University.

Dr. Jon Anton is with the Department of Cunsumer Sciences at Purdue University and a researcher in the Center for Customer-Driven Quality. He has assisted over 400 companies in reengineering their customer service by implementing customer relationship measurements systems. Jon Anton has a doctorate and a masters of science from Harvard University.

Dr. Jon can be reached at 765-494-8357 or at DrJonAnton@AOL.com.

Dr. Natalie Petouhoff, (pronounced pet-a-hoff) alias "Dr. Nat," is a Director of Content for BenchmarkPortal, Inc. As a principal investigator working with Dr. Jon Anton, she writes books and white papers that provide companies mission-critical information to enhance their customer service strategy through inbound call and e-business centers using the latest in telecommunications (voice), and computer (digital) technology. Dr. Nat specializes in using the Internet for external customer access, as well as Intranets and middleware.

Dr. Nat Also specializes in change management, re-engineering, and business process mapping. Dr. Nat and Lisa Schwartz co-created the SP3M process, which enables companies to measure, market, and manage the people, process, and the technology in the ever-changing world of customer contact centers. Their unique blend of the Successful People Process (SPP™), SP3M™, and solid backgrounds in technology allow them to reduce the adoption resistance so often experienced when companies change how they deliver service via enhanced technology solutions. Reducing the adoption resistance results in technology implementations that are within budget, on time, and within scope, leading to a larger return on the technology investment, increased customer lifetime value, larger profits, and revenues.

Dr. Nat's background ranges from technology to human resources. She has firsthand experience at companies like General Electric, General Motors, Hughes Electronics and Universal Studios as well as Internet start-up companies. She believes that customer call centers are the ambassadors of a company, as they are generally one of the first customer encounters. Her signature speech, No People, No Business™, demonstrates her commitment to helping companies understand the value of the human asset when benchmarking.

As a former Change Management consultant for PriceWaterhouse Coopers, Dr. Nat evaluated and installed call centers, ERP systems and designed customer access interfaces. Through this front line experience at companies like Warner Lambert and Sony Pictures Entertainment, she was able see the challenges companies face when implementing new technology solutions and changing workflow processes.

Dr. Nat is currently working on a Human Potential ROI Calculator. This will help companies see the value of training and developing employees, as well as a way to quantify Human Capital as a corporate asset. Dr. Nat has come up with a credible way to calculate how the degree to which people accept change can allow for the full return on investment for expensive technology. Dr. Nat also specializes in helping companies reduce the employee resistance that always accompanies change.

For her outstanding work in technology at Hughes Electronics, Dr. Nat received three awards, namely: 1) the Leadership Achievement Award for leadership in the face of resistance, 2) the Superior Management Award for quick technology solution implementation with a tiger team, and 3) the Peer-Selected Award for demonstrating exemplary behavior towards peers.

Dr. Nat has published 10 technical papers in industry journals. In 2001. Dr. Nat, as the editor, completed a book on call centers entitled Recruiting, Training and Evaluating Call Center Employees for the American Society of Training and Development (ASTD). *Integrating People with Process and Technology: How to Optimize Employees' Acceptance of Technology Initiatives*, Anton Press, 2001. She is a popular speaker as evidence by being asked again to speak again at the Women and Technology Conference in Santa Clara to an audience of over 6,000 technical women who will hear about her latest ideas in technology as applied to customer service and career development.

Dr. Nat's formal education is in technology. She was awarded the General Motors Fellowship to complete her Doctorate of Engineering from UCLA where she did her thesis research at Oak Ridge National Laboratory and Hughes Research Laboratories in Metallurgy and High Energy Particle Physics. She also has a Masters and Bachelor Metallurgical Engineering from the University of Michigan financed by five scholarships.

She lives on the beach in southern California with her cat Tushka and is an avid student of yoga.

SECTION 1:
Operational CRM—
Accessibility

Thinking Outside the CRM Box

CUSTOMER RELATIONSHIP MANAGEMENT: REDUCING THE CHAOS TO ORDER

The dream of any leader is to be able to predict the future. The only way to do that is via Customer Relationship Management (CRM) because in the end, if there are no customers, then there is no business, and no future. Companies today are spending more on CRM than they ever have.

> The percentage of companies that will spend more on CRM in 2001 vs. 2000: 74 percent.
> —Harte-Hanks, *Jupiter Media Metrix,* July 2001

In our technology consulting, we started to ask:

- How smart is the spending?
- What kinds of technology are being purchased?
- Does that technology really manage the customer relationship?
- What is the return on investment for the technology?

- Is anyone measuring ROI? If not, is that being fiscally responsible?

- What and how are they measuring?

- When CRM does not produce the results expected, what went wrong?

- Did the salespeople overpromise or might it have something to do with how the change in providing customer service affected the people who deliver it and the organization?

- Was the human element (the people providing the service) considered a strategic part of the technology implementation or were change management, training, communication plans, and the like still being cut out of large technology budgets as a cost savings measure?

In today's fast moving and highly competitive market, products come and products go. For companies large and small, the most important real asset, with measurable long-term value, is loyal, one-to-one customer relationships. CRM *implemented* is the ability to see the future and act on it to create these loyal customers. This book is about how people, process, and technology can help not only to predict the future, but with the information from that triad, can drive the success (or failure) of a business.

> *Sugar is made of three molecules: oxygen, hydrogen, and carbon. Where is the sweetness? In the relationship!*
>
> —Fritjof Capra, *Tao of Physics*

Using Frijof's analogy, CRM is also made of three parts: customers, relationships, and management. The R (relationships) in CRM seemed to be the least understood and written about in CRM books. While this book covers many parts of CRM, its focus is to understand how to make the combination of these three aspects sweeter (illustrated in Figure 1.1).

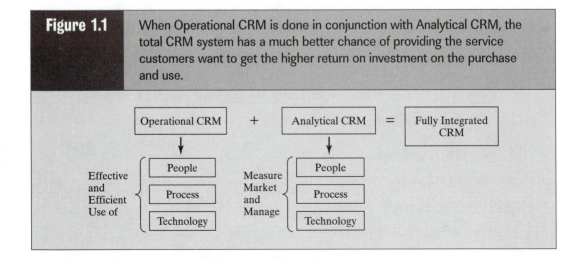

Figure 1.1   When Operational CRM is done in conjunction with Analytical CRM, the total CRM system has a much better chance of providing the service customers want to get the higher return on investment on the purchase and use.

To do that, this book is divided into two sections:

1. The ability to provide accessibility to your service through people, process, and technology, or Operational CRM

2. The ability to measure how well you are providing that service, through measuring people, process, and technology, or Analytical CRM

Operational CRM

Within the Operational CRM section we look at the effective and efficient use and management of:

- People, CRM, and change

- Process, CRM, and change

- Technology, CRM, and change

The key symptoms of nonworking accessibility or operational CRM factors are:

- Low morale of human capital assets

- Customer dissatisfaction

- Customer disloyalty

- Customer attrition

How accessible are you? How much do you know or focus your CRM technology to correct and optimize these factors?

Analytical CRM

The second half of the book is analytical in nature, where we examine what your technology is doing and how it is doing it. Are your people using the information that technology can deliver and integrating it back into satisfying your customers? Are you measuring the customer service index, measuring the employee's performance (via a tool like Centerforce), benchmarking the customer service center (BenchmarkPortal.com) for people, process, and technology best practices as well as helping employees to accept change and to provide the best service they can (LMRAssociates.com)? In the Analytical CRM section, we examine tools and case studies to help define:

- How to use technology to measure the delivery of service via people

- How to use technology to measure the process of delivering service

- How to use technology to measure the technology you are using

How Many Ways Can You Spell ERP?

Despite the legacy of horror stories surrounding the many never-ending implementations of Enterprise Resource Planning (ERP) systems, companies seem eagerly poised and ready to spend millions of dollars on the latest TLA (three letter acronym), CRM. Much like the ERP craze, CRM seems to take its roots within the C-level executive group. From there it is typically delegated to the appropriate technology professional, and the shopping begins. The typical CRM implementation cycle begins with the acquisition of technology and ends when the agents figure out that it is simpler to print information and post it in their cubicles than to utilize the overly complex process provided to them by someone who has never visited the department.

Our view on technology is a little different than what most people have considered to this point. Our view is that technology is not CRM, but that it is only the enabler of the people, process, and technology triad (Figure 1.2). After hearing countless stories about how companies had bought a big hardware/software package that was not really being used, we concluded that something was not working and we wanted to put the pink elephant on the table.

It seems that the big gold rush that started approximately 6 years ago with ERP packages followed by Y2K and now with CRM may be part of what has created the downturn in technology stocks. When the big technology boom came with the promise that technology could do everything except clean the kitchen sink, everyone was buying it. And although the costs of ERP and CRM were in the $2 million to $50 million range, the expenditures were there. As technology consultants and implementers ourselves, we watched the huge rise in purchases accompanied by equally large expectations. Then we watched the downturn in the results.

—Implementations that were promised in 6 months took 2 years. Some are still not completed.

—Technology never talked to legacy databases like it was promised.

—The people using the technology still do much of their jobs in the old way, ignoring the technology or in some cases sabotaging it.

Only 6 percent of 500 companies surveyed considered their ERP systems to be effective at helping them collaborate with partners, while 79 percent said their ERP systems weren't effective.

—Forrester Research

In a study of 100 large companies, only 52 percent reported achieving their business goals and only 37 percent could point to a tangible financial impact for technology solutions.

—Boston Consulting Group

The triad of people, process, and technology and questions will determine if all three areas satisfy your customer.

Figure 1.2

—Did our CRM strategy start with people?
—Did we consider both our employees' and customers' needs?
—How do we know we have hired the right people?
—What behaviors are the most important to getting and keeping our customers?
—How do our employees react to change?
—Do we know what drives their behavior?
—Why have we left this to chance?
—When we ask them to do something, why don't they?

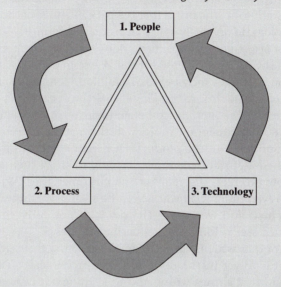

1. People

2. Process

3. Technology

—Did we map out our process for service? (If not, do this now.)
—Are all the steps we have in our process necessary?
—Do we have more than one group doing the same thing?
—Are the groups working together?
—Have we done any business process mapping and/or re-engineering to take out the redundancies?
—When we have replaced people with technology, is that still providing the service the customer wants?
—When we make service level agreements with internal and external customers, do we have a way to measure whether they are implemented?
—Is there a good way to market the results of the service level agreements to make people accountable, visible, and therefore keep the CRM system on track?

—Is this the last step in deciding on a CRM strategy? (If not, go to the people section and begin again.)
—What do we really want it to do?
—Does it really work?
—Can it integrate with the current infrastructure and legacy databases?
—How long will this take?
—Will the people really use it?
—How much will it cost?
—What is the ROI? How is that measured?
—Did we ask our technology vendors the hard questions—to share their failure and success stories?
—Can our vendor provide references of 10 companies that are happy with the system, the implementation, and the ROI?

Because of the overzealous promises of these technology solutions, buyers of technology are starting to get more skeptical. And the budget expenditures on technology are now starting to be questioned, with CFOs working more closely with CIOs, though in many cases they still might not really understand what's not working. The technology sellers sound very factual and in most cases are. What still goes underestimated is the amount of change an installation of a technology solution brings to a company and that the underestimated change and the lack of expertise in managing it is what makes these technology solutions so expensive. Managing change is an art and few have practiced the skills to do it without leaving many dead bodies in their path. In Chapter 4, we will explore leadership styles that empower people to lead change optimally.

There are several possible reasons why technology stocks may be seeing a downward turn. The first is that the balance sheets of the companies buying the technology do not really reflect an accurate accounting—what is left off is the extra cost of technology implementations, many times exceeding the cost of the initial sale by 10 percent to 100 percent. A system that might have been priced at $2 million essentially increases to $20 million. Companies are continuing to spend and not getting close to breaking even. In most cases they won't break even until 2010, especially when the cost of customer attrition is added to the P&L sheet.

Another reason technology stocks may be faltering is that buyers have lost confidence in the products. When one telecommunications vendor approached a current customer wanting to show them their latest and greatest new product, the reply of the customer was, "Why would we want to spend even more with you when the stuff you sold us earlier is not fully implemented and working?" The result of not delivering short-term technology successes is long-term reduction in sales.

Another issue is the way large consulting firms generate revenue. Their model is to get in the door and then never leave. They are geared to continue to find things wrong and to keeping adding on work. While no one can fault their wish for continued business, if the goal is not really to get in and get out, then it makes sense that the implementations take much longer. Large firms need to be held accountable to an ROI; without it, it is doubtful the money spent will result in the returns expected from the investment. If the Big 4 firm's business model was based on providing the customer the highest ROI, you would see a much different approach.

Though the buying shift went from ERP and Y2K packages to CRM, the disappointing return on investment (ROI) data on CRM technology implementation is starting to look very similar to the ERP and Y2K results.

- 69.3 percent of CRM installations failed to meet all goals

- 45.3 percent were late

- 36.8 percent were over budget

- 31.7 percent did not produce meaningful results

—Selling Power, CSO Forum

In *Enlightened Leadership*, Ed Oakley states that 85 percent of all CEOs are disappointed with the results of change management and reengineering programs. Of the $96 billion spent on these programs in the last year, they felt that $82 billion that was spent amounted to a waste of time and energy.

Consider this: If someone asked you for advice on a large investment they were considering and told you that the chances of it being successful were only 12 percent to 15 percent, what would you advise them? How quickly would you want to put some of your own money into this "hot" opportunity? Probably you wouldn't want to very soon. Yet every day, business leaders who should know a bad investment when they see one invest time, money, and the workforce in opportunities offering just such a probability for failure. While their intentions are good, the returns are not.

Even with the writing on the wall, Dataquest reports that the worldwide CRM service market generated over $19.9 billion in revenue in 2000, a 28 percent increase from 1999. The average budget for end-users of CRM is currently over $1 million. This spending is expected to double over the next 12 months and IDC is predicting that CRM investments will reach $125 billion in 2004. Says Kevin Scott, marketing analyst at AMR Research, "This rise in expenditures is not surprising, given that top management is buying deeply into CRM right now. With the downturn in the economy, they are turning to see how they can make marketing more efficient, how they can retain customers and how they can get more revenue from existing customers."

There is one common denominator in this CRM/Y2K/ERP trend and that is that the technology is being implemented without giving equal consideration and spending to the people part of CRM.

We tend to meet any new situation by reorganizing. And what a wonderful method reorganizing is for creating the illusion of progress while producing inefficiency and demoralization.

—Petronium, Greek Philosopher, 210 B.C.

What we also found was that companies generally are not sure how to collect, measure, and understand the interrelated, non-linear relationship between how the CRM system can provide the service and the results they want, first, without the finger-pointing so that they can deal with the real issue very quickly and solve it and second, to see how to change the operation to turn it into a profit center.

If insanity is continuing to do the same thing but expecting different results each time, then the spending on technology without having a field book like this at your side is really crazy. This book is dedicated to helping you to avoid falling into the financial and implementation gaps that happened in the ERP gold rush. Its purpose is to raise questions and red flags and to give you the tools to understand what you are buying in the world of CRM as well as to determine if they meet your business needs and objectives.

We don't want to knock technology companies, we just want everyone to be able to really understand what it is they are asking the technology company to do and whether a particular vendor can deliver that. Then we want the buyer to understand the costs associated with it and how best to get a return on the investment. Educating the buyer is in the best interest of everyone. Technology companies that can deliver what they promise, within budget and scope and on time, with a measured ROI will be the leaders of technology and the ones with the highest stock prices. The driver of the change in how technology providers market their capabilities must be the savviness of the buyer.

When executives really see the customer service center or customer interaction center as a tremendous source of data about customers for capturing the customer experience with the full enterprise, then the paradigm will shift from just measuring a customer service index to using the raw data from the customer service center to make analytically-based business decisions. The data is there—use it.

The shift we want to evoke by providing a section on measurement is just that: the customer service center is the brains to the data executives need to predict the future and to stay ahead of it with factual information.

The data can provide executives with *Forward Intelligence*™ and the ability to predict the future. And we feel that this shift in management paradigms is pretty powerful. Thinking outside the box and seeing the customer care center as the central brain for executive decision making can enable you to gain the ROI of the CRM solution you've chosen.

In our section on Analytical CRM we include some of the case studies from our upcoming book *Forward Intelligence*™. The company with the most information wins. It is about how to increase your customer base and profits via your customer service center data, where we show how raw data turned into management information has saved products, services, and ultimately, customers. We show exactly how this can be done. The results are astonishing—the CRM data answers the questions:

- Why customers are upset

- Which product has a problem

- Which part of the world or country has the biggest concern

- What is wrong with the product

All of this helps to facilitate a quick resolution and that's how you get the best ROI from your technology implementation. If your technology isn't doing this, what is it really doing? That's the question we urge you to think about. Our book is nudging a revolutionary new paradigm in managing a company, one that all executives need to know if they truly care about keeping customers.

This book is a detailed look at the bottom-line effects of customers and the employees who serve them. It is an insightful look to help you transform your company, no matter where you are on the threshold of new

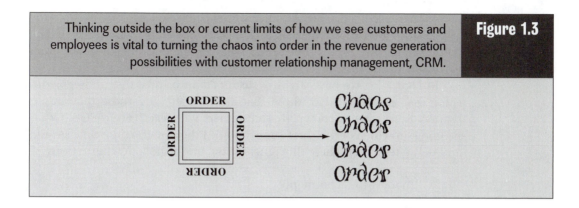

Thinking outside the box or current limits of how we see customers and employees is vital to turning the chaos into order in the revenue generation possibilities with customer relationship management, CRM.

Figure 1.3

paradigms in CRM. In this first chapter we start with some brain candy: hard-hitting facts and questions to motivate you to understand where you are in the continuum of CRM. With those new insights you can then think outside the CRM box (Figure 1.3) to find new ways to turn the chaos into order of choosing and measuring CRM implementations.

The business of business is getting and keeping customers.

—Peter Drucker

Fact 1: Customer Attrition Needs to Be Added to the Profit and Loss Statement

If a company lost 10 percent of its inventory to theft, swift action would be taken to stop the loss. But if a company is losing 10 percent of its customers to competitors, no one might even notice it, much less actually do something about it. This happens daily in thousands of companies. Is it happening in yours? In terms of customer attrition, Figure 1.4 shows there are really only three possibilities: You deliver more than expected, as expected,

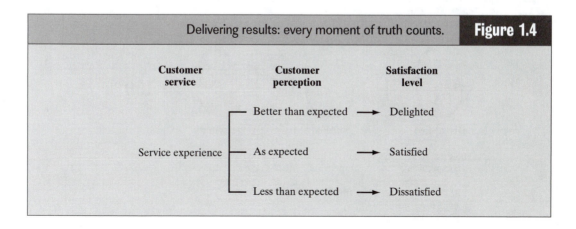

Delivering results: every moment of truth counts.

Figure 1.4

or less than expected. The customer will subconsciously grade or score the relationship after each experience, no matter how subtle, and the accumulation of all these scores determines whether the customer will buy from you again in the future.

In Figure 1.5 we have divided customers into three distinct segments: those that are dissatisfied, those that are satisfied, and those that are delighted. Research has shown that customers will react very differently depending on which of the three states of mind they are in at the time (Anton and deRuyter 1991). These differences show up in the following actions:

1. Willingness to recommend

2. Intentions to repurchase

3. Positive word of mouth

According to an often quoted study by the Xerox Corporation (Freedman 1993), customer loyalty and willingness to repurchase is not a linear relationship as is clearly shown in Figure 1.6 (Reichheld & Sasser 1990). Delighted customers can result literally in generations of repeat customers—for example, the John Deere Company likes to measure customer loyalty in terms of generations of farming families that have used its products.

Why doesn't the company's financial system account for this critical asset: the customer?

Fact 2: Customer Dissatisfaction Is Expensive

If you think losing a customer or two here and there means little, or that you are better off without those nitpicking, piddling complaints, then consider this: If just one customer a day who usually spends $100 per week stops

| **Figure 1.5** | Customer segments. |

Dissatisfied + Satisfied + Delighted = 100%

Dissatisfied	Satisfied	Delighted
High risk of loss to competition	May jump to competition if opportunity occurs	Will tell others and repurchase your product or service

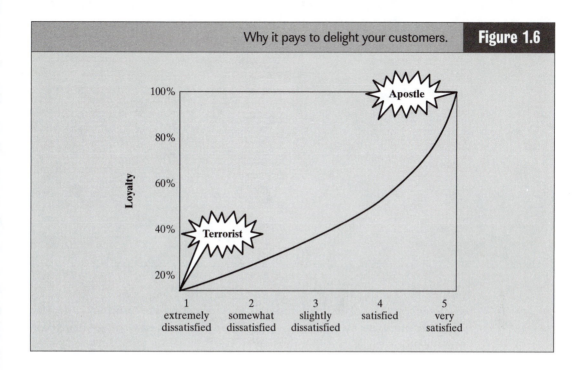

Figure 1.6

Why it pays to delight your customers.

doing business with your company, you will lose $1.9 million in annual revenues. This does not include the additional potential loss due to bad word of mouth from dissatisfied customers, (Figure 1.7). It is important for loyal customers to say good things (positive word of mouth) about your company and its products/services. The figure shows the results of a study conducted by General Electric's market researchers (Clemmer 1993) indicating the overwhelming importance consumers place on the opinions of friends before making a purchase decision.

When customers are asked, "Why did you change products or suppliers?" Figure 1.8 shows a whopping 68 percent replied, "I had a problem with

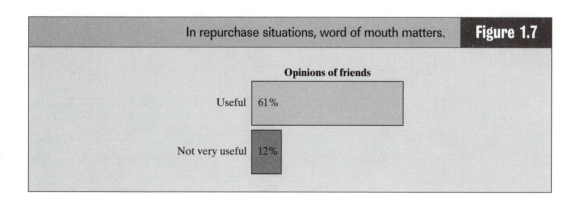

Figure 1.7

In repurchase situations, word of mouth matters.

Figure 1.8	Reasons for customer disloyalty.

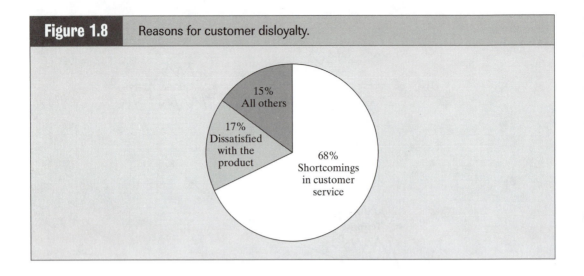

customer service!" The most important relationships are terminated by how we treat our customers. That's a people, process, and technology issue. Voting with our feet is the American Way.

In comparing and contrasting unhappy customers with happy customers, the U.S. Office of Consumer Affairs (Knauer 1992) produced the data summarized in Figure 1.9. Surveys of unhappy or dissatisfied customers become an important link in continuously improving customer relation-

Figure 1.9	The value of customer satisfaction.

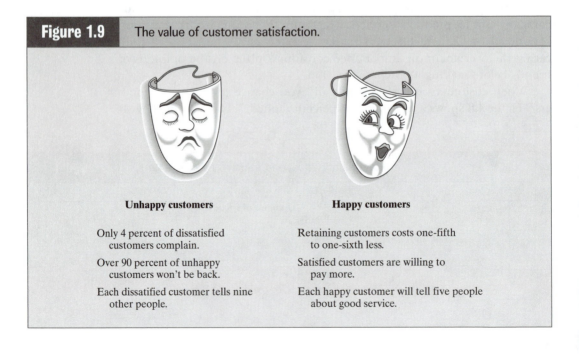

Unhappy customers

Only 4 percent of dissatisfied customers complain.

Over 90 percent of unhappy customers won't be back.

Each dissatisfied customer tells nine other people.

Happy customers

Retaining customers costs one-fifth to one-sixth less.

Satisfied customers are willing to pay more.

Each happy customer will tell five people about good service.

ships. According to Tom Peters in *Thriving on Chaos* (1988), the actual business impact of customer dissatisfaction is as follows:

■ It cost five times more to get a new customer than to retain a current one

■ Twenty-six out of 27 customers fail to report a bad experience

■ Customers don't report it because they feel you won't do anything about it

■ Ninety-one percent won't return

■ Thirteen percent will tell 20 or more people, further polluting your reputation

■ Eighty-two percent to 95 percent come back if the situation is resolved well and in a timely manner

■ A well-handled problem usually breeds more loyalty than before the negative incident

A person only complains if he or she can conceive of something better, or has experienced something better. Therefore, we should always ask a complaining customer for his or her opinion of what would be a "better way." You'll be amazed what you find out—a gold mine of opportunities. Each complaint is a way to serve a particular customer differently, and as such, is an opportunity. Customers often have valuable suggestions to improve a process, even though these suggestions frequently sound like complaints. Complaints are really just mistakes we've made in the eyes of individual customers. Our focus in this book is on developing a customer relationship measuring system to enhance the management process so we can tune in to every wish and need of individual customers.

Research reveals that delivering high-quality service is closely linked to profits, cost savings, and market share in many industries. Studies have found that increased profits are due to several factors:

1. Fewer customer defections

2. Stronger customer loyalty

3. Long-lasting customer relationships

4. More cross-selling of products and services at higher margins

"When you build a plant, it starts depreciating the day it opens. The well-served customer, on the other hand, is an appreciating asset," says McGarvey (1995) in *Entrepreneur*. In Figure 1.10, you can see the real magic of customer retention, and the real reason for you to focus on managing your customer relationships. When you can increase customer loyalty, a beneficial "flywheel" kicks in, powered by:

■ Increased purchases of the existing product

■ Cross-purchases of your other products

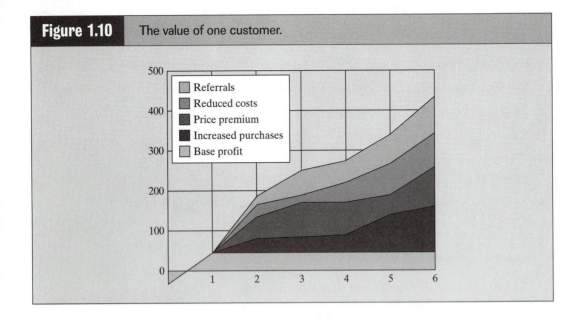

| **Figure 1.10** | The value of one customer. |

- Price premium due to appreciation of your added-value services

- Reduced operating cost because of familiarity with your service system

- Positive word of mouth in terms of referring other customers to your company

AT&T did a six-year study comparing their market share to customer-perceived value and found the results shown in Figure 1.11 from *Bank Marketing* by T. Lian (1994). The figure shows a period of time during which AT&T was reengineered completely to make the customer number one. Notice how exactly market share parallels customer-perceived value. Research has shown that customer-perceived value and satisfaction are excellent leading predictors of next year's revenue, market share, and profits.

Why is so much of our marketing budget spent in attracting new business vs. serving the needs of our current customers?

Fact 3: We Continue to Underestimate the Value of the Human Capital Asset

We want to start driving home the importance of dealing with the people part of business. Even venerable management consultants and business seers readily admit they have not understood the true value of the human capital asset.

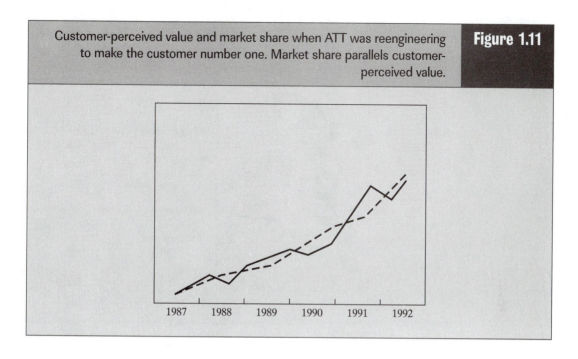

Customer-perceived value and market share when ATT was reengineering to make the customer number one. Market share parallels customer-perceived value.

Figure 1.11

We forgot about the people part of the reengineering process that has impacted business change for the past decade. We were not sufficiently appreciative of the critical, human demand of the enterprise.
    —Dr. Mike Hammer and James Champy, authors of *Reengineering the Corporation: A Manifesto for Business Revolution*

CUSTOMERS ARE PEOPLE

Customers are people and they want a personalized relationship with the company they are buying from. The components that make up a satisfying relationship are shown in Figure 1.12. When technology can really provide that kind of relationship then expectations will meet reality. Until then we need to understand that technology is an enabler of the customer service process and not a replacement for the people aspect of business.

Many of the big consulting firms/technology implementors enticed C-level executives to buy technology solutions. They felt that by replacing people with technology, they could reduce their administrative costs of service and save money by reducing head count, thereby streamlining their business operations. While this idea is good in theory, those kinds of service delivery models rarely provide the cost savings they promise. The reason is because what really shows up on the balance sheet is not the whole picture.

The percentage of users satisfied with customer service online is 41 percent.
    —Harte-Hanks, *Jupiter Media Metrix,* July 2001

| Figure 1.12 | Customers want a relationship with people and will accept technology solutions that make their life easier and enable that relationship. |

- Responsiveness

- Knowledgeable people

- Promptness

- Promises kept

- Understanding

- Security

- Follow-up

- No surprises

- Accuracy

- Communication

- Accessibility

- One-to-one interaction

The cost of poor customer satisfaction or attrition does not show up on the balance sheet, while the reduction in head count does. If companies are using CRM customer satisfaction as a marker to justify their expenditures of CRM, then they need to really start worrying about customer satisfaction and why it is not at 99 percent.

What we want to stress here is that by a traditional accounting view, you have saved money via headcount reduction. But if we start to add, as we saw in the beginning of this chapter, customer dissatisfaction costs, then we begin to see the whole picture. One of the reasons accounting had not added these kinds of figures to the balance sheet is few had figured out how to account for this and it stayed in the soft-skills area and off the balance sheets. It is only now, after the technology implementations, when we interview the customers, when we see their disappointments and changes in their buying habits, that we understand the full cost.

Now that we have nearly 6 years of data that is pointing to reduced customer satisfaction via technology solutions, we encourage CFOs to start reevaluating their accounting methodologies. In Chapter 7 we provide formulas for calculating customer lifetime value and market damage due to poor customer relationships. Several references that will be helpful in calculating and adding customer value to the balance sheet are *Listening to the Voice of the Customer: 16 Steps to A Successful Customer Satisfaction Measurement Program, Call Center Performance Enhancement* and *Call Center Management By The Numbers* by Jon Anton as well as *The Loyalty Effect: The Hidden Force Behind Growth, Profits and Lasting Value* by Frederick F. Reichheld.

We encourage accountants, CPAs, accounting firms, and the Generally Accepted Accounting Procedures (GAAP) Committee to reassess what needs to go onto a balance sheet. We also encourage professors of the MBA schools, accounting schools, and business schools to start teaching the new paradigm in accounting principles we stress in the book. And we ask technology companies and consulting firms to also begin to offer customers ROI in their proposals. We encourage customers to measure their return after the implementation and then pay the implementor the full amount when the ROI is obtained. Without this, no one can obtain the real value of CRM.

EMPLOYEES ARE PEOPLE

Not only does a company need to track and react to the needs and preferences of its customers, but it also needs to consider the desires and preferences of its employees. This is especially true for the ones that provide customer service, whether they are serving customers directly in a customer service center or in a store or indirectly as managers of a customer service center or integrators of technology solutions.

Ask yourself, "Can the machines run themselves? Does the process know how to follow itself?" No people, no business!™ People are the glue that holds the technology and process together. And the critical aspects of employees providing excellent customer service are shown in Figure 1.13. Later in the Analytical CRM section, we will look at the economics of the human capital asset and how you can calculate ROI to provide better customer service.

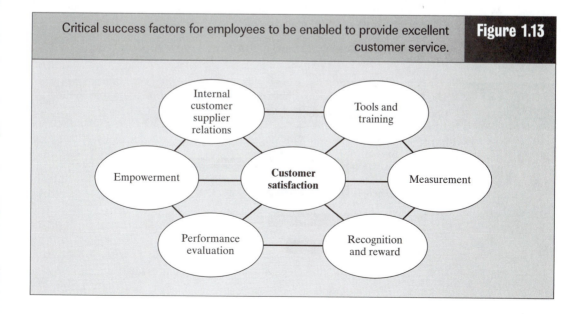

Critical success factors for employees to be enabled to provide excellent customer service.

Figure 1.13

Fact 4: Customer Loyalty Is a Bottom-Line Issue

Although everyone has not figured out how to implement it, the economics of customer loyalty and retention have become a science. Figure 1.14 is a survey conducted by the accounting firm of Ernst and Young of 750 CEOs. It shows that top management has awakened to the importance of satisfying the customer, and the importance of motivated employees. Of *Fortune* 500 companies responding to a study conducted by Purdue University researchers, 87 percent specifically mention customer satisfaction in their corporate mission statement. Ironically, however, only 18 percent had in place a viable method of measuring this elusive metric, and none based compensation on customer satisfaction.

Customer satisfaction is the link between short-term success and long-term growth and prosperity. Corporations of all sizes are realizing that customer satisfaction:

- Is a critical strategic weapon that results in increased market share and increased profits

- Begins with the commitment of top management

- Involves the entire organization

- Can be quantified, measured, and tracked

- Has fundamental organizational structure implications

An example of customer loyalty economics from Frederick F. Reichheld's book, *The Loyalty Effect*:

- If a credit card company can increase its retention of customers by 5 percent each year, then total lifetime profits from a typical customer will rise an average of 75 percent.

- This retention translates into a company's growth potential.

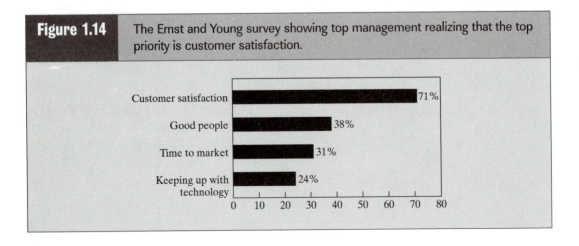

| **Figure 1.14** | The Ernst and Young survey showing top management realizing that the top priority is customer satisfaction. |

If Company 1 has a customer retention rate of 95 percent and Company 2 has a customer retention rate of 90 percent, the company's growth rates are sizably different:

Company 1: 5 percent loss of profit per year

Company 2: 10 percent loss of profit per year

If both companies acquire new customers at the rate of 10 percent per year, Company 1 will have a 5 percent net growth in customer inventory per year, while Company 2 will have none. Over fourteen years, Company 1 will double in size and Company 2 will have no real growth at all. And other things being equal, a 5 percentage point advantage in customer retention translates into a growth advantage equal to doubling of customer inventory every 14 years. An advantage of 10 percentage points accelerates the doubling to seven years. In order to accomplish these kind of bottom-line effects, the leadership strategy must focus on how to create loyalty among its customers, which also means retention of its employees who serve those customers.

> *The goal of loyalty-based management is to find a way to plug in the human asset leak in your corporate balance sheet to thereby improve your productivity, cash flow, and profits.*
> —Frederick F. Reichheld, *The Loyalty Effect: The Hidden Force Behind Growth, Profits and Lasting Value*

> *Why aren't executives focusing on loyalty-based leadership to decrease the human asset leak?*

Loyalty-Based Management

Loyalty-based management is about your people: your customers, employees, and investors. Loyalty is based on motivation and behavior, not about marketing, finance, or product development. At companies where loyalty-based leadership is predominant, employees are proud that they treat their customers and each other the way they would want to be treated. Their work experience is balanced between their own goals and the organization's dedication to serving the customer. Work that sacrifices personal principles drains employees' energy. When work is congruent with personal principles, it is a source of energy, and pride results. Pride is therefore a powerful source of motivation and energy.

Pride doubles the economic advantage inherent in a loyalty-based system. In Chapters 3 and 4 we'll look at a tool (CRM Successful People Profile—CRM SPP™) that connects employees' goals to the customer service goals so that both the company and the employees are served. With this tool properly implemented, their jobs then become congruent with personal principles and work is a source of energy that transforms service providers into loyalty-based employees. It is also a tool that can help transform managers into loyalty-based managers and executives. But first, let's look at a quick example of the economics of pride to further convince you of the value of people.

An example of a company that knows the economic value a loyalty-based management brings to a company is USAA, the San Antonio insurance and investment management firm that serves active and retired military officers and their families. Under the leadership of CEO General Robert F. McDermott, who insists that, "Customers and employees are both precious resources," USAA grew from $207 million in assets to $34 billion in 26 years. With this hundredfold increase in assets:

- The company's employee base has only expanded by a factor of five

- Employee attrition rates shrank from 43 percent to 5 percent

- The customer retention is 99 percent

McDermott, with a background as a professional educator, turned the theory of loyalty-based management into an applied science. As a first step, the company changed its focus to people first, then to process and technology. With the focus on people, they invested $130 million in technology to enhance service and loyalty to create measures to monitor progress in those areas. With a company focus on understanding the economics that underpin loyalty-based management, they built that understanding into all their decision-making processes. They refined their ability to learn from failure (from customer and employee attrition) and to achieve continuous measurable improvement in the creation and allocation of value.

Our book will review tools for you to to learn to select, hire, and grow your employee base so that you can get the return on your human capital asset and transform your culture into a loyalty-based organization. It is based on how you communicate with each other. Without a tool to understand how communication is currently done and where the gaps are, you can't begin to create this kind of culture.

Why do we still think of things like people's loyalty or motivation as soft skills and not respect the effects they have on the bottom line?

Operationalizing a Business Revolution: People, Process, and then Technology

The goal of this book is to draw upon the ideas of thought leaders and management theories, and our own practical experience and to provide a book that will operationalize a business revolution through people, process, and then technology. One of our favorite mentors is Albert

Einstein, not just because he thought about science differently than all physicists of his time, but also because of his philosophies on change and human nature (see Figure 1.15). While many people are familiar with his work in science, few know that he was a philosopher (*Essays in Humanism, Living Philosophies,* and *Einstein on Peace*) and a very good friend and colleague of Freud. The two wrote papers together on human potential. We wanted to expose that part of him, not only because of the significance of his theories on change, but also because he represents to most of us the hard data, equations, and the facts of science. Often, when someone thinks of implementing CRM, that is what they ask: "What kind of hardware/software do we need to buy?"

> *The significant problems we face today cannot be solved at the same level of thinking we were at when we created them.*
>
> —Albert Einstein

What we wanted readers to know is that even behind the most solid, concrete number crunching is a precursor to the success of the hard data, to the hardware and software. It is that creative, intuitive side researchers use (but don't talk much about) to ask, "What if?" It allows them the freedom to think beyond the current limits, to see into the future and design something that has never existed before: television, Coke, Apple computers, the Internet. It is this soft side of an intellect that fuels the imagination and the spirit to create innovation and pride, which is what truly keeps customers coming back for more.

We want to begin to shift the paradigm that so that the softer sides of CRM (people and process) have as much or more value than the number-crunching facts and data organizers (technology). When the three (people, process, and technology) are used in combination in a corporate culture, that is where the real success can be found (Figure 1.16). You have an invitation to think outside the box and connect that creative side to the numbers as Einstein did, and have your business zoom as you collect and keep your customers happy.

PEOPLE

Prior to the creation of the mass marketing, outlet chain, mail order, and e-commerce world we live in today (referred to as the MO-ME age), individual proprietors created the ultimate CRM. They weren't equipped with multi-channel, data warehouse, and videoconference capabilities. What they did have was a strong personalized relationship with their customers. In the 1800s a blacksmith knew the name of each of his customers and what their needs were. He had knowledge of who was buying a new horse, and who was building a new house. It was a small environment where this knowledge was readily available from neighbors or simply by observation. Today our world is larger and the blacksmith is dealing with 100,000 customers, not 100. Personalization is typically not possible. But interestingly enough, the data is still readily available. Companies simply do not utilize

Figure 1.15	Albert Einstein was not only a great scientist but also a great humanitarian.

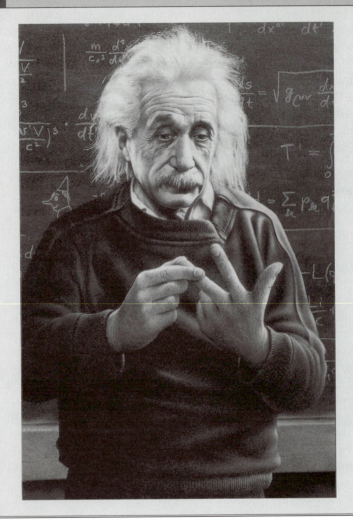

Imagination is more important than knowledge—Albert Einstein

For more information on Einstein's ideas on human potential and philosphies on change see:

- *Albert Einstein: The Human Side* (Banesh Hoffman, Princeton, NJ: Princeton University Press, 1954)
- *Philosopher Scientist* (Paul A. Schlipp, Boston: Open Court Publishing, 1988)
- *The Joys of Research* (Walter Shropshire and Albert Einstein, Boston: Smithsonian Institute Press, 1982)
- *Eintein on Peace* (Albert Einstein and Otto Nathan, NY: Simon and Schuster, 1960)

SIDEBAR: HOW THE BENZENE RING WAS DISCOVERED

Kekule was a German scientist who liked to sip wine after dinner in front of the fireplace as he relaxed and thought about his day's experiments (Figure 1.16). He was working on a new compound with six carbon atoms and hydrogen. As he stared into the fire he began to visualize how the atoms in the molecule could be connected to each other and still satisfy the laws of how atoms bonded together. Each individual flame flicker became a carbon atom. As he watched the fire dance, he started to see individual parts of the flame join hands and dance in a circle. Hence, a eureka moment came to him: Of course, the carbon atoms were joined in a circle! This was different than most molecular structures of the time because they were linear molecules, with the atoms lined up in a row.

Allowing the mind to dream creates great discoveries. How much is that worth to you?

Kekule in front of the fire, dreaming about what the structure of the benzene molecule looked like. Picture of benzene ring (inset).   **Figure 1.16**

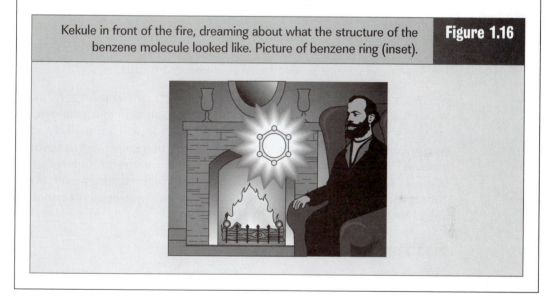

the data appropriately. Today's CRM solution requires a clear strategy and the support of the appropriate technology. Creating the same customer relationship that was created in the 1800s can still be accomplished.

You'll see later in the book that not only the order of people, process, and technology is important, but that *how* we are suggesting to do the people part is different than you've ever seen before. We will provide a way to understand and shift human behavior that not only changes how employees, managers, and executives do their job, but that leads directly to increased revenue, profits, and customer retention. We will provide return on investment calculations for things that have been traditionally thought of only as expense and non-revenue generating.

PROCESS

In addition, the Schwartz-Petouhoff Measure, Market and Manage Model (SP3M™) will change how you create, implement, and market (yes, market) the results of the service level agreements (SLAs) to measure, prove, and monitor how your dedication to customer service is affecting bottom-line result. By implementing the Schwartz-Petouhoff 3M process, everyone will have the early warning signs before an issue becomes a huge problem and you fly right into a mountainside or a storm. A quality-monitoring SLA system is a tool that will tell you if you are really making things better or if quality was just one of the executive's initiatives for the year to qualify for a bonus.

TECHNOLOGY

What we want from technology is to enable people and process. Specific uses of CRM technology are to:

- Provide Service
- Measure service
- Learn and change service based on measured results

With the new outlook on people and process, the reasons for buying technology, and which technologies will enable you and your employees to provide the customer service you want to provide will most likely shift. You'll see examples of technology that enables the people and the process parts of CRM. In addition, you will have concrete reasons for buying certain kinds of technology. You will understand why many of the products out there cannot deliver what you need and you won't overspend on capital or underpurchase in capability.

Fish Stinks Most at the Head

Shifting how your company approaches CRM will show employees that the customer service quality initiative is not the new management initiative du jour. What we have seen is that management decides to do something, assigns people to do it, and then rarely goes back to see if it worked before it makes another mandate. The CEO reads something in a trade journal on an airline flight and feels the need to keep up with the competition. Arriving back at the company, the CEO calls the CIO and says, "Get right on this." The CIO naturally starts the project by looking at the technology solutions available, assigns a team to work on it, and away they go. What we observe is the point where the CRM chaos begins.

Which Side Is Up?

In our work developing, implementing, and operating CRM programs for our clients, we have observed a very typical scenario. Companies have begun the CRM initiative with an emphasis on technology and data, not the customer.

This error is compounded by the vendor population selling hardware and software CRM solutions. The correct approach is to begin with the customer, the person making the contact. Is your company meeting the customer's needs? The customer wants a seamless, painless transaction across any communication channel. Providing that "unified face" to the client is the most critical step. The process and the technology required to create a seamless relationship with the customer is secondary to the actual creation of the relationship.

If CRM starts with technology, it is bound to turn into a costly and unsuccessful mess. It must start with understanding the customer needs and how to provide acceptable solutions. The days are over for technology to push decisions. Instead, in the CRM initiative the technology will be pulled by the CRM objectives defined by the customers' needs. But we feel that this distinction is only starting to be realized by the highest levels of decision makers. We felt that we needed to reflect to our readers what the collective technology buyer is experiencing. One of the reasons there is still a pink elephant about technology solutions is that few want to admit they spent all the money and it did not work. We want to make it ok to tell your war stories. In fact, we invite you to send them to us!

Vendor Push-Customer Pull

One example of vendor push versus customer pull is that today's CRM market is saturated with vendors applying the latest technological advances to the CRM industry. Features like voice over internet protocol (VoIP), streaming video, and co-browsing all sound great and make for some terrific demonstrations.

> Unfortunately companies may not have asked themselves the most basic question before issuing a purchase order. Will my customers use this technology? The latest statistics available indicate that over 50 percent of all households now have a personal computer. How many of these computers have the configuration required to support these technologies? They must have a microphone for VoIP, and significant processor speed and memory for either streaming video or co-browsing. In the appropriate situation these technological advances are wonderful tools. A widely dispersed sales force that can access a centralized data center for training or meeting can benefit from VoIP or even streaming video. Unfortunately the technology is being pushed to industry as a mainstream product that everyone is using! Do not be pushed into purchasing what your customers will not use; ask the vendors to supply what you need to achieve your customer relationship management goals.

> —John Roberston, Vice President, Edcor, CRM Leader

In one company CRM celebration meeting we attended where C-level executives were announcing the success of the CRM solution and giving employees accolades, one employee stood up and said, "All this is very nice, but when are we going to really implement it? The customers aren't using all this technology." A hush came over the room, executives blushed and whispered on stage and then one had the guts to stand up and ask the hard question,

"Can you tell me more about what you, as a customer service employee are experiencing?" In that very brave moment, a true leader opened up the celebration to an open and honest forum where the feedback flowed freely.

It is in the details of the implementations whether something makes a difference on an everyday level or not. Management may ask people to do this, but you also need to get the data once it is installed and working to see that it is making a difference. One of the things we experience when we help CRM centers benchmark is that they do the benchmark, create a report, and then say, "Great, we can check that box off our list. We have done our benchmarking for this year." It is not enough to benchmark or measure and think you are done. On the contrary, that is just the beginning of using CRM data to improve your customer service. We will provide concrete examples of how to work with the data in section 2, Chapter 8, of this book so that you will know whether your CRM process is adding any value at all. Most often we see that it is not.

We also want to stress that not only should you measure your employees and hold them accountable, but also measure and hold accountable the managers and executives. Our premise is that "the fish stinks most at the head." If you are an executive, you'll want to read this book before all your employees so that you can begin leading them into the brand new world of CRM. It is the distinctions and methodologies about people, process, and technology that will determine whether your CRM implementation will return the investment and the customer revenue you were promised.

This book is written not only for those wanting to buy or upgrade a CRM system, but also for consultants who help others buy and install systems. Our collective experience in technology implementation and through interviews with respected consultants and executives is shared in an honest assessment of where the field of CRM is, where the gaps are, and where it is headed. We feel that in the future it might become fiscally irresponsible to steer a company without the perspective and knowledge on people, process, and technology. Now that is a new management theory that will give you something to think about!

Executive CRM Strategy: A 30,000-Foot Look at CRM

Sit back by the fire and imagine what your company would look like if it was as successful as you can imagine. Allow yourself to think like Kekule for a moment. Sit back in your chair, kick up your feet and see it; the most amazing customer service center.

What if you had data at your fingertips, within minutes, to know:

■ How your customers feel about your products and or services

■ Which products are doing well

■ Which products or services are in trouble and why

And that the changes that you are about to make will have:

- Won quick approval because you were able to calculate the return on the investment

- Ample payoff

- Benefits via a combination of increased revenue and expense reduction

- Included strategic advantages that help you beat your competition by:

    - Maximizing service delivery

    - Optimizing productivity

    - Increasing market share

    - Avoiding unnecessary costs

    - Streamlining bureaucracies

See your company standing out from the pack by offering extraordinary service that makes it hard for customers to look elsewhere.

Wouldn't you feel like a smart, proactive, in-control business executive or manager? Many times the process of understanding why one is even setting up a CRM practice goes underinvestigated. Once you understand what it is that you want to deliberately create with CRM, then comes "how does one actually accomplish that?" That is where the strategy of CRM becomes important. In this age of product likeness, in which the market fails to perceive any profound difference between products or companies and any product advantage today is copied by the competition tomorrow, quality customer relationship management is the only thing that can place one company head and shoulders above the rest. The mindset for developing a competitive customer service strategy must be different.

CRM Is Change

The reason why companies that set out to reach a goal don't hit the target is that they probably don't understand the process of change or how to manage it. Hence the CRM implementation is very costly, time consuming, and does not yield the results initially sold in the proposal stage.

Insanity is doing the same thing, but expecting different results.

If we had started the chapter by telling you that the definition of CRM is really managing the changes you are making to providing service, you might not have understand that conceptually. To illustrate this point, take a look back at the example in the last section, the Kekule moment, where you were dreaming about how your customers felt about your products, services and your company. Then take a look at where your company scores on any one of the items in the CRM dream list (discussed further in Chapter 4). Most likely there is a gap in "where you are" and "where would like to be." That's normal. What the gap means is that, in order for you to get from the "as is" state to the "could be" state, something will have to change.

If you want to go from one state to another in a way that is purposeful, then you need to manage the change very carefully so that you end up with the desired result. Hence CRM is change and that change needs to be managed. And that is the value that change management brings to a technology/process change. It manages the change so that you get the results you expected and the ROI. We also wanted to include a chapter on the human reaction to change because the ability to manage the change is based on preparing the employees who are going to be implementing the system for handling change.

MEASURING CHANGE

People usually think of a customer relationship as a continuous activity, an intangible that cannot be measured. Thus the first challenge in creating a customer-focused culture at your company is defining a customer relationship in a way that it can be measured and therefore managed. We encourage you to read Dr. Anton's book, *Listening to the Voice of the Customer*, to learn how to create customer surveys that really measure satisfaction.

We want to stress the importance of establishing a recognizable method of measuring the health of customer relationships and changes in them, whether good or bad. With the focus on the customer, leading companies today are still trying to overhaul their traditional financial-only measurements of corporate performance, and seeking new metrics (both internal and external) that include customers' perceptions and expectations. Financial measurements are straightforward mainly because there is a unit of measure, namely, the dollar. The relationship measurement techniques discussed in this book transform qualitative—that is, "soft"—numbers into statistically sound numbers and indexes for decision makers.

Start with the People

CHANGE BEGINS WITH YOU!

Even the brightest can't see what they can't see until someone else beats them at their own game. In Joel Barker's book, *Paradigms: The Business of Discovering the Future,* he uses the following examples to illustrate how we negate ideas through our own filters of how we see the world. We oftentimes see the world only from our own limited perspective and the result is that we miss the boat completely. Don't lose your customers because you have clouded glasses.

The Earth is the center of the universe.

—Ptolemy, astronomer, 300 B.C.

The phonograph is not of any commercial value.

—Thomas Edison, inventor of the phonograph, 1880

Who the hell wants to hear actors talk?

—Harry Warner, Warner Brothers Pictures, 1927

There's no reason for anyone to have a computer in their home.

—Ken Olsen, president of Digital Equipment Corporation, 1977

Light bikes? What are people going to do, ride them or carry them?

—President of Schwinn Bikes, 1980

We wanted to add one to this list with respect to CRM.

The call center has nothing to do with making sound business decisions.
—This could be you!, 2001

Earlier in this book we said that when the paradigm shifts and executives really see the call center as a tremendous source of data about customers for capturing the customer experience with the full enterprise, then the value of the CRM implementation will increase exponentially. It is not just the place that inbound or outbound calls are made. It is your warehouse of raw data to make analytically-based business decisions. It is the key to your future. Use it.

Be the change you want to see in the world.
—Chandi

TO AVOID MAJOR PITFALLS IN CRM IMPLEMENTATION, START WITH THE PEOPLE

The status quo in approaching CRM is to start by looking for technology solutions, (Figure 2.1). We found it imperative to start with people, then go to processes and then pick the technology based on the people (customers' and employees' needs) and the process (how the work will get done) (Figure 2.2).

TRUE COMPLAINTS OF TECHNOLOGY IMPLEMENTATIONS THAT DIDN'T START WITH THE PEOPLE

Wanting to read the pulse of the audience of our book, we asked people what really happened when they started a CRM implementation with the technology, hardware, or software they had chosen. You may see yourself in these comments, and note they were universal for nearly every client we spoke to.

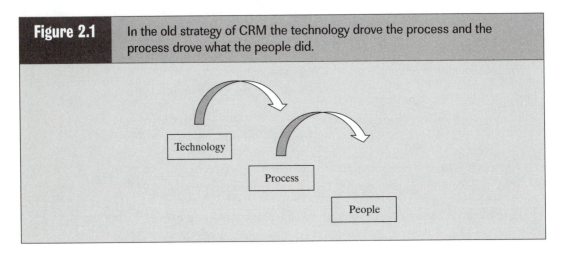

| Figure 2.1 | In the old strategy of CRM the technology drove the process and the process drove what the people did. |

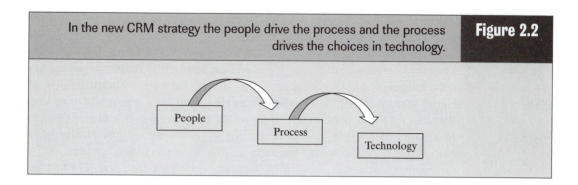

In the new CRM strategy the people drive the process and the process drives the choices in technology.

Figure 2.2

People → Process → Technology

Issue 1: Understanding the Culture and the Users' Expectations

"In our company the HR department helped people pick everything from their doctor to which stock they should purchase on their 401K plan, so basically there was no real process for HR benefits. We did not understand that in order for the technology to do what we wanted, we had to establish and map out all our transactions and interactions. We thought all they had to do was talk to a few vendors, and pick out something that would allow us to put the administration HR system on the intranet. When we figured the costs for the extra time to do this and the cost in Full Time Equivalents, we were astonished. They seemed to have forgotten the cost of the people needed to make this happen.

"We did not know in the initial cost estimate that we would need to add business process mapping (BPM). The salespeople only talked about turnkey technology. We had never done business process mapping, so those on the CRM implementation team had to learn business process mapping. It was then that we found a lot of redundancies in the process or no consistent process for benefits so we reengineered the process. We did not see any point in adding technology for redundant steps. It was not a simple mapping of the process—as we went along we realized that departments critical to the process had not originally been included in the CRM team: finance, payroll, IT, facilities, etc. By the time we did include them, they were upset and came with an attitude. All of this greatly expanded the timeline and the cost of the project. Most of us had full-time jobs and were expected to do this on top of an already exceedingly heavy workload. Did we see our families during the two years it took us to do this? Not on your life; this project sucked the lifeblood out of all of us.

"Once we got a clear picture of what we wanted the software from the BPM to do, we went back to the vendors and that's when the price really went up! It was not that the salespeople had knowingly lied, but that the people selling the technology were not the ones installing it—so when we got to the place we could ask those detailed software/hardware questions, the vendors brought in technical people who got the bid closer to reality. The bid went from $250K to $2 million. Unfortunately, the CFO had approved the $250K, and was quite angry several months later when we came back with the $2 million figure.

"The other thing we did not really know about was change management. What we learned was the value it would have brought to the success of the implementation. It did not occur to us that we needed a communication plan to tell the employees that their hand-holding HR department was now turning into machines and that personal interface would be gone. We also underestimated the amount of detailed training needed for the employees and HR staff to learn to use it. We had scheduled some early training for the HR staff, but because the implementation took so long, by the time the system was installed, they had forgotten what they learned in the training and needed to repeat it. When we announced the opening and invited employees to use the new system, we ended up with more employees in our office than we had ever had before. They got stuck, did not like it, wanted us to hold their hand while they tried to log on. We had more work to do with the technology than we had before."

—from an HR call center implementation in an entertainment company

Issue 2: Understanding the Difference Between Strategy and Reality

"When the consulting firm sold us on the call center, they talked at the 30,000-foot level about the financial benefits of transforming the administrative functions of HR, finance, etc. into a shared services group. They explained that by using technology to automate the administrative parts of HR, the HR staff could then focus on the real issues in HR such as creating and developing knowledge workers.

"The two problems that came up with this were first, we were never given a real ROI; it was only implied to close the sale; and second, we did not understand at the time we bought the system that most of our HR people had an administrative mindset and skill set.

"When the CFO asked for the ROI documents, there were none to substantiate the changes. What there was did not take into consideration that we had to fire most of the HR staff because they were not qualified to develop knowledge workers and had to be replaced by much more expensive, HR-capable people. The two costs were the severance packages of the outplaced HR staff and the more expensive HR people."

—from a CRM implementation in a pharmaceutical company

Issue 3: Understanding Vendors—Functionality versus Hardware/Software Purchases

"We realized we had a blind spot in trying to compare various vendors' products. At first we were not sure what we really needed, and then when we tried to compare apples to apples in terms of functions of the product they were all so different it was nearly impossible. Assessing different vendors became a nightmare. We had heard stories that salespeople promise everything, so we knew to be wary of that and had brought in our IT people. But even they had a difficult time understanding what technologies would result in the kind of enhanced customer service we wanted to provide. A lot of it sounded good, but who could tell if it was marketing hype or for real?

"When we started, we did not have a defined, detailed plan of what we wanted to accomplish with the technology. Because we were very inexperienced at technology buying, what we said to them was always at a very high level. We did not really consider what the customers were going to want in terms of everyday use. When we started to understand more, we realized we would be very disappointed in what a turnkey system could do.

"We learned after meeting with so many vendors the issues with interfacing with a legacy database. Then the truth about turnkey systems came out—we found that we would have to purchase $500K more in hardware/software and professional services. We found out we could have tested the hardware before buying it, under user loads to make sure it would be compatible with other legacy systems without additional costs."

—from a CRM call center implementation in the airline industry

Issue 4: Departments Arguing Over the Best Thing to Do

"Part of the increased cost for us was hooking up to legacy databases. The HR department did not want to replace everything they had because of costs. But the IT department ran into problems trying to find pieces for the Web and e-mail that could hook together and into the old payroll system. We explained to HR that in some ways it would have been better to replace the old payroll system than patch it together with code, but we were under tremendous time schedule restraints. The payroll department did not want to reinvent themselves—they had a typical HR mindset—slow to change, outdated like the dinosaur, and burdened by rules they followed blindly."

—from a customer service center implementation
in an automotive company

Issue 5: Understanding the Work Load and Amount of Staff and Expertise Required

"In our technology implementation we underestimated the need for professional services. I guess we thought the IT department could do it all and we would just have an internal chargeback to IT. But when the project got going, IT had too much on their plate just doing what they do. Adding a whole new 1 to 2 year project and in many cases needing people fulltime had not been part of the staffing plan for the year. They had not anticipated that we would need so much help and had not hired people to do so. We had to weigh the cost of hiring contract employees internally versus paying the consulting company for their professional services. What we needed was a team of people to install, test, and retest the equipment, then run the legacy system in parallel with the new system for several months to make sure they were stable and to get the bugs out. And because it never works the first time it had to be tested under real loads such as employee benefits sign-up, where everyone in the company is signing on, to understand whether the system could scale up.

"Although it is sold as though you flip a switch and magically you have a new system, we finally realized it is not like turning the key in a new car and driving off. We wish the consulting company had forewarned us."

> —From a customer service center implementation in a consumer products company

We share these stories so that you will know you are not the only one out there experiencing this kind of disappointment. We also wanted to emphasize that most of the issues in these implementations were a result of poor communication, poor planning, or poor strategy by the people involved. We don't mean to admonish the people, but rather to point out that the weak link in a technology implementation ultimately boils down to the people. There are many more stories like this that we have heard, but this begins to set the stage for that pink elephant to rise up and be seen, and for us to present some solutions to all the weak links in CRM.

The Secret to Risk Management of CRM: People

THE CRM IMPLEMENTATION = CHANGE

Almost all companies are continually changing how they do their business to keep up with customers' demands and the global market competition. New technologies accelerate the demands for change, including faster communications, more detailed and timely information about customers, and more precise measurements of cost and quality to provide excellence. These increases are driving the need to consider the triad of people/process/technology to maximize the return on investment (ROI) for implementing start-of-the-art technology. We see more and more companies getting caught up in buying the best technology available, only to find later that all the bells and whistles are not being used, much less the basic functionality of the system. What we have found in our consulting is that the maximum ROI occurs when a comprehensive change management program guides the change in the workplace.

The reason for a comprehensive change management program is that CRM really is all about change. For example, when a company decides that they want to either add a CRM program to their existing customer service strategy or upgrade their existing CRM practice, what they are really saying is that they want to *change the way they are providing service.* The operative word that we want to emphasize is **change.**

> *If the word excellence is to be applicable in the future, it requires a redefinition. Excellent companies don't believe in excellence—only in constant improvement and change. Excellent companies will know how to cherish chaos and thrive on change.*
>
> —Tom Peters, *Thriving on Chaos*

We want to help you thrive on change. Most CRM books deal with the various parts of CRM technology or process. What we found that went unaddressed or underestimated in implementing CRM is the effect change has on the people, process, and technology. The bottom line is that when you change the way you are providing service, it means people have to change what they were doing. Practically ignored in almost all CRM projects is that the nature of humans is to resist change. They resist any change: not just technology, but any change. Humans resist change, even when it is a good thing. We will learn more about why later in this section.

We wanted to be thorough in this book and to address what clients were telling us about unsuccessful CRM implementations. When we worked with companies to upgrade or change their CRM practice, what we found across the board that impacted the success of the CRM project was how they dealt with change. And while the issues with changing technology, workflow, or process are important to the success of a CRM implementation, nothing had more effect on the implementation than how the changes were dealt with on the interpersonal level. We also found that many executives' and managers' attitudes about giving consideration to this human aspect ranged from denial to skepticism to downright indignancy. We also found that leaders with those attitudes were the ones who were the most disappointed with their CRM implementations.

> *Error number no. 8: Not anchoring changes in the corporate culture. Change sticks when it becomes, "the way we do things around here." Until new behaviors are rooted in social norms and shared values, they are only temporary and a waste of time and energy.*
>
> —John Kotter, "Leading Change: Why Transformations Efforts Fail,"
> *Harvard Business Review*, 1995

The reasons we are covering change so early in the book (authors who have addressed it usually leave it for the end of a book) are because dealing with change is the precursor that makes or breaks a CRM implementation, and to present the stepwise methodology of successful CRM implementations, which begins by dealing with change.

CRM PROCESS STRATEGY

"Strategy! We don't need no stinkin' strategy!" The typical organization never addresses the overall commonsense relationship management strategy; more typically the various strategies are developed under the various departments. IT develops the Web strategy, customer service develops the call center strategy, nobody addresses e-mail, and what about good old-fashioned mail? Has anyone checked the mailbox lately? Meanwhile marketing is coming up with an entirely new approach to reaching customers, but have they thought about how the customer will reach us?

If you did not actually do the CRM strategy dreaming in Chapter 1, it is important for you, as a leader, to spend the time dreaming about what you want the CRM implementation to provide. Then, when you create your CRM implementation team, have them contribute to this dream and vision. The reason for this is very simple. First, they will buy into it if they are creating it. Second, if you understand what services you want to provide, then it becomes clearer when you look at your "as is" and "could be" states where the gaps are in who is providing the services (people), how the services are provided (process), and the vehicle by which they are delivered (technology).

When expectations are not clear, then the reality of the CRM implementation is bound to be disappointing. Without assessing various technology solutions to determine if they will do what you envisioned them doing, you will not only be missing the big picture, but you'll also not have a clear understanding of all the little details that go into making the big picture happen. In order for a CRM implementation to deliver what you dreamed, it takes the ability to translate the big picture service model into the little tiny details. Those little tiny details are what determine the kind of technology you need to provide the service you want your customers to have.

Mapping out your processes, i.e., how the work gets done, is the best way to translate the big picture into the little tiny details of the service process. Once you have mapped them out, then you can begin to describe the functionality that you want the software and hardware to have. This process is known as business process mapping (BPM). You may even find that you'll want to eliminate some of the steps in the process or that there are overlaps in various departments, thus leading you to do some business process reengineering (BPR). With a new look at the processes you'll use, you can then pick the technology that will really deliver this new kind of service. Most people start with telling vendors they want technology without understanding that they themselves need to detail what they want technology to do.

The scope of a CRM project is typically all-inclusive when implementation begins. This creates an extremely lengthy startup period, as design meeting after meeting is held to determine what the technology should look like. Quite often the team is designing phases of technology that are not scheduled for implementation until the second or third year of the project. The issue is the lack of obtainable goals. Any team requires a process by which they can accomplish something and gain job satisfaction. No one wants to work on a project that never ends. Defining goals and projects in small achievable projects is crucial to the long-term success of any CRM project. Understanding what Utopia looks like is important—it keeps the project going in the right direction. Understanding whether or not you are succeeding along the way drives further achievement and brings clarity to the final goal with each step.

The truth is, there is not a turnkey technology system, no matter what any vendor might intimate. Part of that is because most technology must be integrated into legacy databases or computer systems and people have to be trained in the new workflow. It is never as simple as buying a black box and being able to turn the key and have really happy, satisfied customers. We will deal with more of the details of how to provide great customer service in the next chapters on process and technology, but next we want to dive right into the first part: the people and change.

The People Affect the Scope, Schedule, and Budget of CRM Implementations

When planning and implementing CRM, there are people involved. Some of the people are your employees who will be doing the planning and implementing. Some of the other people are the ones who will be using the CRM center: the customers. Understanding the impact of change on these two groups is important. Here is a short list of why we are going to be covering the people part:

1. Installing CRM or improving part of an existing CRM practice means that you are going to do business differently.

2. Doing business differently means you've changed the jobs of the people who do the work, from executives to managers to call center agents.

3. Changing their jobs means they will need not only to accept the change, but also get training and skills to be able to do the job in the new way or they won't be able to follow the new process or use the new computer system.

4. Once you have established a new way for the employees to provide customer service to your customers, you must communicate that to the customers who need to use the new system, then monitor their reaction, incorporate their feedback, and make more changes to the technology, process, or people part of the business.

It's not so much that we are afraid of change or so in love with the old ways, but it's that place in between we fear. It's like being in between trapezes. It is Linus, when his blanket is in the dryer—there's nothing to hold on to.

—Unknown

HUMAN REACTION TO CHANGE

Change can be seen as *Crisis or Opportunity*, as we know from the ancient Chinese symbol, (Figure 3.1). It just depends on how you see it. If you are able to shift your paradigm about change, then you can be on the road to opportunity. When change is viewed as opportunity, the exhilaration of change can be a booster for your rocket ship. But if change is seen as a crisis, then it is an energy sink that will sabotage and hinder the success of any project or implementation. When people view change as a crisis, it is why most things don't really change. Whether someone sees change as a crisis or an opportunity has a lot to do with whether they are a proactive or reactive person. Forty percent of the workforce has a behavior work style that is reactive and slow to accept change. Change can be scary because it is the unknown.

> The earliest surviving book is by some accounts the ancient Chinese Book of Changes, *I Ching*. It proposes a matrix of 64 distinct circumstances and recommends actions to capture the greatest benefit or minimize difficulty. The 64 distinct circumstances tend to flow freely into one another. If you get out your calculator and compute the permutations when one circumstance can flow into another, you will see what the ancients felt they were up against. Conditions are no simpler in business change today.
>
> —The PWC Change Integration Team, *Better Change*

WHAT HAPPENS IF YOU DON'T DO THE CHANGE PART?

The consequences of not doing the change part well or at all have large impacts on the cost, schedule, and scope of the implementation, Figure 3.2. We found that most companies, when reviewing the budget for a technology implementation, will spend thousands to millions of dollars on the software and hardware, but start to cut out things like business process

The Chinese symbol for change is a combination of the symbols for crisis and opportunity.	**Figure 3.1**

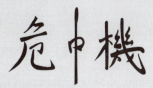

Figure 3.2	The exponential effect of not dealing with the human reaction to change is increased scope, increased costs, missed time deadlines resulting in increased project risk, and reduced return on investment as well as reduced confidence by both the employees providing the service and the customer receiving it.

Scope: Unending   Implementation Delayed and Timeline Extends   Higher Implementation Costs   Project Risk

∞ × ⧗ × $ = [High / Average / Low]

mapping (BPM) and reengineering and almost always greatly reduce or minimize the budget allocation for change management functions like training employees or communication plans. Technology implementations are very costly and it is a wise decision to cut costs wherever possible. However, the one place executives overspend is on the technology, with tons of bells and whistles that sound really great; they tend to underspend in the area of training people to use these new, complicated technology systems.

The willingness to accept the validity of soft skills again goes back to what we have traditionally viewed as value added. Capital equipment, software, and the like are tangible and have a cost associated with them that fits nicely into a spreadsheet. However, until recently, people's motivation, training them, etc., did not have direct costs associated with them because people did not know how to calculate them to show the bottom-line effects. What this book does is to calculate the people part of the equation so that you can add it to the P&L sheet. This will help in transforming how leaders value the human potential of their companies. In Chapter 10 on Analytical CRM, we provide a case study where training had a 1400 percent ROI.

Leaders feel their most critical issues in business are service, quality, profitability, cost control, productivity, and overall performance. These issues show up as poor quality, declining profits, productivity drop offs, sales downturns, and unacceptable customer service. These show up on the balance sheet. However, these issues only represent the symptoms of the underlying root cause. Leaders tend not to dig deeper to find their root cause. Part of that is a paradigm in how business is done and part of it is that leaders place importance on hard issues because they seem to be based on fact. Factual matters can be debated, proven, and strategized upon. Yet addressing hard issues just because they seem more tangible and measurable is like being the proverbial drunk who looks futilely for his keys half a block from where he lost them, reasoning that "there isn't a street light down there." Focusing on the hard issues because the means to address them seems clearer does not make the problems go away. It only temporarily cures the symptoms.

> We've spent the majority of our energy in the eighties and nineties working on the hardware of American business because that hardware needed to be fixed. But the hardware has limits. The Japanese, on the other hand, have the software, the culture, which ties productivity to the human spirit, which has practically no limits. That's where we have to turn in the new millennium—to the software of our companies—to the people and the culture that drives them. We must touch every single person in the organization every business day.
>
> —Jack Welch, former chairman and CEO of GE

AN EXAMPLE OF NOT DOING CHANGE WORK

Sometimes CRM can be employed to aid internal customers or employees. In one particular company, the HR department was changing the way it provided administrative HR benefits to employees. During our discovery process, we found that employees came into the HR department with their requests, for example, for a 401K choice, written on stickies or scrap paper. The information was then translated onto various forms with the help of an HR professional. In a move to reduce the headcount in HR, management decided to implement an intranet online service for all HR benefits. In this process of changing their HR benefit service delivery model, they neglected to educate the employees on the change. Brochures and e-mails were sent out, but it was not until the employees went to use the system that it became clear that the limited communication plan did not explain they would not longer be able to get personalized help via the old hand-holding HR department, or be able to write 401K choices on stickies.

The consequence of not providing detailed communications and training for the employees was an employee (customer) population that was very confused and angry. The employees lined up in the HR department with complaints and questions. The HR staff had been only minimally trained on the new system, so when any detailed question came in from the already angry employees, they had to defer answering the question until they could get help understanding the issue. That meant that they had to go back to the software implementer and pay for their time at professional services rates.

After several weeks of this, one of the senior HR leaders said, "Why didn't we receive training on this stuff? When you (the vendor) presented the pitch for this new HRMS system, it sounded so automated and easy." The vendor replied, "Remember when we were doing the budget? The consensus was the cost of the detailed training was too high and you cut it out of the budget." The look of remorse filled the room, as they all realized they were spending more money than the original training would have cost. Plus, they had lost the confidence of the employees. The word on the street from the employees was, "The call center was another stupid decision by management." Feedback sheets from focus groups revealed their anger: "You call this 1-800-HR-Focus; well it should be 1-800-F_ck-You." We think that says it all.

While customers will just buy from someone else, employees (internal customers) may not leave but just become more disenchanted by management and therefore less productive. We see this a lot—when management installs technology that doesn't really serve employees, the employee response is, "They don't really care about ME! Why should I show up on time or go the extra mile? I come in, I get my paycheck and I go home. Did I tell you I just started this business on the side . . . ?" And there goes the energy you need to keep your business strong. Your employees feel apathy and are now entrepreneurs for themselves. Wouldn't it have been better to include that energy on the CRM team and to have created a solution that really served your employees?

Lessons learned from this experience are to educate your customers (employees) on how they will be receiving the new service and educate everyone who provides the service to the degree that they can solve real problems. If you don't pay up front to provide for these change management pieces, you'll pay double later to clean up the mess, if you are lucky enough to be able to recover from the mess.

THE IMPORTANCE OF MANAGING THE HUMAN ASPECT OF PROJECTS

To illustrate the importance of how the human aspects of a CRM project affect cost, schedule and scope, we provide stories of how other companies have done work to reduce the issues leading to failure. The performance risk management tools and ideas that will be covered in this chapter and in Chapters 4 and 5 include:

1. Stakeholder analysis and how to get their buy-in

2. The CRM SSP™ that helps individuals understand their reaction to change and how and why they are important contributors to a team

3. The phases a team goes through and the ways to counterbalance the issues in team dynamics and long-term project implementation

WHY DO WE NEED TO THINK ABOUT STAKEHOLDERS?

Let's start first with the people who have the most to gain or lose by a CRM implementation. We are calling them stakeholders. Stakeholders can include employees, executives, managers, customers, or vendors. They are essentially anyone, no matter their level in an organization, who has the ability to influence the successful implementation and the use of CRM systems. Stakeholders form the framework of relationships that surround any change effort and are the keys to the acceptance and support needed to get through implementation. If the human aspect of the stakeholders is not dealt with from the very beginning of the project, studies show that the benefits of the program are not fully realized; implementation is delayed and higher costs result. This risk can be mitigated through a series of change management steps.

As leaders of CRM implementation, you need to do everything you can to get the support of stakeholders. You want to include several call center agents. Oftentimes the lack of full implementation is because the agents were not involved in choosing the new system and they don't use it. Then it comes down to $12/hr agents being in control of whether your $5 million CRM expenditure works or not.

Stakeholders (people) are the keys to the resources and the energy needed to overcome resistance and experiences associated with past change efforts. On average, 20 percent of people are natural supporters. The other 80 percent of people generally have some resistance or may be cynical, fearful, or even angry that this project is getting support while an initiative they were associated with earlier did not. In other cases they might have fears about:

■ Being outsourced themselves

■ Losing control of their department

■ Having their mistakes or decisions held up to criticism in the process of mapping out how business is currently done

■ Having an ongoing internal critical dialog with themselves in general

■ Being criticized by a boss who sees mistakes as failure versus the opportunity to learn and grow

The list of fears can go on and on. And sometimes bosses think that criticism will motivate someone to do a better job. Sometimes it might, but studies show that this drives very few work styles.

When an employee or manager understands his or her own work style and the other person's, the risk of insulting or demotivating someone is much less. We'll talk more later about how to understand not only the work styles and drivers of motivation of individuals but how those individual styles create a collective culture of accepted behavior. Sometimes the current behavior styles increase productivity and sometimes they leave employees with so little morale that hardly any work gets done. The bottom line is, when employees don't get their work done, the business is losing money. CRM work style profiles that are part of the Success People Process™ are key to reducing resistance and increasing productivity, that is, increasing the human potential of the individuals and the team. We provide a "how-to" section on managing teams and stakeholders in Chapters 4 and 5.

HOW EMPLOYEES REACT TO CHANGING WHAT THEY DO ON THE JOB

To illustrate the effective use of change management, we will look at how employees on a CRM implementation team reacted to the changes in providing service. Figure 3.3 shows that changing delivery of service can impact

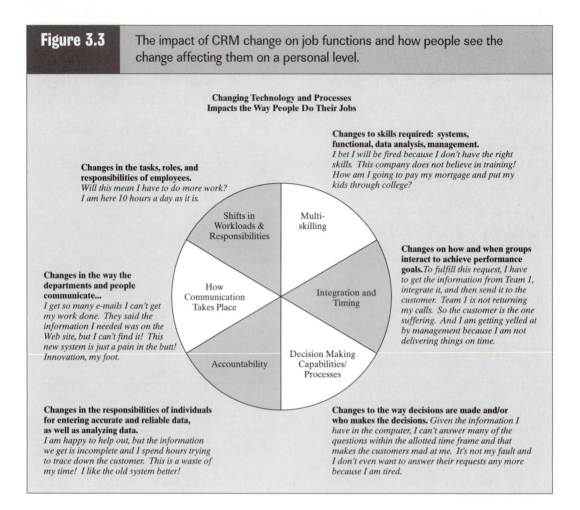

Figure 3.3 The impact of CRM change on job functions and how people see the change affecting them on a personal level.

Changing Technology and Processes
Impacts the Way People Do Their Jobs

Changes to skills required: systems, functional, data analysis, management. *I bet I will be fired because I don't have the right skills. This company does not believe in training! How am I going to pay my mortgage and put my kids through college?*

Changes in the tasks, roles, and responsibilities of employees. *Will this mean I have to do more work? I am here 10 hours a day as it is.*

Changes on how and when groups interact to achieve performance goals. *To fulfill this request, I have to get the information from Team 1, integrate it, and then send it to the customer. Team 1 is not returning my calls. So the customer is the one suffering. And I am getting yelled at by management because I am not delivering things on time.*

Changes in the way the departments and people communicate... *I get so many e-mails I can't get my work done. They said the information I needed was on the Web site, but I can't find it! This new system is just a pain in the butt! Innovation, my foot.*

Changes in the responsibilities of individuals for entering accurate and reliable data, as well as analyzing data. *I am happy to help out, but the information we get is incomplete and I spend hours trying to trace down the customer. This is a waste of my time! I like the old system better!*

Changes to the way decisions are made and/or who makes the decisions. *Given the information I have in the computer, I can't answer many of the questions within the allotted time frame and that makes the customers mad at me. It's not my fault and I don't even want to answer their requests any more because I am tired.*

Wheel segments: Shifts in Workloads & Responsibilities; Multi-skilling; How Communication Takes Place; Integration and Timing; Accountability; Decision Making Capabilities/Processes

basic job functions. Figure 3.4 shows typical reactions of these employees to the changes being suggested. Many times when leaders have not led change projects, they may be surprised by what we call Reptile Talk™ or the negative reactions that come from the part of the brain that reacts to change by being threatened or upset. This human dynamic and reaction to change, left unaddressed, is what causes implementation to go awry, resulting in the Valley of Tears (the decrease in productivity of team members) and increasing the project's risks.

Just as the software/hardware implementation of a CRM project has a life cycle, so does the human aspect of a project. Figure 3.5 shows a typical life cycle and the level of support the CRM team gives during the implementation. In the beginning when the project is first announced and team members are chosen, the level of excitement and expectations is very high. As they move forward into the next stage, the amount of work the project is going to take on everyone's part starts to become clearer. Many times employees are asked not only to do the tasks required for this new project,

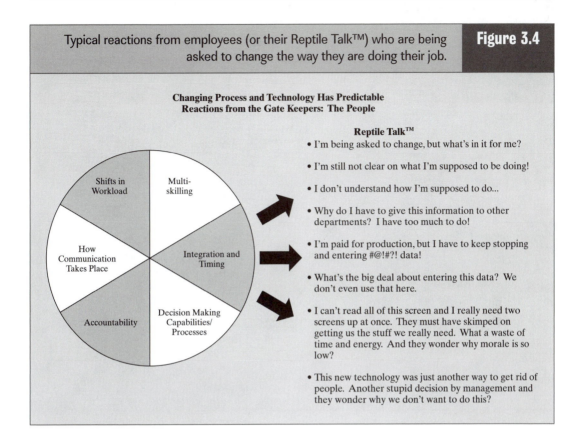

Typical reactions from employees (or their Reptile Talk™) who are being asked to change the way they are doing their job.

Figure 3.4

Changing Process and Technology Has Predictable
Reactions from the Gate Keepers: The People

Reptile Talk™

- I'm being asked to change, but what's in it for me?

- I'm still not clear on what I'm supposed to be doing!

- I don't understand how I'm supposed to do...

- Why do I have to give this information to other departments? I have too much to do!

- I'm paid for production, but I have to keep stopping and entering #@!#?! data!

- What's the big deal about entering this data? We don't even use that here.

- I can't read all of this screen and I really need two screens up at once. They must have skimped on getting us the stuff we really need. What a waste of time and energy. And they wonder why morale is so low?

- This new technology was just another way to get rid of people. Another stupid decision by management and they wonder why we don't want to do this?

Wheel labels: Shifts in Workload, Multi-skilling, How Communication Takes Place, Integration and Timing, Accountability, Decision Making Capabilities/Processes

but also maintain the responsibilities of their current job. This in itself can send most into the despair mode, realizing that the commitment to make the new project work and still do their other job is not only unrealistic, but they probably won't see their families for the next several months to a year.

Near the end of a project, the light at the end of the tunnel starts to show through and the level of support for the project increases. However, because the change was not dealt with, the net effect is to expend more time, money, and effort. When a CRM project is led by a correctly managed change management program, it optimizes the efforts. Figure 3.6 shows how it elevates the support as the life cycle curve moves up and to the left. In Chapter 5 we will share with you a technology implementation at Braun's CRM center, where this phenomenon of the human reaction to change was actually measured and managed. We will also share how the team leader and employees dealt with the various stages in the life cycle of the project (Figure 3.7) to increase the effectiveness and efficiency of the implementation. And probably most important, at the end of the implementation, because people were handled so well, their support and pride for the CRM system carried over into their everyday use of it. Sometimes after the implementations, teams are left

Figure 3.5	Typical emotional life cycle of a project (Human Capital Life Cycle, HCLC) and the level of support the technology team gives during the various stages of implementation: analysis, design, construction, and implementation. In the construction phase, teams go through what is called the Valley of Tears.

Without People Management or SSP™

+ High expectations

Support for the Project (employee productivity)

Realization of effort and complexity

The Valley of Tears

Light at the end of the tunnel

Despair

−

Project Implementation

Analysis   Design   Construction

with such a bad taste in their mouth, the very idea of having to use the system sends them into a spin. ROI in that case? None.

THE CAUSE OF THE VALLEY OF TEARS: THE AMYGDALA

You might be wondering why the Valley of Tears even happens. Why do teams dip in emotional support in the middle of a project, as shown in Figure 3.5? It has such an impact on a CRM implementation's success we wanted to spend some time on this. Learning this information will help you to gain management support and budget to deal with this team experience that all teams go through. Whether they are implementing technology or working at a charity, the emotional response on teams is the same. This information has helped others to understand the scientific reasons for the phenomenon.

By understanding the scientific explanation, we hope it will validate the reality of this and how much it affects your business. By measuring it and giving it a name, we hope that we have provided you with concrete enough evidence to motivate you to deal with it. Across all companies, we ran into many managers that wondered why, when you ask an employee to do something, they don't do it? After years of running departments, running companies, and consulting, we found that employees don't come to work and try to ruin your day by not doing their job. Most of them truly

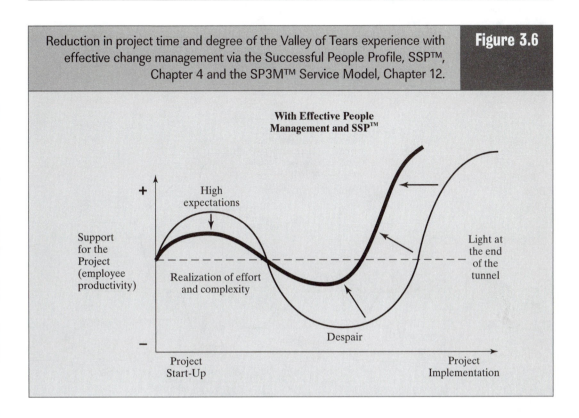

Figure 3.6

Reduction in project time and degree of the Valley of Tears experience with effective change management via the Successful People Profile, SSP™, Chapter 4 and the SP3M™ Service Model, Chapter 12.

want to do the right thing; however, something happens that stops them. Part of this is that it is not so much that employees resist change; it is more that they resist *being* changed.

After visiting the Institute of HeartMath™ in Boulder Creek, California, Dr. Petouhoff had a better understanding of the brain's function in change. HeartMath™ has been measuring the human reaction to change and has 15 years of data that proves the theory of the amygdala and its reaction to change. The book *From Chaos to Coherence*, by HeartMath's Doc Childre and Bruce Cryer, details the reaction of the human brain to change. Science shows that what we bring to a situation is what we expect to experience. What we expect to experience is based on our past experiences and that is what shapes our attitudes and values. If we have been yelled at for doing something wrong, we expect that if we do something outside the norm (change how we are doing something), we will get into trouble. If we have been congratulated and supported for doing something out of the ordinary, we expect that by taking a risk, regardless of the outcome, we will receive praise and support.

All this really means is that we are programmed neurophysiologically to subconsciously seek to prove through our experience that we are right. Our mind likes being "right"; it seeks evidence to support the story. This need to be "right" stems from millions of years of an old habit. That habit started in the cave days; if a tiger were chasing you and you interpreted the situation

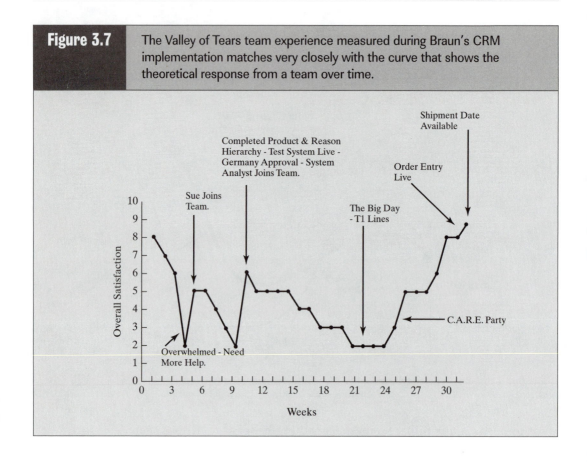

Figure 3.7 The Valley of Tears team experience measured during Braun's CRM implementation matches very closely with the curve that shows the theoretical response from a team over time.

incorrectly, you were eaten alive. Being "right" meant life or death. Now our choices don't result in such dramatic outcomes, but the response in our brain has not evolved much from those times when lions and tigers and bears were chasing us.

UNDERSTANDING SURVIVAL MECHANISMS

Change is something that can evoke a survival response of freeze, fight, or flight. The three-F response is actually the pushback, resistance, and sabotage leaders and managers are feeling from their employees when they introduce change. This happens many times in the first team meeting after the leader finishes introducing the project and asks for questions. The room literally "throws up" on the leader with all kinds of Reptile Talk™ about why they can't make this happen. That's why in the very first meeting we want you to give an assignment to the team to go home and think of all the reasons why the project would not, could not happen. In the second meeting you allow them to put them up on the wall on flipcharts (anonymously) and then give them 20 minutes to solve one reason that is not theirs. This not only gets out the Reptile Talk™, but it also lets them realize the value

---

SIDEBAR: WHAT REWARDING TAKING A RISK DOES

A small boy tried to pour a glass of milk from a large pitcher. Being little, he was not able to balance the pitcher, and milk went all over the counter, himself, the chair, and the floor. His mom walked into the room and smiled. She said, "Let's see how much fun we can have playing in the milk." They sat down next to each other on the floor and played in the spilled milk. They laughed, and when they were done, the mom said, "Let's go outside." She brought a pitcher and a glass with her, turned on the hose and filled the pitcher. Then she said, "If you are going to learn how to pour milk, you will have to practice your pouring skills." The little boy smiled and began pouring. This little boy grew up to be the founder of the Dow Chemical Corporation. Sometimes spilled milk is much more than just spilled milk.

---

of having other people on the team who see things from a different perspective. Let's take a look at the brain and its biochemistry to understand this response to change.

The research by Dr. Paul McClean and other neuroscientists at HeartMath™ shows there are at least three brain structures within our brain that have evolved over time. Each part of the brain has a different function and all three brain parts, functioning as a team, are necessary for optimal human performance. Figure 3.8 shows the three parts of the brain that we know about. The goal is to have all levels of the brain working together to make good decisions. But what we know about humans is that oftentimes when they get a new assignment their reaction is to freeze, flee, or fight. Key to all of this is the amygdala. It is an almond-sized structure in the subcortical areas of the brain. It "eavesdrops" on information received through the thalamus, looking for an emotional match to a previous experience to determine if it is a "lion, tiger, or bear" or if it is really safe. Working at high speed, if a match appears to be found, it communicates it to the higher regions of the brain that control decision making.

The first brain area governs reflex and instinct and is responsible for many basic functions necessary for survival. The second brain area exhibits control over the first level and is capable of hindsight and that is an aspect of the development of memory. Emotional information appears to be processed here, yet it is not where we first experience the physical manifestations of feelings. Positive feelings are experienced around or near the heart, whose electromagnetic field is forty times stronger than the brain's. Negative feelings are experienced near the solar plexus or the gut. The second brain area's functions and basic drives are seen in Figure 3.8. The third brain area, constituting roughly 80 percent, has the highest level of control and is capable of foresight and many other important functions.

Capabilities like creativity, language, self-reflection, complex problem solving and the ability to choose what is appropriate behavior are believed

Figure 3.8	The first brain is the low-level brain whose function is control via reflex and instinct. The second brain is mid level, where the mechanism is hindsight. The third brain, the high level, is where control is accomplished by foresight. The amygdala is an almond-sized structure in the subcortical areas of the brain. *Souce:* Institute of HeartMath® Research Center, copyright 1998.

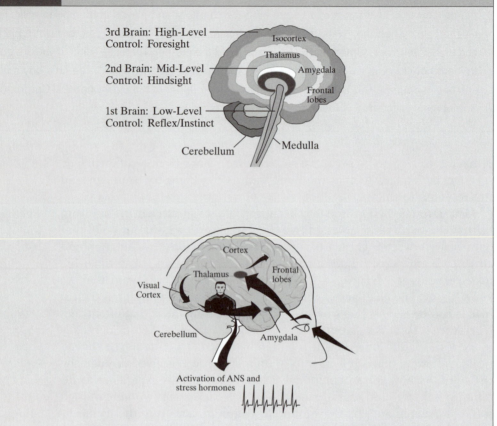

to emerge from the third brain area. A company hires employees for what it believes it can gain from the third part of the employee's brain. However, this third part of the brain can be jammed by the reaction of the first and second brain regions. Conversely, when we feel harmonious and balanced, our third brain function is enhanced. Hence, companies that want to take advantage of the full capacity of their employees need to be concerned about how employees feel and how the three parts of the brain are operating as a team. If change is handled well in a CRM project, then most of the time employees can manage the change from the third brain region, spending much less time in brain region one, reacting to the change.

When there is an outside stimulus, such as a boss suggesting that there is a better way to do things, the brain team goes to work to respond. As brain area one assesses the situation, it determines the danger factor in unison with the other brain areas. If it assesses that the need for protection is not there, the thoughts move predominantly on to the other parts of the brain. The employee is able to hear the manager's request and responds with feedback and suggestions. But if brain area one senses something is at risk (Figure 3.9) its territorial nature to protect the psyche responds in one of three ways:

- Freeze (like a reptile does to blend into the surroundings when you walk up to it)

- Fight (kill the intruder)

- Flight (run away from the intruder)

Some people get stuck in brain area one and become fearful, defensive, and respond as a victim either by freezing, fighting, or fleeing. A victim or negative response occurs when there is destruction or obstruction of the brain team.

- **The fight response** manifests itself in these kinds of behaviors in your organization: fighting, gossip, resistance, pushbacks, looking for a scapegoat, put-downs, screaming, blame, and judgment.

- **The flight response** manifests itself as: compliance, denial, workaholism, pulling away, self-medication (drugs or alcohol abuse), or suicide.

- **The freeze response** manifests itself as: sabotage and non-compliance via passive-aggressive behavior.

Figure 3.9

When employees sense something is at risk, they may respond in one of three ways with Reptile Talk™—almost as if their brain has been taken over by monsters. These ways include freeze (like a reptile does to blend into the surroundings when you walk up to it), fight (kill the intruder), and flight (run away from the intruder).

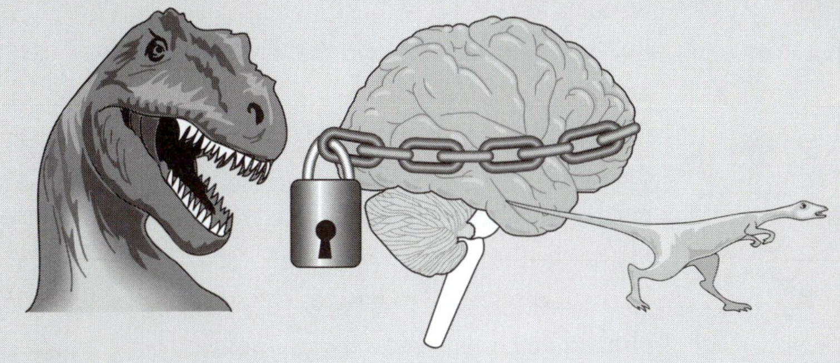

These responses can lead to further feelings of isolation, fear, loss, rejection, and hoarding and create excess stress and lower self-perspective. Many times when a merger or acquisition is announced, a company culture that once was normal can exhibit these behaviors because employees get scared about what is going to happen to them. When the brains of employees work as a team, the employees feel opportunity, possibility, and abundance. Effective change starts with each individual, their feelings, and their ability to face change via their emotional intelligence.

Edward de Bono, best known for his 6 *Thinking Hats Process* for teams to think outside the box, has worked with major corporations and government in 52 countries over the past 35 years. As a Rhodes scholar and as faculty at Oxford, Cambridge, and Harvard, his medical research on the brain shows how the nerve networks in the brain allow incoming information to organize itself into patterns and sequences. The key is perception: the brain organizes the incoming information triggered by what we see and feel around us. How we react to that information has everything to do with our attitude towards it. The key to managing change is knowing how to help employees manage their perception and expectations.

An example of the perception part of thinking and reacting is given via falling snow, (Figure 3.10). Snows falls. It just did what snow does: fall. The snow did not do anything to the people in the example, but their reaction to it falling might seem as if snow had some terrible motive. How people react to falling snow depends on what they value, how they see the situation, and how it impacts

Figure 3.10	This chart demonstrates the range of reaction of various individuals to the fact that it snowed.

Situation: It's Snowing

Person	Reaction
8th grader	Happy that schools are going to be closed for the day
Father	Upset because the roads will be icy and the drive to work will take twice as long
Ski lodge operator	Relieved because if it did not snow soon he would have to file bankruptcy
Farmer	Concerned that it may get too cold and ruin the crops and he'll lose the farm
Store Owner 1	Delighted because he can close the store and finish the book he started last night
Store Owner 2	Frustrated because today was the unveiling of a big, profit-making product line

them—this is their perception of the situation. Our attitudes add all the rest of that stuff: happy, upset, relieved, concerned, delighted, and frustrated.

The same reaction can be had when the call center manager announces that the group will be taking part in a CRM implementation project. You can see now how the reactions to job changes (Figures 3.3 and 3.4) created extended scope, budget, and time to implement (Figure 3.2). All employees are doing is participating in improving service to please their customers, but their reaction to those changes seems much more personally severe than what is on the surface. Hence, most managers are surprised at the pushback. There does not seem to be a logical reason for the pushback. And that is why we have spent part of this chapter on this; to show you there is a logical reason and that there are things that managers and executives can do to shift from a threatening experience to an enlightened one by increasing their emotional intelligence. The best place to begin managing the emotional intelligence of your team is the CRM SPP.™

> *The world we have created is a product of our way of thinking.*
> —Albert Einstein

We need a new way of thinking and a new way to enhance the emotional intelligence of our organizations. Emotional intelligence is one of the last reservoirs that will give us the competitive edge to stay in business in this new millenium. Perception, the lens through which we view life, is at the root of our Reptile Talk™. The CRM SPP™ helps to facilitate through the "lions and tigers and bears, oh my," and we find, on the other side of the pain, there are choices. We just need leadership to help see them, if we are not already able to do so ourselves. That is why it is so important to have a person specifically dedicated as the change manager on your team. Generally, because of internal politics, it is better to have a neutral outsider who is skilled at managing change to play this role. As Victor Frankl, a Holocaust survivor and author said so eloquently, "Everything can be taken away from you, but the one thing that can not be taken is our freedom to choose our attitude in any given set of circumstances."

THE VALUE OF INCREASING THE EMOTIONAL INTELLIGENCE

So if employees with higher emotional intelligence (EI) make better decisions, are more productive, and contribute more, how can an organization increase the emotional intelligence? Some of the most significant feelings that reduce EI are associated with stress: anger, anxiety, frustration, alienation, depression, victimization, self-judgment, and intolerance. These feelings emotionally highjack the brain's ability to work as a team.

The reduction of stress in the workplace is one of the factors in increasing EI. Stress is characterized by the flee, flight, or fight response, where the production of hormones like adrenaline is increased. If negative emotions such as fear, anger, worry, or anxiety are present, research shows there is a decrease in productivity, normal sleep patterns, and health. This is one of the key reasons why yelling at employees or using the command and control type of leadership, which usually makes employees feel threatened, is contrary to good business.

> How do we create organizational coherence, where activities correspond to purpose? How do we create cultures that move with change, that are flexible and adaptive and expansive? How do we simplify things without losing control and differentiation? Is there a magnetic force so attractive that it pulls all behavior towards it and creates coherence?
>
> —Margaret Wheatly, *Leadership and the New Science*

Using a process like the CRM SSP™ with a highly skilled change agent, work environments that are supportive, nurturing, and positive are shown to increase the well-being of employees and their productivity. If employees are in a positive state, less stressed, then the production of hormones such as DHEA is increased, as are the feelings of well-being and success. Research shows that the most successful people are those who have learned to manage their emotional reactiveness, neutralizing and transmuting negative emotions. This may be one of the reasons managers who use the relationship-based, loyalty-based management style are so much more successful than those who use the hierarchichal, pedantic leadership style.

The Human Heart and Increasing Emotional Intelligence

The human heart provides the key to managing EI. The reason the heart is key to EI is that the heart has been found to be central to a whole array of processes that affect brain function. The heart communicates to the brain through two sets of nerve pathways. It radiates an electromagnetic signal that reaches every cell in the body, including the brain. Although the heart and the brain each radiate electrical frequencies, the heart's amplitude is 40 to 60 times stronger than that of the brain. The coherence of the heart's rhythms can change the coherence of the brain wave pattern (EEG). The heart continuously sends information about one's emotional state to the cardiac center of the brain stem, which in turn feeds into the thalamus and to the amygdala, which is directly connected to the base of the frontal lobes. This is happening as you read this page.

Emotional states affect the heartbeat's rhythm and subsequently affect our brain's ability to work as a team to think and process information. Dr. Karl Pribam's (a preeminent neuroscientist) work at Stanford has shown the coherence of the heart's rhythm can change the coherence of the brain wave pattern (EEG). This means a negative reaction to an unpleasant supervisor's screaming would cause erratic rhythms in the employee's heart (Figure 3.11) and inhibit the employee's brain's teamwork. The common result is poor decision making, impulsive communications, and reduced

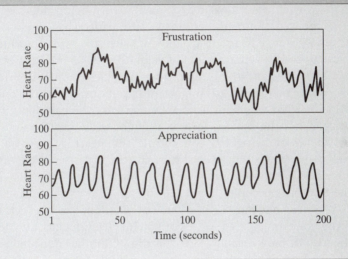

Figure 3.11

These are graphs of employee heart rhythms. When the heart rhythm changes, it changes the brain's ability to process information, including decision making and problem solving. A jagged path from someone who is frustrated (the top graph) represents an employee who has limited ability to process information, including decision making, problem solving, and productivity. Smooth rhythms are associated with an employee who feels appreciation and is thus clear, calm, and able to handle work in a proactive manner. *Source:* Institute of HeartMath® Research Center, copyright 1998.

creativity or problem solving ability. It then takes energy and time for the employee to get back on track, if at all. They may just tune out for the rest of the day, week, or year. The result of continued negative exposure is an apathetic, resigned, and demoralized employee population.

HeartMath™ studies show that a 5-minute period of recalling an angry experience caused the suppression of the substance IgA, responsible for good immune responses, for 6 hours. In contrast, five minutes of sincerely feeling care or compassion boosted IgA for 6 hours. What is the return on the investment for treating your employees well, saying thank you, job well done, we really appreciate your efforts? It's almost a whole day's worth of work (6 hours). As the gap widens between how people feel and how they want to feel, despair or resignation fills the gap. Is the energy of your organization frazzled or coherent?

Remember several pages ago, where we gave an example of "It Snowed" and we saw the various perceptions and reactions of different people? It is important to remember that we have control over this whole process we experience. Our perceptions and the underlying reactions we generate create a cascade of events either enhancing or limiting effectiveness. Perceptions generate thought and emotions, which result in measurable effects such as heart rate, hormonal balance, and immune strength. The physiological effects affect the neural circuits, which affect our perception. This is a feedback system. When we are in a bad mood, a distorted perception can generate negative thoughts and emotions, causing physiological imbalances in the heart, immune, and hormonal systems, that reinforce the negative cycle. This is why you will want to curb the Reptile Talk™ in the very beginning of the project. You don't want to go immediately into the Valley of Tears. Research has shown that the most successful people and teams are the ones that learn to manage their emotional reactiveness, neutralizing negative emotions and turn the situation from lemons to lemonade. That is why we put the creative vs. reactive charts in Chapter 4. With this understanding of the brain, those upcoming charts will add value to your team. Emotional intelligence can be taught and the human heart provides the place to start.

While people say it is important to put our hearts into our work, to have pride in what we do, or to speak our truths, the paradigm in corporate settings is that the heart is seen as a sign of weak, irrational, or emotional behavior, or of being too soft. While the heart is the vital controller of well-being, we have dismissed it by creating a corporate culture that believes emotions are inappropriate at work. Meanwhile, heart disease has become the number one killer in the world.

So now you can begin to see that emotion, not intellect, is the fuel that drives your company to success or not. Intellect provides the direction, but not the fuel. In most organizations, this distinction has not been activated, so the fuel used is hardly high octane, but more like kerosene. You are paying the price. How a company reacts to its employees and customers and how it prepares its people for change are bottom-line issues. Truly intelligent organizations understand this and are taking action to generate coherent emotional intelligence that unleashes the tremendous power reserve that lies waiting for a enlightened leader to give permission to make this part of "how we do business."

> *In the age of chaos, organizations rise and fall more due to the lack of management of emotions within a culture, than mere product success or process improvements.*
>
> —Daniel Goleman, *Emotional Intelligence*

REACTIONS OF EMPLOYEES TO A MANAGER'S REQUEST FOR CHANGE

When an employee hears a request to do something in a new way (change), their reaction is to become threatened and to think:

- "I must be doing something wrong."

- "I might get fired if they don't like the way I have been doing this."

- "I can't believe they are changing my job. I was good at that. What if I don't do this new thing well enough?"

The research shows that the primary reason that so few programs result in the expected results is that the consultants or managers *tell* them what they need to do differently versus spending the time to enroll and engage the employees in an interactive dialogue, where managers ask employees what they think. The telling is what puts people into the threatened mode. Being told traditionally does have a certain appeal. It seems easier when someone else, especially an expert, just gives us the answer. The problems come later when resistance develops and someone else's approach does not work for us. Asking versus telling is one of the keys to reducing the resistance to change.

Traditional Steps to Managing CRM Projects

The traditional methodology used for implementing CRM projects takes these steps:

1. Identify the problem

2. Bring in an expert

3. Tell people how to do their jobs differently and better from the way they have been doing them

4. Spend tremendous amounts of time, energy and money trying to
   a. Overcome the resistance caused by step 3
   b. Recover the decreased morale

Can it be any surprise that it takes companies 3 to 5 years to implement a new CRM system? Most of their time is spent on step 4—convincing resistant employees to try something new and making sure they follow through.

A trade magazine featured a glowing article about a beverage company that had spent hundreds of thousand of dollars with a respected consulting group to meticulously revamp the company's quality assurance program, including the CRM process. The article praised the company's leadership for being proactive in doing this. It also mentioned that after 18 months of changing most of the system, the consultant and managers were beginning to conduct sessions with employee groups to generate enthusiasm and commitment for the new programs. The consultants and executives expressed hope that by using slogans, banners, and meetings to motivate people, they would begin to embrace the new program within another year. The article did admit there was resistance from the employees and now they were trying to overcome that. They clearly saw the people part as a thing to deal with later.

What we consistently see is that it does not need to take 3 to 5 years or even 18 months to realize substantive, enduring results from CRM programs.

The long implementation time happens when the project begins with technology first and then deals with the people part later. Trying to fix the people problems late in a change process is like the antiquated and expensive method of fixing a bad product at the end of the manufacturing process. Dr. Petouhoff, once an engineer, remembers the days at a large automotive company before concurrent engineering. The engineers were working on changing a car design. All worked separately on their systems—the engine group, the transmission group, the chassis group—then after six months of designing, they all brought their parts into the chassis area to start fitting them together. Guess what? There was not enough room for the engine or the transmission to fit into the space designed for the engine compartment. All groups had to go back to the drawing board. Another six months was wasted because they had not talked to each other and worked as a team. Engineers don't traditionally like teaming or talking—they want to engineer—but when the people interaction of the engineering process of designing a new car is left out, it delays the schedule and increases scope and costs.

Only when a critical mass of the people have taken ownership and responsibility for the needed changes as a team can the organization assure a competitive advantage in today's very challenging marketplace. In *Enlightened Leadership*, Ed Oakley states that when change management dealt with the mindset of employees from the beginning they saw:

- A manufacturing firm went from 5 consecutive years of loss to a profitable quarter and the upturn has continued

- A company with an ugly history of union unrest turned months of negative profit-and-loss statements into record productivity within 60 days and ended the year with the highest profits in 28 years

Customers Are People, Too

Everything that we have learned about employees applies to customers. What customers want most is a real relationship with the companies whose products and services they buy. The customer's needs (Figure 1.12) are simple, but the corporate challenge and gaps in delivering this kind of one-to-one relationship are where the real skills of change agents are important to be able to deliver a customer experience that exceeds expectations (Figure 3.12). Figure 3.13 shows the many elements that are included in customer relationships, and also emphasizes the complexity of managing this important asset of your company.

In this book we will focus mainly on describing simple and cost-effective ways to measure and manage each relationship with the goal of discovering continuous improvement ideas as guided by the customers in each specific relationship, that is, being customer-driven. The typical customer relationship cycle includes at least the steps depicted in Figure 3.14.

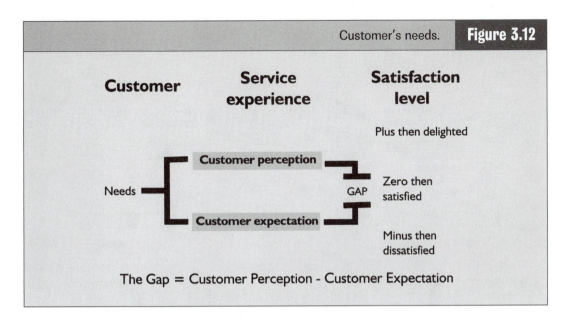

Customer's needs. **Figure 3.12**

The chain of events that leads to customer satisfaction begins with design decisions and runs through marketing, all of manufacturing and field sales, and culminates in after-sales support.

—John A. Young, the former CEO of Hewlett-Packard
at a high-tech conference (Clark 1993)

The question is, can you do that? Listening to customers and seeing their perspectives, providing reliable, excellent service, having the information

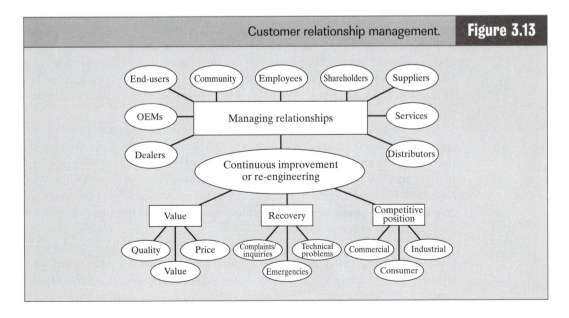

Customer relationship management. **Figure 3.13**

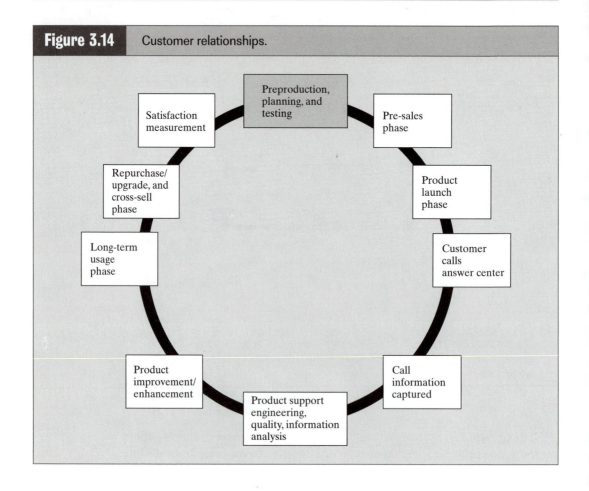

Figure 3.14   Customer relationships.

technology installed to make sure that the service strategy happens, being able to recover on the fly when you do make a mistake, delivering service above and beyond the expected, developing a spirit of teamwork, listening to employee perspectives, and having management that leads by example are all keys to success.

The customer relationship phases that should be measured and consequently managed to achieve success are shown in Figure 3.15. This shows the typical company as an integration of multifunctional, multidiscipline workgroups, each with a purpose and a product/service to provide to the customer. Figure 3.15 sets in motion our investigation of which processes are ripe for improvement or reengineering because of their importance and impact upon the external customer.

The steps of managing customer relationships, differentiating customers, defining expectations, and measuring quality all deal with effectiveness. They answer the question "Is the organization doing the right thing right for the customer?" When companies embark on improving an activ-

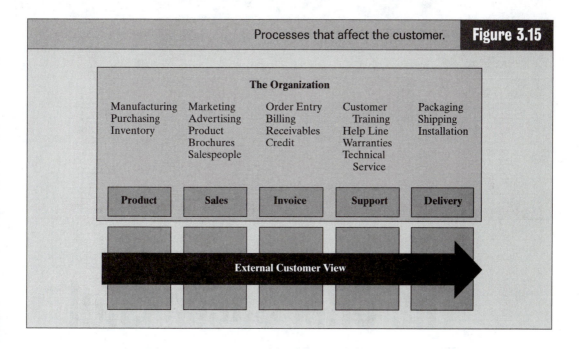

Figure 3.15 Processes that affect the customer.

The Organization

Manufacturing	Marketing	Order Entry	Customer	Packaging
Purchasing	Advertising	Billing	Training	Shipping
Inventory	Product	Receivables	Help Line	Installation
	Brochures	Credit	Warranties	
	Salespeople		Technical	
			Service	

Product	Sales	Invoice	Support	Delivery

External Customer View

ity, most look at changing how they do what they do (their processes). This is an area of great opportunity, but the wrong place to start.

A company can create a wonderfully efficient, error-free process but still produce something its customers don't want. The fact is that customers generally don't care how a company does its work. This focus on internal activity encourages producer-centered thinking. Starting with effectiveness is key, then followed by efficiency. In a later chapter, we provide a benchmarking case study that shows how this can be done.

The CRM Successful People Process™ (CRM SPP): The Key to Opening Up Employees to Change

PEOPLE ARE THE KEY TO IMPLEMENTING CRM CHANGE

Tom Peters shares two customer service stories about when bad things happen to good customer contact centers and the anger and anguish of real business owners at defects in products and services. Both companies were having problems with customer service and quality. After an influx of negative customer service calls, each company organized meetings to deal with the situation.

Company A

A company that made cabinets was having a high failure rate. Their approach to a problem was to analyze everything. How many doors fell off? What percentage of doors fell off? How much would it cost to stick 'em back on? What were the chances of getting sued? How much advertising would it take to counteract the bad publicity? Not once did they actually talk about the doors, the hinges, or why the doors fell off in the first place. It became clear that they were not interested in solving the problem; they just wanted to manage the mess.

Company B

Coleman Stove had some boilers that were cracking. The executive committee assembled, with the usual small talk. Then the service department came in with the reports, the clipboards, the yellow pencils, and everybody hunkered down for a service discussion. Well, you know how long that meeting lasted? About 30 seconds! Old man Coleman sat up right in his chair and exclaimed: "You mean we've got goods out there that aren't working? Get 'em back. Replace them and find out why." And that was the end of the meeting. There was no financial analysis. There was no legal analysis. There was no customer-relations analysis. There wasn't any analysis at all. The issue was the integrity of the product—which meant there was no issue at all. Their bottom line was, "We stand by what we make and that's that."

MAKING CHANGE HAPPEN

So for the manager of CRM the real question becomes: once people leave that room, how do we make that change happen? Saying, "Go fix it!" is easy and it's easy to want to accomplish the fix, but it can be hard to actually implement it. Why?

Fixing the situation means that people have to change what they were doing and do it differently. If you are not familiar with the human reaction to change, you might not understand why change doesn't happen. This part of the chapter is dedicated to helping you understand change, your employee's reaction to it, and why or why not the customer service might be getting better. It seems very simple that if you tell someone to do something, they should just do it, right? If it involves change, then it is probably not that simple and is a good reason why most managers get frustrated with their employees.

When change happens, whether it is at work or on a personal level, the normal human experience of change usually includes stress and discomfort, and if managed well can possibly include happiness and elation. In creating stretch goals or reengineering the current way of doing something, it means that we have to stretch ourselves beyond our current comfort zone to achieve this new level of performance. That ability to emotionally stretch must be included as part of the criteria in selection, hiring, and training customer service center employees.

In selection, one needs to assess candidates for flexibility and openness to change. In the training process, customer service center managers need to include and communicate the human dynamic issues that occur when change happens. Additionally, because customer service centers are such an integral part of a company's business, employees who embrace change and continue to provide excellent customer service need to be rewarded as part of the performance evaluation process. We'll look closer at how to assess these work style assets.

Getting people to do their job requires knowing who they are and how to address them without firing up their amygdala to respond with one of the 3-F responses. We will start by looking at what a change management program is and the details of dealing with change and people. The first place we'll look is at a process called the CRM Process (CRM SPP™) which gives managers the know-how in understanding their employees and how the employees deal with change, what drives employees to be productive, and how to assign tasks to employees. One of the biggest issues in a company is when key team members leave the company—along with them goes the brain trust. Attrition costs money. We'll go over how to calculate attrition in Chapter 9, but for now, know that it eats deeply into the company profits.

We'll also look at various types of leadership styles and which ones have the most success in projects. We also address the differences between reactive and proactive decision making as well as time management. All these factors are included because without a good understanding of them, they are what contribute to the inefficiency of people and thus the increased scope, budget, and implementation time of projects. Many managers' reactions to this can be, "I don't have time for all this people stuff. I've got a schedule and a budget and I have to get this CRM system up and running before the competition beats us to it. Otherwise, my boss will have my head." Here's the bottom line: Scope, budget, and implementation time are the very things that will slip if you don't do the people things. You really don't have a choice if you are being true to what you say you want to accomplish.

HOW TO DO CHANGE WELL: CHANGE MANAGEMENT

A change management program must include:

1. Gaining the support by management for the change management program, financially as well as in the timeline

2. Understanding who the stakeholders are and making sure they are all chosen to participate on the team

3. Profiling the readiness and capability of the employees to change the way they do their work

4. Creating a communication plan around the timeline and changes to the technology and workflow processes

5. Outlining the current processes that the technology supports and mapping the changes to the process that new technology would create

6. Creating an implementation plan and schedule to realistically transition legacy systems to the new system, running the old systems in parallel for a period of time to assure seamless transition

7. Creating a lessons-learned process, so that once the new system is running improvements and updates can easily be made and employees can be trained on the changes

Stakeholders and the Value the CRM SPP™ Brings

A stakeholder is any individual or group who has influence over the successful implementation of changes to the customer service center, such as informal and formal leaders who are directly involved in designing the new system, using the new system, or those who control human, organizational, or facilities resources needed to implement and maintain the system as well as the customer.

> *There is a consistency and predictability to the quality of behavior in the very best organizations.*
> —Margaret J. Wheatley, *Leadership and the New Science: Learning about Organization from An Orderly Universe*

Margaret makes very interesting observations about the workplace by comparing them to science. In the book just mentioned she goes on to say that, "Great organizations trust in the power of guiding principles or values, knowing that they are strong influencers of behavior to shape every employee into a desired representative of the organization. These organizations expect to see similar behaviors show up at every level in the organization."

Overall, the stakeholder profile and interview has two purposes. The first is to gain the information to make the business case for change. The second and less obvious purpose is to gain buy-in with the people who can give or decline support for the project. This is best accomplished by identifying, assessing, and responding to stakeholder issues. If the stakeholder feels as though you have their best interest in mind, they are more likely to support suggested changes down the road. If they do not feel heard, they can block the project altogether, even if the changes make good business sense. Assessment of the stakeholders and stakeholder issues is not a one-time event—it is necessary throughout the project's life cycle (see Figure 3.6). In addition, by periodically interviewing stakeholders it allows us to determine if responses to their issues are adequately addressed; if not, then a different approach can be tried. It also allows us to determine what new issues may have arisen.

When a project starts, everyone generally has a team meeting of all the people who might be involved in the project (stakeholders), including all the executives, managers, and employees who might participate. The purpose of this first meeting is to create a feeling of teaming and participation among the stakeholders, where all individuals are heard and acknowledged. If this takes place in the beginning, much less of the leader's time will be spent placating the people involved. One might spend some time outlining the vision, and then ask participants to come back with two lists. The first list entails their input to what a dream CRM system would look like. The second one is all the reasons why the company or they could not make the changes necessary. Those could include: budget, time, FTEs, management support, never done that here before, etc. In the next meeting collect those and we'll show you how to use them later. This list of "why it won't work here" is a way to manage the Reptile Talk™ constructively so the next meeting does not turn into a complaining session.

When you get down to it, implementing CRM means each and every person on the team needs a goal. And their action on the goal must lead to positive results. Evaluation time is usually the only time we look at whether people do the stuff that either accomplishes their goals or not. Many times when we start out assigning a goal, it seems like the employee is on board. It is only later when the rubber meets the road that we see whether they are or not by whether the goal gets accomplished. Accomplishing the goal depends on whether they are driven to follow through (values) and how they do it (work behavior).

Understanding How People Behave at Work: CRM SPP™, the Successful People Process™

We have found a way to achieve a high rate of return on your investment when kicking off a CRM project. In organizing and selecting a new CRM project team, start with engaging in a CRM Successful People Process (CRM SPP™) with each team member including key influencers on the project. The profiles that are part of the SPP are available online from *LMR Associates*, www.lmrassociates.com.

The ROI of the CRM Successful People Process™ training, when used with an online profile, is very easy. The SPP creates the opportunity to know others on the team (communication building) and identifies functional strengths to be used on the project. The CRM SPP™ targets *specific CRM project related* areas of improvement and highlights each individual's importance in creating a successful CRM project.

Remembering Figure 3.5, the sine-wave like curve presenting the level of emotional support for a project, we show how the CRM SPP™ can be used to reduce the depth of the Valley of Tears and move the curve to the left, shortening the time for CRM implementation (Figure 3.6).

As the project progresses, the results of the CRM SPP™ short training sessions reduce turnover, increase customer service, and secure the success of the implementation, thereby increasing profits and sales. The CRM SPP™ adds ongoing value to the culture of the company because once employees are exposed to this they keep using it. Thus, the return on investment can be in the 1000 percent range.

The Gallup Organization, in their book *First Break All the Rules*, details the important behavioral talents that are the key to organizational success. The data is based on in-depth interviews of over 80,000 managers in over 400 companies. Their findings show that those managers and colleagues who focused on turning each employee's behavioral talents into performance had the greatest productivity, job satisfaction, and retention. To transform the ideas from the Gallup book into action, employees and managers need the how to tools. Most managers read that book and then say, "Ok, that's not me, and I may want to consider being that, but I have no idea how to become that."

The key is to give managers a tool so that they can develop those characteristics. CRM SPP™ is the key to transforming work behavior of managers. CRM SPP™ training tailors information so that employees can reach business goals that impact the bottom line. In addition, a tool like this helps employees be more of who they already are, both professionally and personally. The resulting changes in the interactions with bosses and co-workers, managing up, laterally, and managing down, are phenomenal.

When employees are not happy, especially in a good economy, they vote with their feet. From an article in *USA Today*, June 2000, on the heels of an announcement of a beverage company adding perks to refresh workers:

> Once again it amazes us that management just does not get it. Adding another holiday or giving employees Friday afternoons off will not satisfy what workers truly are yearning for. Employees are people and people want to be cared for. They want to be recognized for a job well done, encouraged to take risks, and guided when they are not sure of themselves. People leave companies because they do not get the attention they need from managers. Until companies understand that they are only as good as the people in management positions, they will continue to experience turnover. Employees leave bosses, not companies!

Dr. Petouhoff's experience at a defense company revealed that one of the employee's main complaints and causes for attrition was that the department managers were not "people" people. Most managers were engineers who got promoted into managing people. The two animals are very different. They attended meetings, did paper work, and occasionally talked to their employees around appraisal time. That is how they saw their job and how many managers of people understand the job requirements of management.

One of the suggestions to stop the outflux of the engineering brain trust was to hire one manager as the technical, meeting-going person and another to manage the people part. While this was a good idea in theory, most managers, even with MBAs, have never been schooled on motivating the human capital asset. It may not be that they did not want to do it or do it well, they just had no idea *what* exactly they were supposed to do. And when many of them tried, they felt they made it worse, they became discouraged, and started avoiding it. It became very clear that one of the most important skills in a manager must be the ability to motivate the human capital asset. This is another reason why the CRM SPP™ is so important. Without a concrete tool to help managers understand who the employee is, they can shut down motivation and decrease morale without even knowing it.

When using profiles in the CRM SPP™, it is important that people do not feel they are being tested, scored, or evaluated, but rather that they'll gain an understanding of their unique talents. There are no right or wrong answers. Each person needs to see him- or herself as special and perfect. The ability of each person to see his or her value is the ability to which they can see the value of others. Their ability to appreciate others increases as does the success of the project and the company.

When Dr. Petouhoff uses the CRM SPP™, which comes with about a 35-page detailed profile for each individual, she uses unique techniques to relieve the team of post-profile jitters. She also employs various techniques to defuse what she calls Reptile Moments™ where participants become self-critical in the training process.

The CRM Work Style Profile allows employees to analyze not only what behavior they bring to the job but also the behavior required to be successful in that job and on a team. This increase in emotional intelligence will serve them the rest of their career and life. Companies even create their own language and culture around the profiles, increasing their everyday use and effectiveness.

Benefits to an employee or manager of understanding the profile are that one can take control of their decisions and:

- Increase the value of life, satisfaction, and fulfillment

- Develop an increased appreciation for the uniqueness of others

- Understand the causes of conflict in communicating with others

- Enhance communication with others so they are understood

- Enhance communication with others so you are able to understand them

- Reduce misunderstandings and conflicts

- Increase the enjoyment of working in a team

Common examples of behavior are:

- How we show up in a meeting or a conversation

- How we solve a problem

- How long it takes us to do a task

- How we react to change

- How we respond to rules and procedures

- How we interact with others

Under Natalie's guidance using the Successful People Process™ we transformed not only our work dynamics and bottom-line results, but we all became better people.

—Paul Rassumon, Director of IT, Universal Studios

Just the Facts: The Tools and Their Validity

There are a number of tools on the market today that profile individuals according to various measurements. The most effective profiling tools we have found contain detailed information in a report format on one's behavioral talents for handling decisions, interacting with people, handling pace (change), and the view on procedures (rules). This profile is based on the DISC behavior model, which has been in existence in various forms since 400 B.C. Dr. William Marston was a pioneer in the history of the DISC language. In 1921, C. G. Jung spoke of four types of psychological functions: thinking, feeling, sensation, and intuition. He divided types into "introverted" and "extroverted." In 1928, Dr. William Marston took this one step further. He was educated at Harvard University with an A.B. in 1915, an LL.B in 1918, and a Ph.D in 1921. He published a book, *The Emotions of Normal People*, upon which the DISC language was founded.

The profile provides information on natural and adapted behavioral work styles. "Natural" refers to how someone would be when they are hanging out at home, watching TV, and eating popcorn. The adapted style is how they shift the way they are "being" when they come into a different environment from home; work, sports, and so forth. This information will help you to easily identify behavioral styles in yourself and others. It allows you to adapt your style to increase communication and effectiveness. It eliminates guesswork in understanding why people do what they do to help you gain a strategic advantage in understanding customers, co-workers, and even family behavior.

What we want to emphasize: "This is not soft stuff." Marston spent years doing research on his theories at Harvard University. He studied the reaction of people to different kinds of situations by hooking up electrodes to monitor their brain response. From this scientific approach he created a behavior theory that when applied in the workplace reduces the resistance to change and creates a very synergistic workplace geared to productivity and results.

For those who are still skeptical or want to know more about the validity of the results, we included some information from *Statistical Comparison Between Style Analysis and the Performax Personal Profile System* by Dr. Russell J. Watson, Wheaton College, 1998. This test was performed to determine:

- Test/Retest—stability of scores over time

- Specific Validity—extent instrument measures a specific trait

- Content Validity—how well instrument measures what is intended

- Predictive Validity—ability to predict performance on another activity

- Comparison Validity—relationship of style analysis to other tests

Using Spearman-Brown "split-halves reliability coefficient," reliability estimates, r, (reliability) are:

- Dominance: r = .92

- Influence: r = .89

- Steadiness: r = .91

- Compliance: r = .90

THE PROFILE PART I: WHAT THE CRM SSP PROFILE MEANS

The graph in Figure 4.1 outlines the various aspects of the profile. Employees come with various styles of behavior. Quality organizations know how to treat and deal with each style of behavior. Successful leaders adapt their style of communication to the behavioral style of their employee or manager. Employees adapt to each other and to their bosses. Often we fail to understand the behavioral styles of others and how they view the world. We tend to react to others based on our own behavioral style.

The success of any communication depends not so much on the actual words conveyed but on whether or not they're really heard and understood. Are you communicating in a style that coincides with the frequency your colleagues are tuned into? If not, you're in for lots of static and probably some trouble—even if the ideas you are trying to tell your employees are right on, and even if employees seem to be agreeing. They may be saying "yes" but internally shaking their heads "no."

We consulted with a CRM call center outsourcer who profiled their customers and realized that they were not selling to them in a way that opened a window to communication and therefore more sales. After profiling the customers, and adapting the way they approach their customers, sales skyrocketed. We suggest that you use these profiles to understand your customer better, also.

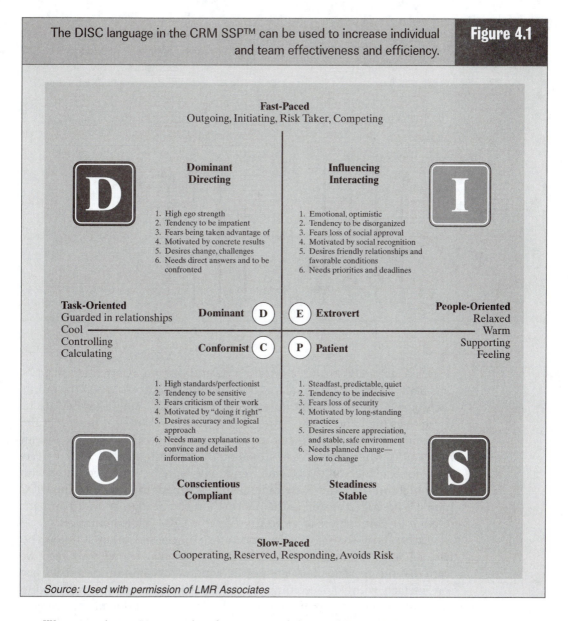

The DISC language in the CRM SSP™ can be used to increase individual and team effectiveness and efficiency.

Figure 4.1

Source: Used with permission of LMR Associates

We wanted to give you a brief overview of the profiles and then give a couple of examples of how this can be used in CRM projects. There are four factors that are measured:

D is for how someone faces challenges (dominating and directing)

I is for how someone interacts with people (influencing and interacting)

S is for how they adapt to change (steadiness and stable)

C is for how much they enjoy rules and procedures (conscientious and compliant)

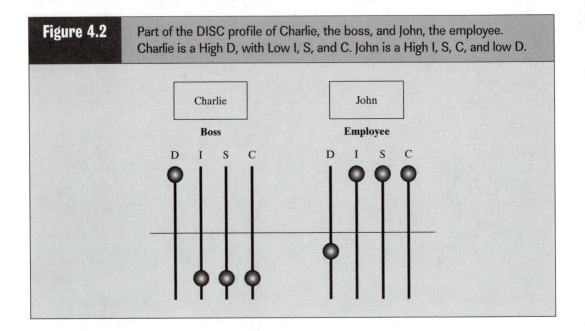

Figure 4.2 Part of the DISC profile of Charlie, the boss, and John, the employee. Charlie is a High D, with Low I, S, and C. John is a High I, S, C, and low D.

Each factor constitutes a certain style and they are referred to as D, I, S, or C Style. These are the graphs of how they adapt at work. When the points occur above the horizontal line, Figure 4.2, in DISC language they are referred to as high and below it are referred to as low. However, the use of the words high and low here is not meant to connote good or bad; it is just an indicator of where that person scored on the continuum of each factor. People who score high on the D and C tend to be more task-oriented; those who score high on the I and S are more people-oriented. Each style in the DISC profile is described as well as the information you need to know if you want to get your point across to a certain style in a CRM implementation.

Each person, through the "nature-nurture" process, develops a unique behavioral design. From Thomas Ritt's book *Understanding Yourself and Others*, we learn that this behavioral design is one's "window" of communication. If a person interacts with you according to your behavioral design, you will tend to open the "window of communication." If a person intentionally or unintentionally interacts with you against your behavioral design, you will tend to partially close, close, or LOCK the "window of communication." When employees and managers are aware of those behavioral styles and talents, they have the power and knowledge to modify their behavior for a maximum effect.

We know from our classes in communication that most of the message does not come from words, although people spend most of their time in preparation there. One's behavioral talents can be adapted to others and ways to adapt them are given below, from the least to the most effective means of communication:

- The words used (7%)

- Tone of voice (38%)

- Body language (55%)

Words only comprise 7 percent of communication, so if you want to be effective when you are talking to someone, using a particular tone of voice will increase your successfulness. You might look at whether your voice is warm, soft, loud, strong, clear. Do you speak in a controlled and direct manner or are you enthusiastic? Different styles like to be talked to in different ways. Next you might look at your body language. This means your eye contact, gestures, head nodding, and posture. A manager that is looking over at their computer or watching who is walking by their office and not looking at the employee doesn't communicate strong listening skills. If you do things the same poor way, you can expect the same poor results.

THE CHARACTERISTICS OF EACH STYLE IN A PROFILE

High D Style

The high D or demanding employee or manager wants it now with no hassles and doesn't care about the details. They are quick to anger, but don't stay mad. Their response to conflict is to fight. They expect you to stand up for yourself and want you to show them if they are wrong. However, many times their bark is so loud that others become scared to express their opinion. They like win-win, result-oriented, bullet points without the long story about what happened and why (18% of the population).

Recognizing a High D Style

Since D style people perceive themselves as being the center of the universe, they tend to take up a lot of room. Ever notice someone sitting at a table with their arms stretched across the chair next to them? That's a D style of behavior. Their walk is often brisk and bold, clearing away anything in their path. If a D style is walking toward you on a mission, move out of the way or expect to be bumped aside. To D style people, their mission or issue-of-the-moment is the only thing that counts. At least in their minds, Ds tend to stand with their weight on the forward foot ready to spring into action. Famous examples of High D styles are Rush Limbaugh, Murphy Brown, Barbara Walters, and Michael Jordan. Magazines of interest to High Ds would be about mountain climbing, marathon running, or something fast and easy to read like *One Minute Manager!* books.

Your Body Language for the High D Style

If you are meeting with a high D person, greet them with a strong handshake. Maintain direct eye contact with them, lean slightly forward in your stance while keeping your distance. D styles don't want to deal with weak people.

They want to deal with strong, confident individuals who know what they're talking about. So provide that perception by how you look and act.

Speaking with a D Style

As you can guess, you will only succeed in speaking with a D style if you are direct and to the point. Your tone of voice must be strong, clear, confident, and direct. Your pace should be fast—give your impatient D the impression that you are quickly heading toward results. The same goes for your actions. Look like you're making something happen, like you're taking definitive action on the important D's behalf.

Words and Phrases to Successfully Communicate with D Styles Include:

Fast	Benefits
Immediate	Bottom line
Now	Leaders in the field
Today	Win
New	Make it happen
Let's do it	Results
Unique	

Dos and Don'ts of Communicating with a D Style:

Dos	**Don'ts**
Be clear, specific, to the point.	Ramble, waste their time.
Be prepared and organized.	Look disorganized, lose things.
Stick to business.	Chitchat, gossip idly.
Present facts logically.	Cloud issues, leave loopholes.
Ask specific (what?) questions.	Ask rhetorical, useless questions.
Take issue with facts only.	Personalize issues.
Provide win/win solution.	Force D into losing situation.
Provide choice of options.	Make decision for them.

High I Style

The high I or influential employee or manager wants to talk about their problems, be accepted, and stay happy. They are very trusting and optimistic. Their response to conflict is to avoid or flee it. When you go to speak to them, they like time for socialization, like to be asked about their feelings and opinions, love to brainstorm, and are motivated by recognition and rewards. They like change and are exhilarated by new ideas (28% of the population).

The I style employee is the person who needs and wants to talk. He has a need for interaction with people and social recognition. Therefore, he will be optimistic, inspiring, persuasive, and trusting in his approach to you. He often speaks with enthusiasm, has a smile on his face, and is hoping for the same from you. They want their problems resolved, but want to have them resolved by people who are friendly toward them. The I style employee isn't a big fan of voice mail since it eliminates the element of human interaction. With this type of employee, relationships are extremely important.

Recognizing an I Style Employee

Based on our perception of how they act in public, examples of I style dominant personalities might include: Bill Clinton, Robin Williams, Oprah Winfrey, Steve Martin, Rosie O'Donnell, and Bette Midler. I style employees tend to smile and talk a lot. As with Ds, appearance is everything, especially physical appearance. They like to wear designer label clothes and jewelry that signify social affiliation. I style employees are into people-related products and would read magazines like *People, Success,* and *Psychology Today.* They appreciate funny cards and collect memorabilia from friends. They appreciate a happening, contemporary atmosphere.

You can spot an I style very easily. They are the ones who stop to talk with everyone and look at everything on their way to the restroom. They might bump into you only because they were paying attention to other things or people. The I style customer is often late. Bill Clinton had to work on his inability to keep his schedule on time in the early years of his presidency. As an I, he was always talking to people and was never on time. I style employees also tend to get off the subject and talk about things irrelevant to the problem at hand, not because they're ditzy, but because they just love the interaction more than the subject. On the phone, the I style will be bubbly, enthusiastic, and engaging.

Your Body Language for the I Style

If you are meeting the I style in person, remember that they respond well to expressive gestures. You need to smile at them and either stand or sit next to them to provide an atmosphere of acceptance. Close is fine with I people; they like you and want you to feel close to them. On the phone, you definitely want to smile when you speak with an I. Your smile will come through in the words you use and your tone. Remember, I style customers are oriented and driven to people and relationships.

Speaking with an I Style

Since I styles are expressive, you need to be expressive and animated in return. That's how you get their attention. Your tone of voice should be energized, enthusiastic, friendly, persuasive, and filled with high and low modulations. You should also sound colorful. I styles love images and word pictures. Your pace should be fast and animated. Your actions should be fast and filled with gestures. These behaviors communicate the aliveness that I styles want to experience.

Words and Phrases to Successfully Communicate with I Styles Include:

Fun	Recognition
I feel	Exciting
You'll look great	The latest thing
Put you in the spotlight	Wonderful
State-of-the-art	Awesome
Everybody	Fantastic
Picture this	

Dos and Don'ts of Communicating with an I Style:

Dos	**Don'ts**
Allow them to discuss dreams.	Legislate or muffle actions.
Allow time for socializing/relating.	Be curt/tight lipped.
Talk about people/their goals.	Concentrate on facts/figures.
Ask for their opinion.	Be impersonal.
Provide ideas.	Talk slowly.
Put details in writing.	Leave decisions up in the air.
Be stimulating, fun, fast moving.	Be too businesslike.
Provide testimonials.	Talk down to them.
Offer immediate incentives for taking risks.	Get trapped and spend too much time.

The High S Style

The high S or steady employee or manager wants to keep things as is, and if change is necessary, he wants to be assured that your solution is logical and will work. They don't express their emotions in their facial expressions, so it can look like they are not upset, but they have as many emotions as the rest of us; they just don't let them show. This can be misinterpreted as cold or unfeeling, when it is just their behavioral makeup. Their response to conflict is to say nothing and to tolerate it. They are like the rock of Gibraltar, steady and solidly grounded. Because they don't like change, they will resist it unless you have engaged and enrolled them into seeing the value of making the change. Without this step they can sabotage change because they feel you did not consider their feelings. In speaking to them, be very patient, draw out their opinions, show how the change will benefit them, and involve them in the planning (40% of the population).

The S style is an accommodating individual. This is the person who, when he is inconvenienced by your work, will make sure he doesn't upset you with his complaint. The S style is patient, relaxed, logical, and systematic. He is adverse to change since he doesn't want anything to upset his process. In working with an S style, it's important to keep this need for stability. If your solution requires a great deal of change on the part of them, you are in trouble, especially if you don't soften the perceived impact of the requested changes. S styles need to be secure in the fact that the solution is going to work and bring closure to the issue.

The S style is a person who works hard to finish a great amount of work, even taking on the work of others. In fact, when you are working with an S style, they may not be the end user but rather someone taking care of the problem for someone else.

Recognizing an S Style

Based on our perception of how they act in public, examples of S style dominant personalities might include: Mother Teresa, Gandhi, Barbara Bush, Walter Payton, Tom Brokaw, and Kevin Costner. Since S styles are loyal and service oriented, they are likely to dress with clothing emblazoned with their employer's logo, and jewelry they received for years of service to their company. They are casual in nature and dress modestly. They like to come back to familiar, reliable places. The moment an S style buys from you, you could have them for life unless you screw up or forget to meet their emotional needs and wants.

Your Body Language for the S Style

If you meet with an S style in person, you will find them to be relaxed in nature and weary of change. You should lean back when standing in front of them and don't rush with your actions. You should appear to be relaxed and not too close for comfort. Use small hand gestures and maintain an atmosphere of calm.

Speaking with an S Style

To facilitate a calm atmosphere, your tone of voice should be warm, soft, calm, and steady. Your volume should be on the low side. Your rate of speech should be relaxed and thoughtful. Your actions should be well paced and relaxed. Think of a baby. If you do something unexpected out of the blue, or suddenly move with a jerky motion, you'll startle and frighten the baby. The same holds true for S styles. We aren't saying S styles are babies. What we are saying is that you can most effectively communicate with them when it's with the same tender and calm manner as you would use with a baby.

Words and Phrases to Successfully Communicate with S Styles Include:

Think about it	Comfort
Take your time	Assure
Trust	You can expect
Guarantee	Conservative
Promise	Certain
Security	Here's what's going to happen
Reliable	Step-by-step instructions

Dos and Don'ts of Communicating with an S Style:

Dos	**Don'ts**
Start with personal comments.	Rush right into business.
Show sincere interest in them.	Stick coldly to facts.
Listen patiently and be responsive.	Force a quick response.
Present your solution logically, softly, and non threateningly.	Threaten or demand.
	Be abrupt and fast.
Ask specific (how?) questions.	Interrupt them.
Avoid hurting their feelings.	Mistake their acceptance of your solution for satisfaction.
Provide personal assurance and deliver.	Promise anything you can't guarantee.
Give them time to think.	Force a quick decision.

High C Style

The high C or compliant employee or manager wants as much detail as possible in order to make a decision and wants to be sure that everything is working according to specification. Their response to conflict is to avoid it. They tend to be concerned with making mistakes, so they don't like to change things or the way they are doing things. When speaking to them, use data and facts, keep on task, don't spend a lot of time socializing, if you disagree, make sure you are disagreeing with the facts and not the person, allow them time to think it over, and avoid new solutions—show them how this is similar to the proven method of doing things (14% of the population).

The C style is your everyday perfectionist. She wants it precise, orderly, and accurate. She is meticulous by nature and diplomatic in behavior. If you are going to satisfy a C style, you'd better be armed with all the facts, figures, and supporting data you can get your hands on. They want all the

Ts crossed and Is dotted before they will accept your ideas. C styles are stick-lers for following rules. If you deviate in any way from your policy or the law, they will let you know. While you may be thanking someone above for only giving this trait to 14 percent of the population, the C plays a pivotal role in keeping the world working with some measure of precision and in keeping all of us honest. If you're trying to cut corners, forget it. The C style will spot you a mile away blindfolded.

Recognizing a C Style

Based on our perception of how they act in public, examples of C style domi-nant personalities might include: Ted Koppel, Jack Nicklaus, Clint Eastwood, Diane Sawyer, and Spike Lee. C styles are great poker players. They always have the same look and you never know what's going on in their minds. They are conservative in nature, as exhibited by their clothing, which is often of good quality. Their jewelry symbolizes professional affiliation and is the "real thing." They love do-it-yourself projects. In fact, they always will ask you questions concerning how they can do it. They love to decorate their offices with charts and graphs. The magazines they want to read in your wait-ing room include *Consumer Reports, Discover,* and technical journals.

The C style will reluctantly move out of the way of an object in his path, at the last possible moment and only after having theorized, strategized, and analyzed numerous possible solutions on how to overcome the obstacle. When they finally stand aside, they're likely to have their arms crossed with one hand resting on the chin as in a thinking position. They are always thinking. C style's sense of humor, when you can find it, is dry wit. Do not expect them to say anything unless they're convinced you have the right so-lution or they are annoyed. Especially on the phone. Forget about engaging them in casual conversation. It won't work. They called for information or a solution. Anything else is a silly waste of time, even downright irritating.

Your Body Language for the C Style

If you talk with a C style in person, don't touch or get too close to him or her. Sit or stand across from them where they can see you. If standing, stand firmly with your weight planted on the back foot. Maintain direct eye con-tact and use little or no hand gestures. Remember, these are extremely ana-lytical people, some to the degree you might consider as being suspicious. Do nothing to suggest you're trying to avoid them or take advantage of them.

Speaking with a C Style

C styles are wary of what you have to say. Therefore, you must keep your tone of voice controlled at all times with little modulation. They are suspi-cious of hype style responses. You must be direct and precise in what you have to say. Your pace should be slow and thoughtful. Your words, vocal tone, and pacing all should convey: Here are the facts you need to get what you want. Nothing more.

Your actions should be slow and deliberate. C styles fit two old sayings, "just the facts ma'am," and, "nice and easy."

Words and Phrases to Successfully Communicate with C Styles Include:

Proven/proof	No obligation
Guarantees	Here are the facts
No risk	Information
Research (or data) shows	Analysis
Take your time	Think it over
Supporting data and analyze	

Dos and Don'ts of Communicating with a C Style:

Dos	**Don'ts**
Be prepared.	Be disorganized or messy.
Be straightforward and direct.	Be casual, informal, or personal.
Look at all sides of an issue.	Force a quick decision.
Present specifics of what you can do.	Be vague and not follow through.
Create time line and measurements.	Overpromise.
Take your time, be persistent.	Be abrupt and fast.
Use data and facts from respected people.	Use emotions or feelings.
	Close too hard.
Give time to make a decision.	Touch them.
Give them space.	

WHAT'S YOUR STYLE?

Besides identifying the behavioral style of your colleagues, it's important to recognize your own behavioral style. Only then will you know how to temper your approach as you deal with the different styles. While the system seems pretty simple, we have seen people become junior psychologists and try to analyze others. We don't recommend this, because people make mistakes in their analysis and then in their behavior towards that person. The best way to find out your style is to do an online profile.

The most comprehensive profiling system we have found for implementing change on CRM projects is an online version used by LMR Associates found at www.lmrassociates.com. It is tailored to specifically help organizations deal with change and team building. The participant logs onto the site and with 15 minutes of answering some easy questions, an approximately 35-page detailed profile is e-mailed back to the participant in minutes. When combined with the Successful People Process used by LMR Associates, the participant learns how to apply the results to a CRM project.

The profile contains information such as:

- General characteristics about your work style and behavioral talents

- Your value to the organization

- A checklist for interacting with others

- "Don'ts" for managers and others when they communicate with your style

- Your ideal work environment

- A planning page for goal setting

We suggest that at the beginning of any project you ask everyone on the team what one thing they would like to work on for themselves (flex from their natural style) and then provide them with opportunities to develop themselves. The planning page is great for this. This way they will enjoy the project more because they are growing and they will feel that you really care about them. In one case Dr. Petouhoff asked this question. One team member wanted to increase her ability to do more detailed work (raising her C) so we gave her the task of keeping the Microsoft project schedule. Another one wanted to bring his I up and so we gave him the opportunity to lead meetings and give presentations.

Each person has a unique blueprint for how they score on the range of attributes for each factor. Again there is not bad or good, it just is who we are. All of us, to one degree or another, have some elements of four different styles in our personality. An individual's uniqueness comes through in his or her distinct mix of behavior. At the same time, all of us are dominant in one behavior style. By dominant we mean that people prefer to behave more in keeping with one style than the others. We all give clues about our dominant style by how we walk, talk, and generally behave.

ADAPTING YOUR WORK STYLE USING YOUR PROFILE

If you are a demanding style, you may need to calm down and be more patient with people, especially those who are S and C styles.

If you are of an I style nature, you may talk too much when it comes to dealing with Ds. And don't forget, Cs don't want to have idle chatter with you, and Ss are looking for security, not social recognition like you.

If you are an S style individual, you must be prepared to change your way of communicating to be heard by the other styles. While you are slow in your pace of speech and low in volume, Is and Ds want you to pick things up, both in speed and volume. They want you to move faster than you are prepared to move. And while you are steady in nature and look for guarantees, the C styles want no risk at all in employing your solutions.

If you are a C style person, show others some emotion. The Is want relationships and smiles. The Ds want decisions and action. The Ss want a stable, relaxed atmosphere with friendly faces all around them.

Hopefully by now you have an appreciation of how better to communicate effectively with others. To ensure you are communicating properly with your employees, focus more on their words, actions, and body language. Think less about your situation. The more attention you pay to your employee, the better both of you are going to feel, and the more effectively you will serve them. By tuning into your employees' individual behavior styles, you will gain a deeper appreciation for and understanding of them and their problems. They in turn will want to listen to you since you will be communicating with them on their frequency. Your interactions will be personal, pleasing, and memorable. And that's what it's all about.

A PROFILE AS APPLIED TO A CRM PROJECT

In Figure 4.3, you can see two graphical results of the profile of a boss and employee. Now let's look at the example of the boss and the employee. When we look at the two profiles we can see they are opposite. That they are opposite can be the reason the team succeeds—it needs that kind of diversity as each profile contributes to the team differently and all are necessary. In the same vein, the differences in style can also be what creates conflict between two people or within a team.

Let's say the boss, Charlie, who is a high D, gives the employee, John, (a low D) an assignment to research all the various vendors of CRMs. Charlie's expectations, based on his work style, are:

1. The work will be done quickly (high D)

2. The employee will provide a bulleted, short presentation with a few facts (high D)

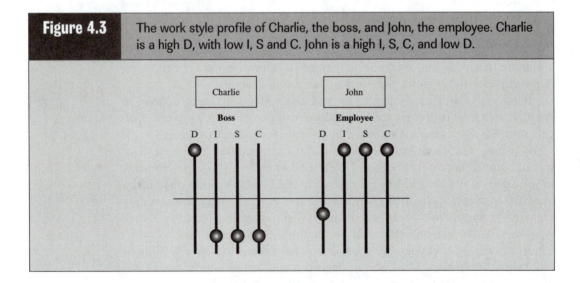

Figure 4.3 The work style profile of Charlie, the boss, and John, the employee. Charlie is a high D, with low I, S and C. John is a high I, S, C, and low D.

3. The solutions will be very out-of-the-box, with the latest and most outrageous (low C)

4. They won't talk very much in the meeting or tell the story about how they talked to this vendor and they said . . . (low I)

Several weeks go by, and Charlie is wondering where the report is. He gave it to John 3 weeks ago; he could have done it faster himself. He marches into John's office in a huff and demands the report. John being a high I, wants some socialization time before he jumps into explanation, and is startled to see the boss in a huff. John begins to tell Charlie the long tale of contacting the vendors, getting the brochures and reading them, and how, when he took them home to read after work, their dog got hold of some of them and they ended up in the pool, so he had to order some more and then it took him awhile to go through all the details and understand them. And that he looked for very stable solid technology; none of that new-fangled stuff.

John can see that Charlie is turning redder and redder and getting madder by the minute and can't understand why, so he figures, "I know, I will pull out the four three-ring binders full of information I prepared and hand that to him. That will impress him!" As John pulls out the binders, Charlie storms out of the room. John feels hurt, underappreciated and de-motivated. He thinks, "Why bother working so hard for Charlie; he is never happy with anything I do." And Charlie thinks, "Why don't employees just do what I ask them? I will go ask Georgia. She'll do what I want." Georgia has the same work style profile as Charlie. What Charlie does not see however, is that since Georgia is a high D she won't be as thorough and they might end up missing the vendor they really need.

So, on a behavioral level, what happened there? If John and Charlie had understood each other's work style behavioral profiles John would have never:

- Taken so long to get Charlie an initial review (Charlie's high D and low S like things fast)

- Given him four binders of data (Charlie's high D just wants a short synopsis)

- Have told Charlie the long story about how he did his work and the dog drama (Charlie's low I and high D do not want to make small talk and want to get straight to the point)

- Would have included some vendors that had the latest in technology even if they had not been in the marketplace a long time (Charlie's low C would want an out-of-the-box solution to stay ahead of the competition)

John's expectations, based on his work style, are:

- The work will be done slowly as he gathers all his teammates' opinions (John's low D)

- That Charlie would want all four three-ring binders (John's high C)

- The solutions will be very conservative and proven (John's high S)

- That Charlie would be impressed with all the work John did and how he took it home after work so he told him all the details he went through in the last three weeks (John's high I)

You can begin to see with one example how not understanding each other's behavior styles can create conflict, slow down work and productivity, and increase the schedule and the budget. And you can also see how if John or Charlie adapted their styles to the person they were working with, they could have resolved the issue quickly and without getting mad at each other.

The Profile Part II: Personal Values Profiles (PVP)

Consciously or unconsciously, every decision or course of action is based on our experiences, beliefs, attitudes, and values. For example, the willingness to make tough decisions or take the time to achieve a difficult goal is based on what we feel is valuable. Values direct our actions and offer stimuli for behavior. Values provide the initiative for the diligent pursuit of a goal or vision. As we learn what truly motivates us, we will have far greater insight into why our work is satisfying, why we are top performers, and why we are thriving.

Values represent the *why* behind what we do. For example, if an employee is participating in a discussion, activity, or career that is in line with their attitudes, they will find value in that experience. But if that discussion, activity, or career is not in line with their values, the result can be indifference or even negativity toward the experience or the person, causing stress, boredom, frustration, etc.

This second part of the profile helps to understand the whys behind your employees' actions:

- What is it that causes them to move to action?

- What are the drivers of their behavior?

- What activities, careers, and conversations inspire their passions?

In the values profile there are six factors:

Theoretical: motivated by knowledge and learning

Utilitarian: motivated when there is a large return on the investment of time or money

Aesthetic: motivated by the beauty; form over function

Social: motivated by helping others

Individualistic: motivated by being in power, in a high position, with authority

Traditional: motivated by ritual, connections to tradition, fighting for a cause for the ideal

So let's say that you have a better handle on your employee's work styles, which tells you how they do their work. Now, with the values profile, you can determine what drives them to do it. If you know this you can motivate them with little effort, and they will be happy because the assignment is in line with their natural motivators. To explain this further, let's look at some of the players' positions on a football team.

What They Like or Value	Good Assignment	Bad Assignment
Throw the ball, get touchdowns	Quarterback	Kicker
Run with the ball	Running back	Defensive end
Crush the other team	Defensive end	Quarterback
Kick the ball	Kicker	Crush the other team

The same goes for employees on a team. When they have an assignment and they don't perform well, they might not know why without the profile. They might think they are stupid or slow or they just can't get motivated, so they force themselves and end up providing poor results. When employees know what motivates them, they won't have internal conflicts and will produce the best results you will ever see out of them. For instance:

What They Like or Value	Good Assignment	Bad Assignment
Learn new things (Theoretical)	Research vendors	Order nice call center seats (Aesthetic)
Help others learn (Social)	Train employees	Research vendors (Theoretical)
Calculate the ROI of the new system (Utilitarian)	Take care of the budget	Train employees (Social)
Lead others (Individualistic)	Team leader	Calculate the ROI (Utilitarian)

The Power of Communication

Ask yourself: Why is it important to learn how you influence people or approach problems? LMR Associates, who has been in the business of training and developing professionals in *Fortune* 500 companies and organizations especially in the area of customer relationship management for over the past 12 years, believes that:

Power is the ability to create a desired effect. Creating desired effects is performance. Performance is maximized when communication is clear and understood.

—Lana M. Ruffins, president, LMR Associates, behavioral analyst and corporate trainer

Conversations in organizations are not just to achieve understanding or agreement on an intellectual level. They are to be in union, both intellectually and emotionally, to accomplish a specific set of actions. Enhanced communication skills allow employees to focus on a core of interpersonal skills to help them reach their individual and team goals. Effectiveness can be improved by having the skills to move others from initial indifference to moderate interest to the full, wholehearted commitment to move to action. The CRM SPP™ is the methodology for developing effective change skills in employees.

Using the CRM SPP™ facilitates specific tasks in CRM team building. When used with CRM teams, selecting people based upon specific profiles is more accurate than blindly assigning tasks to volunteers. An example of selecting the team members means looking at who would be natural advocates for change. As we know, part of the increased cost of CRM can be integrating new systems with legacy databases. Remember back to an example we gave in Chapter 2 where the IT department was describing their issues with the HR department and the communication broke down? Management (high D) did not want to replace everything they had, but then they ran into problems trying to find pieces for the web and email that could hook together and into the old payroll system.

In some ways it would have been better to replace the old payroll system than patch it together with code, but we were under a demanding time schedule, and the payroll department did not want to reinvent themselves: typical HR—high S and C people—S (slow to change) and C (rules—they follow them and can't see anything else).

If the IT department had done the CRM SPP™, they would have understood who they were talking to (HR), their styles, and how to present their idea so that it would not create so much pushback.

Lasting changes don't happen by official pronouncements. Change takes place slowly inside each of us by the choices we contemplate in the quiet, wakeful moments in the early dawn.

—Peter Block, *The Empowered Manager*

Uses of the Profiles

- Dealing with change
- Sexual harassment and diversity awareness
- Customer service
- Sales
- Enhance communication
- Getting peers to understand what you need them to do
- Managing up
- Coaching employees to solve performance issues
- Improving employee-manager relationships
- Selection/Recruiting (competency identification)
- Team building
- Telemarketing
- Career planning

- Skill gap and competency building
- Conflict resolution
- Goal setting
- Layoffs, outplacement
- Executive development
- Coaching employees
- Performance evaluations
- New manager/supervisor/ team leader development
- Presentation skills
- 360 degree feedback
- Strategic and tactical planning
- Return-on-investment for development

Example Business Problems the Profiles Can Solve

Type of Profile	Business Issues It Addresses
1. Employee-Manager	Improve productivity, reduce conflict
2. Personal values	What drives the passion in an employee
3. Customer service	Increase customer satisfaction
4. Sales	Increase execution of all steps in sales process
5. Time management	More efficient use of time and cost savings
6. Executives	Create a more competitive company
7. Team building	Turns groups into high performance teams
8. Interviewing	Hire the right people
9. Job competency	Competency building

Stakeholders' Work Styles—Reactive or Proactive: Which Are You?

The nature of a CRM project is about change and the success of it requires a proactive thinking style. With the information we have from the profile let's take a look at proactive and reactive behavior toward change. The style you are using may not be serving you. The graph in Figure 4.4, shows the relationship between thinking styles, reactive versus creative, and performance, with performance increasing as the thinking style becomes more creative. Let's examine what makes up each of these thinking and decision making styles. Figure 4.5, shows the thought process and behaviors associated with the reactive and creative work styles. Many times even if someone has a natural creative style, because of the nature of business (not enough data, fire fighting, risk adversity) employees and managers turn into reactive decision makers. When you understand your work style, it may make more sense about where you are on the spectrum of reactive and proactive thinking. If you are not thinking proactively, this may be something to work on so that you don't feel internally conflicted during the whole CRM implementation.

> Customer loyalty is built on a solid foundation of perceived value, rather than satisfaction, or even delight. Satisfaction is a passive, *reactive* relationship with the customer, while retention and loyalty require more proaction, closer contact, and greater anticipation of customer needs.
>
> —Michael Lowenstein, *Customer Retention*

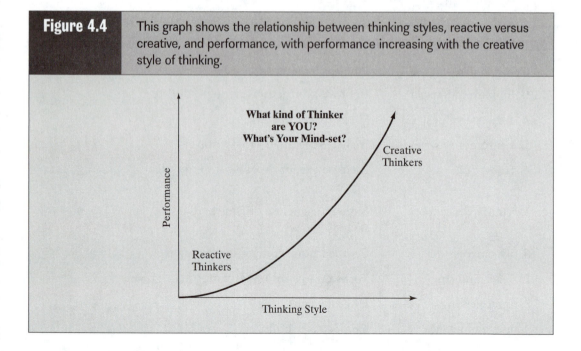

Figure 4.4 This graph shows the relationship between thinking styles, reactive versus creative, and performance, with performance increasing with the creative style of thinking.

Comparison of reactive thinkers' behaviors to creative thinkers' behaviors, showing why the creative thinker has better performance.	**Figure 4.5**

How Do You Respond to Change?

- 20% think change is great (Creative Thinkers)
- 80% think change is bad (Reactive Thinkers)
- Most successful people are Creative Thinkers

Reactive Thinkers	**Creative Thinkers**
1. Resist change	1. Open to change
2. Only see reasons they cannot do things	2. "Can do" attitude
3. Focus on problems	3. Build on successes and strengths
4. Get stuck and lose momentum	4. Seek new opportunities
5. Blame others and avoid taking responsibility	5. Take responsibilities for their actions
6. Are bad listeners	6. Are good listeners
7. Run out of energy quickly	7. Have lots of energy
8. Find it difficult to make decisions	8. Feel in control
9. Get results sometimes, but with lots of hard work	9. Get results with ease
10. Suffer excessive inner stress	10. Enjoy an inner calmness
11. Cannot let go of the past	11. Are future oriented
12. Are dictated by the past	12. Learn and grow from mistakes
13. Have low self-esteem	13. Have high self-esteem
14. Focus on what they want to avoid	14. Focus on results they want
15. Do things right	15. Do the right things

Time Management

Figure 4.6 is a time management grid. Whether you are reactive or proactive affects your time management which, of course, affects budget, scope, and costs. If you find yourself in quadrants 3 and 4, always fighting fires, then you are most likely in a reactive culture. The goal is to transform your time allocation to quadrant 2. This requires that you and your team look at whether they are reactively or proactively thinking; if they are reactive, then the goal would be to make an effort to transition the team's attitude toward being proactive. A professional trainer may be used to help evaluate where you are and facilitate your getting to where you want to be in the area of time management. CRM SPP™ uses this as a step in applying this type of time management grid so that you can work more easily from quadrant 2. Your time management skills greatly affect the scope, time line, and therefore the cost of CRM projects.

Do the first things first.
                    —Stephen Covey, *7 Habits of Highly Successful People*

Figure 4.6	Time management grid, where the goal is to streamline the business and behaviors to be able to spend as much time as possible in quadrant 2.

Time Management Grid

	Urgent	Not Urgent
Important	1 ■ Crises ■ Pressing problems ■ Deadline driven projects, meetings preparations	2 ■ Preparation ■ Prevention ■ Planning ■ Relationship building ■ Empowerment
Not Important	3 ■ Needless interruptions ■ Unnecessary reports ■ Unimportant meetings, phone calls, e-mails ■ Other people's minor issues	4 ■ Busywork ■ Worthless phone calls ■ Time wasters ■ Irrelevant e-mails ■ Avoidance

Change Creates Conflict

The smartest warrior is one who does not need to fight.

—Unknown

Physics has taught us that to stay in alignment, the nature of systems requires constant assessment, feedback, and change. It is the change, however, that naturally creates conflict. One of the other reactions to CRM projects is conflict. Recognizing that asking for change causes conflict allows you to analyze the best way to handle it. When doing that, we have to question our intention. Is it to resolve the conflict or to be right? How managers handle conflict is paramount to success.

There are five ways to resolve conflict (see Figure 4.7). As a change agent, I see my responsibility to take change, which is normally thought of as crisis, and transform it to opportunity. In order to do that yourself, you might need to have a clearer understanding of what makes the conflict better and

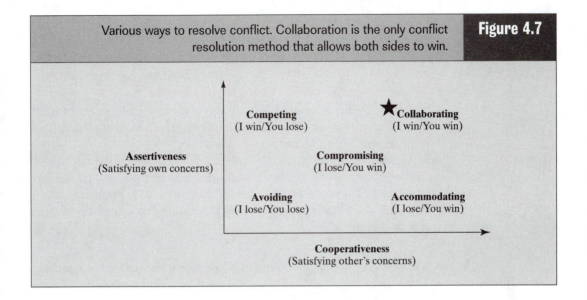

Figure 4.7

Various ways to resolve conflict. Collaboration is the only conflict resolution method that allows both sides to win.

what makes it worse. The five conflict management styles are: avoiding, accommodating, competing, comprising, collaborating.

- Which one do patriarchical managers use? Competition
- Which ones do weak managers use? Avoiding, Accommodating, Comprising
- Which one creates opportunity, reduces Reptile Talk™ and reactivity? Collaboration

Change Conversations and Communications

The language and tone of change conversations is very important. Communication occurs via body language (55%), tone of voice (38%), and only 7% is based on our interpretation of the words themselves, so it is important that our body language, tone, and words all match the message and environment we want to deliver. Research at the University of Maryland psychophysiology laboratory, the Institute for HeartMath™ and other institutions, suggests that every cell in the human body responds to each emotion and spoken word and that the heart's feelings can be measured—from up to five feet away, in fact. In a dialogue, the listener is not only absorbing the message and responding intuitively to the speaker but is also, in a sense, connected to or one with the speaker. We have a responsibility to respect that interactive power of feelings.

Human beings are designed for learning. The rate at which an organization learns may become the only sustainable competitive advantage.
                    —Peter Senge, *The Fifth Discipline: The Art & Practice of The Learning Organization*

W. Edwards Deming, Quality Expert, says our prevailing system of management has destroyed our peoples' intrinsic motivation, self-esteem, and their curiosity and joy to learn.

In a learning organization, where mistakes are seen as positive, feedback is considered information to create with, not rejection. When giving employees feedback, it is necessary to consider their work style and what might threaten them. You might ask yourself before talking to someone, for that particular conversation:

- What's at risk? What happens to this person when there is something at risk?

- Who will lose? What will be (perceived to be) lost?

- Does the unknown threaten them?

- How do they respond to loss of something they really like, value, or desire?

- How can a risk (request) be framed to create possibility, not crisis?

Knowing this and taking the time to prepare a conversation means less resistance and pushback.

CONVERSATIONS TO MAKE CHANGE HAPPEN

How you say something has everything to do with whether someone takes action or becomes passive and procrastinates. One of the most important aspects of making a request is whether you ask or tell. The key is to ask, not tell.

You might have some really good ideas, but when you introduce the idea of doing something differently, know that it might create fear in someone else, even if they have mentioned they are tired of the way things are where you work. If you wish that you could get them implemented, here are some thoughts on how to approach a conversation that entails changing things.

The secret to suggesting change is a four-step process.

1. *Creating Your Reputation*

    First you must be a top performer in your field of expertise. How exactly you gain the expertise is up to you, but generally it is a combination of degrees and real-world experiences, successes, and failures.

2. *Creating Relationships With the People in Power*

Once you have established your work ethic, your ability to lead with a clear head and contribute (without complaining), you are then in a position to establish a relationship with a "big boss." You can do this by asking a big boss if there is anything they need help with. Executives always have projects to do and not enough time to implement them, so they welcome help. In this first encounter you want to build a relationship based on trust, dependability, and your ability to meet or exceed the expectations of the executive. This gives you credibility in their eyes. If they can trust you with one thing, they will be inclined to offer you other opportunities. Many people see this as brown-nosing. It is really establishing a relationship based on aligned trust and establishing your ability to contribute on a more executive level.

An executive's jobs depends on their ability to execute decisions that further the company's success. The risk is high—if they make the right decisions they rise, if they don't, they fall. The higher they go, the higher the stakes. So put yourself in their shoes—if they had been working with you and found they could trust you to carry out an assignment, when a new assignment came up, who do you think they would choose? If their salary, bonus, and position is dependent on the successful completion of a project, they will pick someone who they can count on.

3. *Presenting the Issue and the Solutions*

Once you have established yourself with the executives as someone who can deliver, you are then in a position to bring them an issue that needs resolving in your area. Before you even think of stepping into their office:

- Do a self-check: What is your agenda? To get noticed or to really solve an issue that is critical to the business success or the morale of the company? Make sure your motive is pure and that you really want to help the company—they will know the difference and support you if you are really coming from a heartfelt mind-set.
- Identify the symptoms of the problem.
- Identify the real root causes.
- Brainstorm solutions with one other person who is in alignment with you, so that you get your thoughts and ideas down solidly.

4. *Who to Go To and How to Say It*

A. Figure out who in the company has a vested interest (something to gain or lose if these issues are not dealt with) and who is high enough to make decisions and champion the solutions.

B. Practice your pitch. Make it short and simple. Most leaders are High D styles. Begin with the issue, tell them why they should care about this. Use a bottom-line, one-sentence approach, and suggest a solution. Then concentrate on the details of what is required to make it happen—a plan, schedule, budget and staff required.

C. Eighty percent of the battle is how you are being perceived when you are delivering the pitch. Have someone else listen to your voice, your choice of words, your tone, and watch your facial expressions and body language. Remove anger, blame, judgment, and resentment from your pitch. Then practice the art of enrollment—pitch with the intention to engage the audience to create new possibilities and include them in the process by saying "and here's how you can help make this possible."

D. Listen to the executives' responses and align yourself with their suggestions (they will have some) by saying, "Thank you for your suggestion. That is a great idea and I know just where we can use that!" Then point to some place in your plan where it can be worked in. Acknowledgment of others is the fastest way to get others to follow you and your suggestions.

E. Understand that being a "change agent" requires that you have room for dissenting opinions and an ability to collaborate on the solutions. Know that you will be faced with resistance. It is your job to create with the resistance; if you fight the resistance, they will fight you harder. When you hear resistance, ask "why" at least five times. When you "unpeel" the communication with this "why" method, you discover what their real fear is and then are in a position to understand the resistance and create with it. You can say, "Thank you for telling me that. Now I understand where you are coming from and I see your point. Could we try this?" or, "What would you suggest we do?"

F. Before you leave that meeting, ask for alignment, support, and the opportunity to solve this.

G. Follow through and keep the executives informed so they stay supportive.

H. When the issue is resolved, let them know the success you had and thank them again.

Types of Leaders

In, *Why Employees Don't Do What They're Supposed to Do and What to Do About It*, Ferdinand Fournies looked at 20,000 managers in a 15-year study. See a comparison of style attributes in Figure 4.8. He found better employee performance when a manager's style changed to people-oriented, relationship based management. This included managers who changed their attitude towards employee-manager relationship from command and control to training and coaching, mentoring, and employee training and development via the CRM SPP™. The conclusion was that skills and attributes for the new culture include collaboration, cooperation, communication, synergy, connectedness, networking, recognition, and celebration.

The two types of management styles and the characteristic attributes of people embodying them.	**Figure 4.8**

People-Oriented, Loyalty Based Management	**Command and Control**
1. Collaboration, cooperation	1. Competition, divide, us versus them
2. Feelings, excitement, passion	2. Reason, indifferent, impassionate
3. Flexible, unconstrained	3. Stiff, decisive, stubborn, rigid, austere
4. Being with	4. Doing to
5. Unity, togetherness	5. Unique, one man is an island
6. Communicate, divulge, enlighten	6. Demanding, conceal, suppress
7. Nurture, train, foster, support	7. Fixing, cast down, embarrass, oppose
8. Kindness, care	8. Stern, unyielding
9. Contribution, recognition	9. Take the credit, discount, stifle

These are similar to those that Daniel Goleman, *Emotional Intelligence* (1995, 1998) and Judy Rosener, *America's Competitive Secret: Women Managers* (1997) are recommending. David Whyte, a corporate poet, says:

■ "We leave 60 percent of ourselves in the car, bringing into work an empty shell of ourselves, yet we complain that "they" are like "that"

■ We are each individually responsible for the culture at work: we are "them"

■ When the mind is abstracted from the heart, we close ourselves off. As we close off the air vents, we gasp for air, and yet we reach to close off the next vent and the next one . . .

The original direction in the mainstream of our cultural evolution was towards partnership but, following a period of chaos and almost total cultural disruption, there occurred a fundamental shift. It went from a society that worshiped the life-generating and nurturing powers of the universe, and via prehistoric invaders who worshiped the power of the blade and its ability to take life, to dominate. While for millennias men have fought wars, the chalice represents the fact that there were always societies of men and women that were not violent and warlike. What surprises most men is that there were very early civilizations led by men that were patterned by a partnership model of leadership. While we might today associate men with war, that was not where we were headed before that period of chaos/dominator/ leadership trend that has continued to lead us into this new millienium. The dominator model now seems to be reaching its logical limits.

—Riane Eisler, *The Chalice and the Blade*

Corporate America is suffocating on this old dominator management model. Evaluate your current position and company and ask yourself, "What is it that you are looking for in a company?" If you could create a company you personally would like to work in, what would that be like? What is required to make a company where people want to come to work every day, where they show up energized and excited, which contributes to their productivity and customer satisfaction? What is the formula to create this company? How does a company be the place that everyone wants to get into and then once they are there, they do not want to leave? How does one create this inward flow of people and intellectual brain trust? How does a company become the magnet? American leaders have the choice in creating the next business culture for success.

> Organizational design and leadership, until now, has been predicated on the seventeenth-century worldview of Sir Isaac Newton. With Albert Einstein coming into the picture, things started to change. Now quantum physics challenges our thinking about observation and perception, participation and relationships, and the influences and connections that are created across large and complex systems. Our corporations are these large and complex systems.
>
> —Margaret J. Wheatley, *Leadership and the New Science: Learning about Organization from An Orderly Universe*

Reasons for Attrition

The graph in Figure 4.9 shows an example of how employees feel about work. In previous times, after the world wars, employees were just happy to have a job. But as the economy has changed and people have evolved, the needs of the worker have escalated. In the last 50 years, the fields of psychology and psychiatry have seen many great scholars, Freud, Carl Jung, etc., who have pioneered the field of human potential. From the scholarly works have come an understanding of cause and effect and many theories on behavior change have resulted. An off-shoot of the scholarly theory and traditional therapy is the field of self-help.

As the human potential movement has gained momentum via a more conscious collective mindset, people like Deepak Chopra, Sondra Ray, Andrew Weil, Carolyn Myss, among many authors, have propagated the self-help field with books on their experiences and ideas on personal change. Everyone from psychologists to physicists have come up with solutions to issues people struggle with.

In the same timeframe, the evolution of personal consciousness among many other things created a gap in the satisfaction of workers in jobs. While workers were getting enlightened via self-help, corporations were still operating under command and control leadership originating from the military and following management practices and processes pioneered

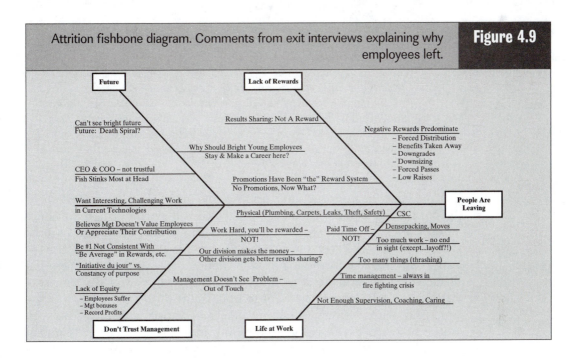

Attrition fishbone diagram. Comments from exit interviews explaining why employees left.   **Figure 4.9**

by Fredrick Taylor in his scientific management theory of the early 1900s. With these systems the goal was to make the middle managers' and workers' activities more predictable and thus more controllable. Taylor wrote, in the early 1900s:

> This, gentlemen, is the beginning of the great mental revolution which constitutes the first step toward scientific management.
>
> It is a complete change in mental attitude: the substitution of *peace* for *war*, of *brotherly cooperation* for *contention and strife*; of *both pulling hard in the same direction* instead of *pulling apart*; of replacing *suspicious watchfulness* with *mutual confidence*; of being *friends* instead of *enemies*. It is along these lines, I say, that Scientific Management must be developed. The idea of *cooperation and peace* is substituted for *discord and war.*
>
> The substitution of this new outlook is the very essence of scientific management. It exists nowhere until after this change in mental attitude of both sides, employees and managers, has taken place.

(Taylor, 1911)

However, that was not really implemented. The wars came to be and the direction of management shifted. The following is a quote from *Fortune* Magazine:

> *America is now peopled very largely by the Organizational Men. They are the middle-class Americans who have left home, spiritually as well as physically*

to take the vows of the organizational life. They not only work for the Organization; they belong to it. Each one of them stands at the center of a deep conflict in American values.

No Standard Pro
Went from indust
materials, and tec
up their own way

Business has institutionalized itself to the point of resembling the bureaucracies it deplores and asked of its growing armies of employees, a total lifelong loyalty.

Perpetuating the "yes-man" culture, it has gotten what it asked for: flabby compliance. That is the revenge of the "company-oriented" man who chants, "love that system" while biting his tongue to hide real feelings. Some executives sense there is something wrong somewhere. They dreamed of bold, imaginative enterprises and instead have a corps of bureaucrats . . ."

You may be surprised after reading this quote that it was written in 1956. In 1956, William H. Whyte, Jr. labeled this phemonemon the "organizational man"—the man who has sold his soul to the corporation. In some cases managers who grew up with this as standard thought and practice are still using the same methodology even though the world around them has changed a great deal. To get a bird's-eye view of where we have been may help leaders to see how they want to lead, Figure 4.10.

Today, with a strong economy, workers are voting with their feet, attrition is high and expensive, and becoming an employer of choice is among a company's largest challenges. Via employee exit surveys, employers are finding that keeping workers, with fast knowledge acquisition, skills, and at-

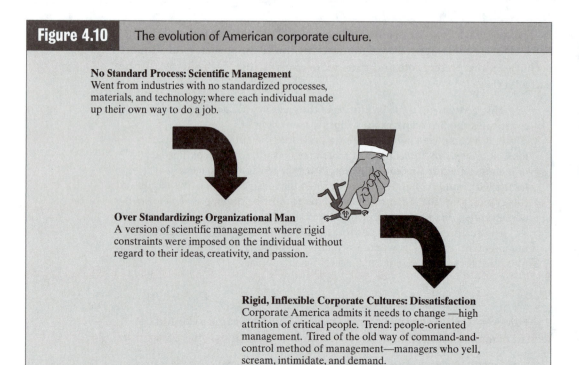

| **Figure 4.10** | The evolution of American corporate culture. |

No Standard Process: Scientific Management
Went from industries with no standardized processes, materials, and technology; where each individual made up their own way to do a job.

Over Standardizing: Organizational Man
A version of scientific management where rigid constraints were imposed on the individual without regard to their ideas, creativity, and passion.

Rigid, Inflexible Corporate Cultures: Dissatisfaction
Corporate America admits it needs to change —high attrition of critical people. Trend: people-oriented management. Tired of the old way of command-and-control method of management—managers who yell, scream, intimidate, and demand.

tributes, greatly depends on how they are treated by management, their work/life balance and the working environment.

> *The most basic task of corporate leaders is to unleash the human spirit which makes initiative, creativity, and innovation happen.*
> —Christopher A. Barlett, "Changing The Role Of Top Management Beyond Systems to People," *Harvard Business Review*

With the need to recreate culture as well as improve technology and processes, the field and billion dollar business of change management was born and has flourished via professional services companies and consulting firms. The objectives and results projected were not realized through the current methodologies applied. Most of this has to do with the concentrated focus of these change programs on technology and workflow process and little or no attention given to the human potential aspect of the change process. At the end of the day, if people don't change, nothing changes. And now for the rest of the change management program, we'll go over some of the other important aspects of managing a CRM implementation.

Communication Plans

It is important to create a communication plan around the timeline and changes to the technology and workflow processes so that no one is surprised and people can prepare. The following is a worksheet to begin the process.

Internal Marketing Communications Plan for a "Change" Program

Objective: The purpose of this plan is to identify existing marketing and communications capabilities. These capabilities may serve important roles in managing the expectations around the changes to the customer service center and to fully address employees' concerns, as well as communicate important information. Existing marketing and communications capabilities may also enable ongoing training and performance support, and as such will play an important role in the design of an effective training strategy. You will want to add to your CRM team someone from the communications department to help with designing and implementing a communication plan.

1. Do you have marketing/communications capability in-house?   yes   no

   If No, please go to Question 4. If yes, please answer the following questions:

   A. What is the main purpose of the marketing/communications function?

   B. How many staff members are responsible for the marketing/ communications function? What is their role(s)?

2. A. What written communications are available at the site?

Internal Written Communications	Yes	No	Frequency of Distribution	Comments
Memorandum				
E-mail				
Newsletter				
Letters with paychecks				
Employee handbook				
Job satisfaction survey				
Bulletin boards				If yes, where?
Other				

Internal Written Communications	Yes	No	Frequency of Distribution	Comments
Brochures				
Other				

In which languages are these communications distributed?

B. What verbal communications are available at the site?

Internal Verbal Communications	Yes	No	Frequency of Distribution	Comments
Plant meetings				
Staff meetings				
Feedback sessions				
Other				

External Verbal Communications	Yes	No	Frequency of Distribution	Comments
Teleconferences				
Other				

Which languages are spoken during these activities?

3. A. What communication materials do you receive from other locations in the company?

   B. Is the customer service center management utilizing the marketing/communications function?

   C. How does the customer service center management view their role in the marketing/communications function?

   D. What message(s) are being sent through this capability?

4. Who can we contact for further information on marketing/communications?

Business Process Mapping

It is also important to outline the current processes that the technology supports and to map the changes to the process that new technology would create. Following are examples of a variety of ways to map out the various processes in a business that provide service.

Figure 4.11a   The following diagrams are various forms of business process maps. This is a very simplified version of a business process map showing the "as is" and the "could be" states of an employee needing to change data such as their address or marital status. With the old system, there are many steps and with self-service technology, those steps are reduced with technology.

"As is" steps in making changes to employee data

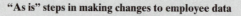

Step 1	Step 2 and 3	Step 4 and 5	Last Step
Collegue has data change	Find and prepare forms	Forms review and approval	HR updates database

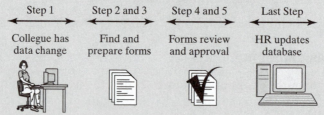

"Could be" steps in making changes to employee data

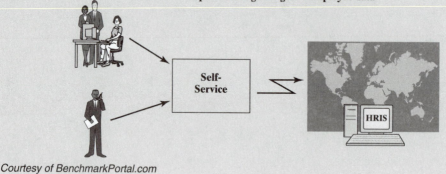

Self-Service

HRIS

Courtesy of BenchmarkPortal.com

This is a business process map of the steps in a company when an employee quits their job. In this process map, there are three main human touch points: the employee or colleague, the manager, and HR. There are numerous processes and technologies that support the process of an employee quitting.

Figure 4.11b

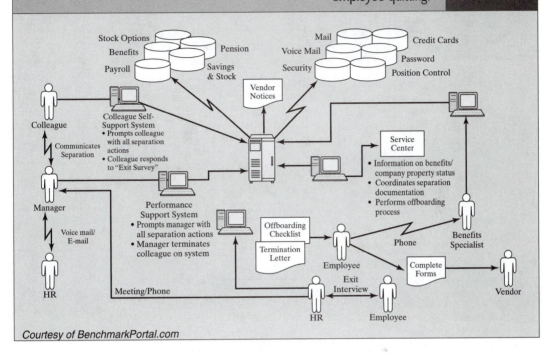

Courtesy of BenchmarkPortal.com

Figure 4.11c This is a business process map of the different tiers in delivering service to customers. Tier 0 is self-service, Tier 1 is the call center, Tier 2 refers to when questions are escalated to a specialist in the call center, and Tier 3 is when an HR consultant becomes involved. This company wanted to reduce the number of interactions in Tiers 1 to 3 and increase the volume of providing service via Tier 0 or self-service technology. It was not until they mapped out their service delivery model that they were able to see what they wanted to change and why it would reduce costs.

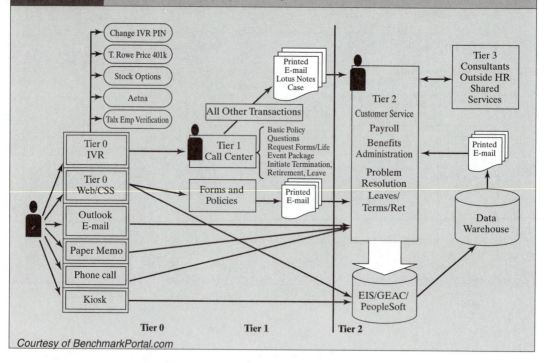

Courtesy of BenchmarkPortal.com

Figure 4.11d

In this last example of a business process map, the steps in the process are represented by a flow diagram. Many times this kind of diagram is then broken down in functional areas of responsibility to see the interactions between various departments and determine if there is overlap, redundant, or unnecessary steps.

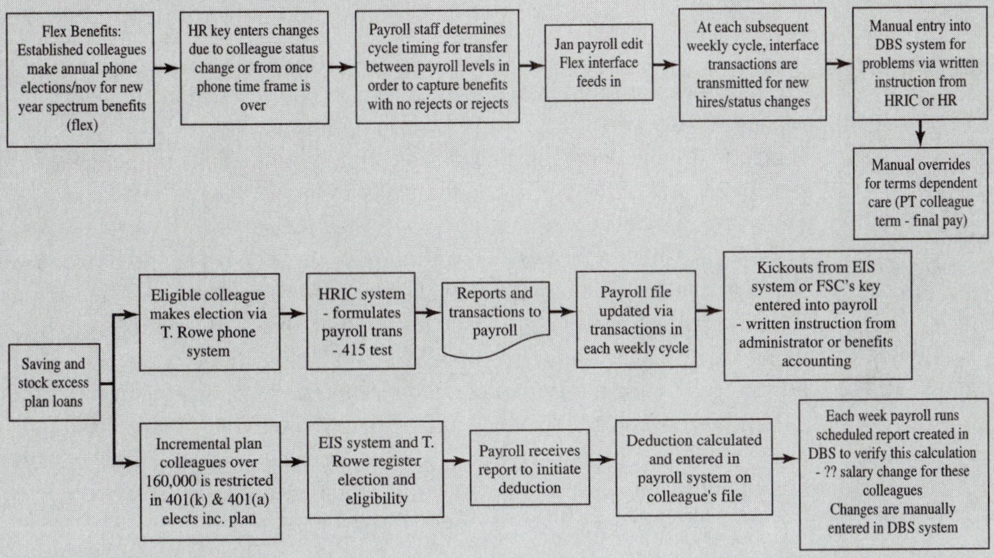

Flex Benefits: Established colleagues make annual phone elections/nov for new year spectrum benefits (flex) → HR key enters changes due to colleague status change or from once phone time frame is over → Payroll staff determines cycle timing for transfer between payroll levels in order to capture benefits with no rejects or rejects → Jan payroll edit Flex interface feeds in → At each subsequent weekly cycle, interface transactions are transmitted for new hires/status changes → Manual entry into DBS system for problems via written instruction from HRIC or HR → Manual overrides for terms dependent care (PT colleague term - final pay)

Saving and stock excess plan loans → Eligible colleague makes election via T. Rowe phone system → HRIC system - formulates payroll trans - 415 test → Reports and transactions to payroll → Payroll file updated via transactions in each weekly cycle → Kickouts from EIS system or FSC's key entered into payroll - written instruction from administrator or benefits accounting

Incremental plan colleagues over 160,000 is restricted in 401(k) & 401(a) elects inc. plan → EIS system and T. Rowe register election and eligibility → Payroll receives report to initiate deduction → Deduction calculated and entered in payroll system on colleague's file → Each week payroll runs scheduled report created in DBS to verify this calculation - ?? salary change for these colleagues Changes are manually entered in DBS system

Courtesy of BenchmarkPortal.com

Integrated Master Plan and Schedule

It is important that everyone is on the same page and this can be done by creating an implementation plan and schedule to realistically transition legacy systems to the new system, running the old systems in parallel for a period of time to assure seamless transition. The following is an example of technology implementation integrated master plan and schedule.

Figure 4.12

These are examples of Integrated Master Plans (IMP) and Integrated Master Schedules (IMS). This IMP and IMS was created in Microsoft Project™. The task names are given an ID number and a duration—that is the "plan part" of the IMP. Then the tasks are listed in with scheduled times and due dates and that represents the "schedule part" of the IMS. From a display of tasks like this, it becomes evident what has to be done first, what tasks are dependent on another task being completed and when the milestones need to be reached for the next phase of the project to be completed. It is a great way to make sure that all team members accomplish their actions items on time. When they don't, it becomes evident to the whole team who is holding up the progress. It can also be used to determine a reallocation in human capital if one area is falling short due to underestimated amount of effort required for particular tasks.

ID	Task Name	Duration	2nd Quarter			3rd Quarter			
			Apr	May	Jun	Jul	Aug	Sep	Oct
1	Program Management	122d							
2	Detailed Design	25d							
3	Key Milestones	89d							
4	Development	54d							
5	Installation & Unit Test	30d							
6	Telephony Testing	22d							
7	BRIT (Business Release Int)	10d							
8	Training	39d							
9	Friendly Trial	24d							
10									

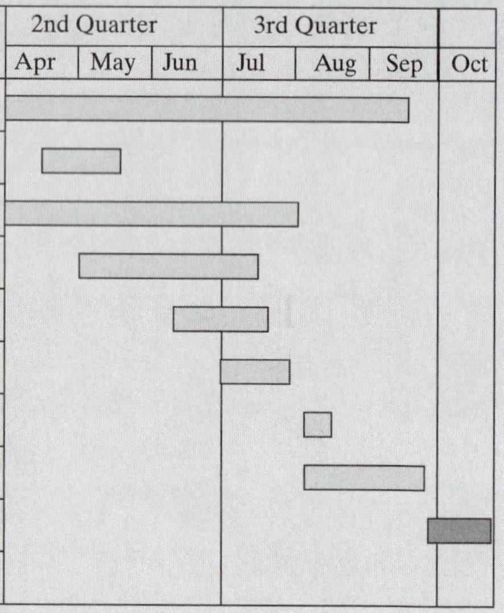

Teams and Their Impact on CRM Implementations

WHERE THEORY AND REALITY MEET:
A GUIDE FOR THE STAGES OF TEAM DEVELOPMENT
AND LEADERSHIP BEHAVIORS

We have managed many major implementations of new technology in call centers and have learned firsthand that implementing the necessary changes to remain competitive in a global market can have a substantial psychological impact on call center employees, which can also directly affect the customer service they provide and therefore customer retention.

This section focuses on the theory of team development stages, the typical behaviors from team members, the productivity of a team's work, and suggested behaviors for team leaders to help the team adjust through the various stages, and compares that to a case study conducted by Julie Kuliopulos of Performix while implementing a CRM reengineering project.

Figure 5.1 compares the various stages of team formation versus what humans experience when they have a loss (the emotional reaction to a loss). The various stages of team development are:

- ???Forming???
- !!!Storming!!!
- ... Norming ...
- $$$Performing$$$
- +++Transforming+++

As a team forms and grows, team theory predicts that there will be various stages of productivity and emotions because teams are made up of people who have predictable reactions to change. Understanding these development stages can keep a team from overreacting to normal group problems and setting unrealistic group expectations that can only lead to frustration. Team theory also states that it takes a team effort to reach the "performing" stage of team development and to stay there. The dip in the

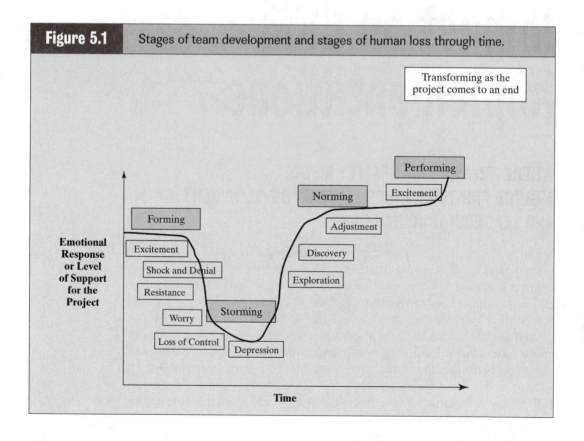

Figure 5.1   Stages of team development and stages of human loss through time.

level of commitment is coined The Valley of Tears describing the decline of support for the project.

In comparing the graphs in the previous section on change and employees, Figures 3.6 and 3.7, to Figure 5.1, we can see that there is a similarity showing that the theory of the Valley of Tears does match reality. In our research and real-time reengineering experiences, we have found *the valley occurs regardless of the technology application or process improvement being implemented.* The valley happens just as commonly in implementing changes in telecommunications equipment, computer hardware, or computer software as in changing the workflow or processes by which work gets done. The reason for this is because changes to technology or process changes what people do at work, and 40 percent of the working population is high S. Their style is by nature adverse to change and change in and of itself is disorienting.

The purpose of recording the emotions through a reengineering project is to document the reality of this human reaction to change. We also wanted to present real data that could document this reaction to change because it would help not only call center managers and employees handle major technology and/or process improvements, but also provide the evidence often needed to convince executives of the need for a change management plan as part of the reengineering budget and plan. One of the reasons 85 percent of executives are disappointed by the efforts of reengineering projects is because they do not know or understand that one of the major factors in failed reengineering projects is how well the human dynamic of change was handled. By sharing our data for the Braun call center reengineering project, we felt anyone involved in a change project would benefit and be even more prepared for the psychological challenges of reengineering and CRM implementation.

THE PSYCHOLOGICAL IMPACT OF CHANGE IN REENGINEERING A CALL CENTER

The psychological impact of change on employees creates emotional ups and downs. Managing these emotional ups and downs can make or break the success of the overall reengineering project. Impacts show up in the schedule, implementation costs, and lower return on investment for the new technology and processes. In most cases when leaders go back to check months or years after an implementation, many of the features of the new technology are not even used by the employees. It is no wonder that after CRM implementation many executives are disappointed with the results. Nobody is really using the system to its full capacity.

To record the existence of the Valley of Tears the leader of the CRM team, Julie Kuliopulos, now at Performix Technologies, kept a weekly diary of how the team felt emotionally about their endeavor every step of the difficult and sometimes frustrating implementation phase. The team used a frustration scale of from 1 to 10. A score of 1 was to describe a very hostile feeling of frustration for the results at the end of the week. A score of 10 was used to describe a very satisfied experience at the end of the week. All the scores between 0 and 10 were used as appropriate.

Braun's Valley of Tears

As you can see in the graph of Braun's Valley of Tears (Figure 5.2), the team started out feeling good about getting the funding for the long awaited reengineering initiative. The funds were approved after weeks of preparation of the necessary justification documentation, including ROI calculations, a functional requirements description, call workflows, plus product and system specification. However, when the Braun team detailed all the tasks that needed to be accomplished in a short period of time, they quickly became overwhelmed and emotionally frustrated. The comments from team members could be summed up in one statement, "How could we possibly do all the work that was necessary along with our normal day-to-day jobs and meet

Figure 5.2   The Valley of Tears team experience measured during Braun's CRM implementation matches very closely with the curve that shows the theoretical response from a team over time.

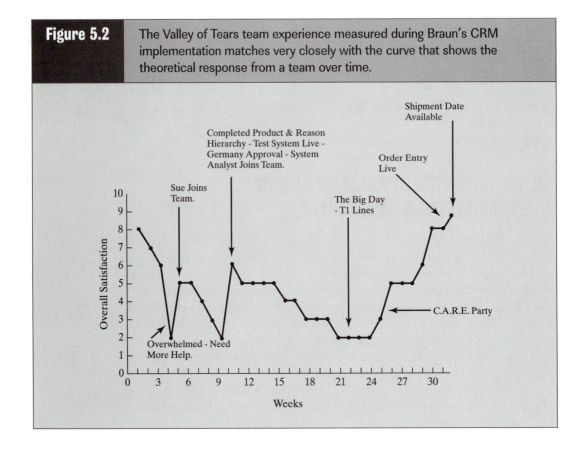

the high expectations that the team and the company had set?" The task at hand seemed impossible and no longer as interesting or invigorating. The goal of a more efficient call center with better customer service was lost in a sea of emotions and unrealizable expectations.

Most important is to note the match of the actual data measured in the Braun call center reengineering project (comparing Figures 5.1 and 5.2 and also 3.5) to the theory on team stage emotional development and productivity (Table 5.1). This particular comparison moves emotional team theory discussion from the theoretical to the workplace, providing proof that the phenomenon of the Valley of Tears is real. And it can directly affect the project's success if not recognized by a team that is led by an experienced team leader who understands the interrelationship of change and human dynamics.

Obtaining skills to do something new brings back memories of an initial high level of enthusiasm and optimism when we first start, followed by stress and frustration during the difficult learning phase, and finally followed by joy and exhilaration upon mastery of the new skill. Whether undergoing a major technology changeover in a call center or a smaller improvement project, it is important to understand that unanticipated and painful surprises are bound to happen and it is necessary to train employees about these issues. By understanding and anticipating the Valley of Tears it will help you and your team members to prepare mentally for difficulties that can occur. A well-trained team can recognize the issues as they are coming up and be proactive about solutions and options, collectively pulling together and remaining productive.

CYCLES INSIDE OF CYCLES

It is also typical to see dips in the emotional response of a team over the lifetime of a project. This means that there can be a cycle of the Valley of Tears within an overall Valley of Tears team development cycle. This "cycle within the cycle" can be created by a range of things in a long-term project. For example, a loss of a team member that is critical to the team, a delay in hardware or software delivery throwing off the schedule, or unpredicted issues that come up during implementation can create a mini-cycle within the larger Valley of Tears cycle. This accounts for some of the extra dips in Figure 5.2.

Suggestions for Minimizing the Valley of Tears Effect

Table 5.1 provides a quick guide to the stage of team development. In each stage are listed the general types of team member emotions, the level of productivity or team-work that can be expected in that stage and suggested types of leadership actions that can help a team move forward through the stages to successfully complete the project. In this case study, the Braun team and leaders did follow this type of program and completed a very successful reengineering project.

	Table 5.1—Stages of Team Development in Relationship to Human Dynamics, Suggested Leadership Behaviors, and Productivity Expectations.		
Team Stages	**Team Members' Emotions**	**Teamwork or Productivity**	**Leadership Behavior Suggestions**
Forming	■ Generally eager ■ Anxious about why they are there, what is in it for them ■ Dependent on the leader	■ Focusing on defining goals and tasks ■ Low task accomplishment	■ Provide information ■ Develop skills of team ■ Clarify roles and goals
Storming	■ Feelings of frustration ■ May have negative reactions to other team members and leader ■ Experience confusion ■ Morale dips	■ Tasks disrupted by conflicts and discontent ■ Slowing increasing task accomplishment and skill development	■ Highly supportive behaviors ■ Listen to team members more ■ Support and resolve conflict ■ Provide positive feedback
Norming	■ Ways of working together become clearer ■ Feelings of mutual respect and trust evolve ■ Feel pleased with task completion	■ Task accomplishment increases ■ Team members understand the task and output increases	■ Decreased direction needed ■ Help team members to develop skills confidence ■ Encourage group to assume more responsibility ■ Communicate more

	TABLE 5.1 (CONTINUED)		
Team Stages	**Team Members' Emotions**	**Teamwork or Productivity**	**Leadership Behavior Suggestions**
Performing	■ Eager to be part of team ■ Feel confident about the goals ■ Work well together ■ Communicate openly and freely ■ Feel positive about team accomplishments	■ High level of output ■ Task feels easier ■ Skill level is higher ■ Work more efficiently	■ Continue to monitor goals and performance ■ Take a less active role in the team's regular operation— let them run things and be in control ■ Support members in taking a leadership role in problem solving
Transforming— Terminating or Continuing	■ Concern about project ending ■ Feel a sense of loss ■ Feel strong sense of accomplishment	■ Output may decrease ■ May be increased output to meet final deadlines	■ Provide support to team ■ Give positive feedback ■ Go through lessons learned ■ Communicate next steps

Team Meetings

IN TERMS OF RUNNING A MEETING:

■ Suggest a timed agenda. Each item on the agenda is given a time, 30 minutes, 1 hour, etc. Adjust it during the meeting as needed, but try to keep to the schedule.

■ Appoint a timekeeper for each meeting to remind the team of time limits.

■ Appoint a facilitator, especially during brainstorming, so the talkers and naysayers are kept in check. If you have a big talker, make them the facilitator.

■ Appoint a scribe so that you can lead the meeting and not write at the same time.

CRM WISH LIST BRAINSTORMING

Some people will not know the rules of brainstorming, so go over them first.

Rule 1—Don't edit any ideas or discuss them, just list them. Elimination is another process at the end. Rule 2—Go through all steps with brainstorming before going back and rehashing anything.

To set up a program like this, it is easy to use a brainstorming process:

1. Who is our customer(s)?

   Make a list without editing or deleting as you list every kind of customer possible: direct customers and indirect, existing customers and those you want, as well as those that do not know exist.

2. What do they need?

   Brainstorm a list for every customer category in number 1. There will be an overlap of the needs of some of the customers, so later we will see that some of the deliverables can service more than one group with a little tweaking to tailor them. For now, lists can stay separate.

3. Exactly how are we going to get "it" to them? By when, within what budget? Make a "how to" list.

   List every way possible to get each one of those customers what they need. Some things will not be possible due to cost, time, or manpower, but some of those things can be given to PR, advertising, done online, etc. Create inter-working team efforts going in the same direction. Again, do this brainstorm without editing, looking for what is possible. List everything that is said.

4. Harvest the best ideas, create scope of team, deliverables, and statement of work.

   At this point in the brainstorming, it is time to harvest numbers 1 through 3. Harvesting means to look at everything and see what is best of the best ideas to service the mission, vision, and goals statements. Then determine the scope of what this team can do, where it wants to focus, and what is being handed off to other teams.

   How to harvest. Look at the customer/need brainstorm list (#2) and group together those that have similar needs, still listing the individual customers. Your list will then turn into a needs list and you will be able to see the list of customers with the same needs. As this list evolves, you will see the scope of your task getting more compact and simple because *many of the needs are the same.* Eliminate those things that are not in alignment with your vision, mission, and goal statement, outside the scope of your team, the budget, or the schedule.

Needs List = Deliverables List

The needs list creates your deliverables—the things that you are actually going to do to meet the customers' needs. You will not be able to fill every need of every customer; the purpose of this is to get a picture of the needs and then figure out to what degree you can service them. It may be at a very in-depth level and it may be more surface level; but the point is that all the important customers are included at some level. Now you know what you have to do.

Statement of Work = Goals of Team

Create the Statement of Work, the checklist of everything you are actually going to do, with a list of goals.

5. Create an integrated master plan and schedule.

The Plan

Once you have the statement of work, you can create a strategic plan to accomplish the goals of the team. Integrated means that each piece fits into the other piece. Some things have to be done before others, so integrating each piece is important. You may also be dependent on other teams for work that you want to happen, but is outside the scope, so those factors need to be considered. Have a headline for each item you want to do and then list every single step to make it happen and who is responsible for it.

The Schedule

Take every single step in the plan and give it a target date. See the examples of IMP and IMS in Chapter 4, Figure 4.12.

6. Measuring success.

Having a series of design reviews built into the schedule to stop and check on the project progress assures things are caught before they get out of hand. Recalibrate the plan and schedule to assure delivery: on-time, within budget, and on schedule with the quality desired. These success reviews can be called Advanced Design Review, Critical Design Review, Delivery Review, and Follow-up and Maintainance Review. You can divide the project into these four phases and celebrate each time the team passes through a major milestone.

The Braun change management program included some of the following actions as part of a change management program to consider before, during, and after a major reengineering initiative at your call center:

- **Department Team Training**—Prepare awareness training about the human reaction to change, ask employees how they feel about change and how they feel they can contribute to the success of the change. Make the change project part of the performance evaluation process so that employees who embrace and push forward the change are rewarded.

- **Department Communication**—Prepare your staff for the changes that are taking place around them—communicate the vision and get buy-in to the project.

- **Team Selection**—Have representation on your team from your internal information technology department, supervision, and representatives from the call center, and your vendor with key stakeholders who have a vested interest in seeing the project succeed.

- **Team Meetings**—Have regular team meetings to communicate and update team members. This may also include the introduction of simple stress reduction techniques that can be done while on the job, including breathing and stretching exercises, visualization, and positive self-talk. Many of these stress reduction techniques are used by major sports teams and players.

- **Detailed Task List**—List all required tasks in the beginning of the implementation and constantly update them, including the responsible team member, the target completion date, and percentage of progress to date.

- **Celebrate**—Celebrate your milestones to give your staff the feeling of accomplishment they deserve.

Recommendations for Realistic Reengineering Implementations

The following are planning issues you might consider when confronted with a major CRM initiative like Julie's Braun team:

- Be ready to compromise. You may not be able to have everything available in your new system on day one. Schedule a phased implementation approach if possible.

- Plan the time during low volume. If possible, time your switch to the new system during a low call-volume period.

- Convert history. In order to do trend analysis, which your stakeholders will want to see, convert at least 18 months of data from your old system.

- Communicate. Keep your organization informed of what the goal is, why it is important, what can go wrong, and how things will change with the new system and the value those changes will bring to them. Constantly articulate a clear vision of what your call center will be like when the final system is in place and how important those changes are to creating and keeping good customers.

- Enhance previous user experience. Find a current user of your new technology and learn from them.

- Expect start-up bugs. Try to work through bugs with a test system, but expect a few things that still need ironing out.

- Involve reps in implementation. They are the closest to your customers—they know what problems exist in the current system and what works. Ask them, involve them, and reward them.

- Get buy-in from major audiences. Before you go too far, make sure you are designing something that will meet the needs of your major audiences (stakeholders, executives, customers).

- Understand the Valley of Tears and get everyone involved in minimizing it where possible!

Here's How the Braun Team Dealt with Change

"In leading change it is important to have some members of the team be naturally optimistic. In our team, as most teams, about 80 percent of the team's reaction to change was negative, with 20 percent or less feeling good about the change. To facilitate the optimism in the midst of the 'Valley of Tears' we added a key customer service representative (CSR) to the implementation team who was an eternal optimist (high I). The value the optimist brought was a wealth of knowledge and enthusiasm to the team, which got us quickly back on track. We then proceeded from that point into the Valley of Tears. The team went straight out, working late hours and weekends. We were feeling the strain, but because the team had had the awareness about the valley, they already expected that it was going to be tough. They understood the feelings that they were experiencing were temporary and normal for a team creating a change project and that there would be a light at the end of the tunnel.

"A huge boost out of the valley occurred each time we accomplished a key milestone. We had completed a large portion of the new system design and had configured a prototype system that was loaded on several CSR workstations. The feeling was great as we walked through the call center and saw CSRs properly testing the new system and enjoying the new features. It truly gave us the feeling that we were really going to make it happen! At the same time, we were able hire a systems analyst, (high C) a newly created position. Having someone in that position for the first time reduced the pressure and relieved the frustration of making sure the system would perform.

"We pushed on with weekly meetings of the process improvement team and our regularly scheduled weekly department meetings. In these meetings we made a point of constant communication of our progress and focused on the solutions to obstacles or what we called our 'show stoppers.' This level of open and honest communication in the teams allowed us to focus on the critical success activities to stay within budget, time, and scope of the project as much as possible. We used the department meetings to keep everyone informed and working towards the same goal. Everyone knew what the goal was and why it was so important to accomplish it. The added advantage of understanding the 'Valley of Tears' phenomenon allowed us to focus on the tasks to be completed versus allowing frustration feelings to overwhelm various team members, which could have easily turned to blame or anger and gotten us off track. The team's comprehension of the valley allowed us to work together in a more professional manner and kept us motivated to work together for the common goals.

> By being in communication with the whole center about the changes, the employees proactively wanted to be involved in creating the new center. In fact the CSRs volunteered for product specialist positions, taking accountability for product categories in the new system and making sure that call workflows were completed for every possible reason a consumer might contact the call center. Each specific product category had to be represented in the new system and all assigned products were properly represented with informational scripts. Other CSRs volunteered to test the new system and to put it through its paces via beta-site testing. There was an incredible team spirit that you could feel just by walking through the call center. This would not have been possible if CSRs had not felt completely involved and in control of the changes that were happening to their job and ultimately to them.
>
> —Julie Kuliopulos, Performix Technologies

Opening Day and the Need for Continued Change Management Awareness

"When the big day came to use the new system, we were ready! We had a new system with well-trained CSRs who were excited and enthusiastic about using the new technology and following the new procedures they had helped to build. Our system documentation was complete and the system vendor was there with us for the opening day. For additional insurance, we even invited extra Braun supervisors and managers (wearing their tennis shoes) on ready-alert to assist with any possible problem as it occurred.

"We had only one real problem: the wait time for customers was 20 to 30 minutes at times throughout the day and the number of customers in queue kept building 15, 20, 25. We knew the new system would have a learning curve associated with it, but this was unthinkable. It took us two days to figure it out, while everyone assumed it was the impact of the new system. We discovered that two T1 lines had gone down the same day we went to the new system (Murphy will always prevail!). Due to this non-system failure, we lost 25 percent of our call handling capacity.

"After the first full month of entering data into the system, we had our first month-end ritual, where we took all the data that went into the system that month and published our first report! With a major milestone under our belts, we celebrated the accomplishment with a party for the entire team! The entire department went to an off-site restaurant and kicked up its collective 'heels.' The vendor was invited to the gala event as well as our senior management. We had balloons filling the room and sweatshirts made up for everyone. With the pictures from the party we created a banner and posted the pictures on the department bulletin board to carry on the feeling of triumph. We found that celebrations during and throughout the implementation of the new system helped to sustain the enthusiasm and pride by the employees, which led to greater productivity.

> We had high hopes for the entire system to go live at the same time, but the order entry system was not added until phase two of the system implementation and reengineering. When our order entry system went live, we really started to come out of the valley. CSRs toggled back and forth between the new consumer contact system and the old order entry system for the first two months (not very elegant!), making sure that the new system could support the requests. While this can be a cumbersome process, running legacy systems along with the new system is common practice to assure good customer service.

> We completed our implementation and were out of the 'Valley of Tears' when we finally had shipment data available in the new system. Shipment data gave us our analytical tool. The number of consumer comments for a product could now be compared to the total number of products that we shipped over the previous twelve-month period, allowing for the factoring out of returns and heavy atypical shipping months, for instance, December. This analytical process is often called 'normalizing' the caller data. Up until this point we were reporting actual numbers, which were of interest, but were not actionable to improve customer service.

> —Julie Kuliopulos, Performix Technologies

Understanding the Stakeholders

You will better understand the value the profiles bring when it is integrated with the information in the following sections. We will look at:

- Understanding the stakeholders
- Stakeholders' thinking styles: reactive or proactive
- Stakeholders' time management

The first question many stakeholders ask is, "How will this affect me?" Stakeholders look at potential wins and real or feared losses. To find out where a particular stakeholder stands on your change effort and to have an indication of their level of support, *ask them.* Talk to them. Ask what they think and what their reaction is to what they have seen and heard. Ask how to make this a win for them and their group (or how to minimize any losses that may occur). Stress how this change will benefit them and/or the company. Make it personal—people take change personally. But remember, the wins must be real and legitimate. Don't promise things you cannot deliver.

HOW TO MANAGE STAKEHOLDERS

There are several steps in managing stakeholders, and they must be repeated often during the life of the project. If you have their profile then you can speak to them in a way that opens their particular door to communication and you will win them over quickly so they will feel acknowledged and empowered.

1. Deal with them as they are and where they are. Find out what they have heard, what rumors exist about the change effort. Do not try to guess what they think, or try to figure out what they should feel—*ask them.* Whatever they are thinking and whatever their current level of support, that is where the process starts. It is not right or wrong—it is the starting point, and the key to discovering it is to talk to the stakeholders themselves.

2. Ensure confidentiality on sensitive issues. Build their trust so that potential barriers to success are identified and responded to. Explain that this interview will be summarized along with many other interviews. Tell the interviewee that, unless requested otherwise, direct quotes will be used in the summary but the name will not be attached.

3. Get their issues in the open. Clarify their issues, fears, and their opportunities. This can help get them past the point of self-interest, or at least temper it, and it may even encourage them to try the change on for size. When people know they have been really heard they are much more inclined to listen, so listen to them first and find out their issues.

4. Tell the truth about the change and the impact it will have. If you do not tell the truth, people will question your credibility. Do not just focus on the positive, or the negative, but be open with both. If the stakeholder is focused on the effort involved in the change, help them to understand what it will be like after the change is in place. The effort only occurs once, but the benefits continue. (If they do not, why are you doing this?)

5. Get them involved. Solicit their ideas, use their input, find ways to get/keep them involved. Above all else, keep them informed and find meaningful and appropriate roles for them whenever possible. Leverage those with positive attitudes and get them invested—visibly if possible. They know what is or will go wrong, and the ways to fix it, so let them help. Very few people are not positively inclined when their advice is solicited and heard.

6. Plan how to deal with and respond to each stakeholder. Use the information and advice you have received to determine how to minimize risks. Plan how to capitalize on those who support the change and control the resources, authority, power, and energy needed to make the change successful. Encourage them to ask questions, and be sure to overcommunicate. Get them actively and meaningfully involved.

7. Help the stakeholders identify how they will know when the change is working well. Choosing selected performance measures and defining how they will change is a great way to make the change real and viewable to stakeholders. This will help them try the change on "for size."

8. Expect setbacks and roadblocks. Be ready for them and address them as they occur. There will always be bumps on the road, so do not put the pressure on yourself or the stakeholders to be perfect. Just deal with these issues as they arise, and learn the lessons they will teach you so you do not have to do it again.

9. Use supportive stakeholders, involve them, and get them visibly involved in representing the change effort and expected results. Have them become personally identified with the change. Having enough stakeholders actively involved, especially powerful ones, makes the course of change irreversible. This removes the question of *whether* you should do the change and shifts it to *how* you should do the change.

The first step in stakeholder management is the most important: get the information and find out what their issues are—and why. Find out what they need in order to become supporters and how this process can be made to be a win for them, as well.

DETERMINING STAKEHOLDER CHARACTERISTICS

1. Stakeholder Type

The breakdown of stakeholder types helps to define the role and impact of the stakeholder and is a key input in assessing the influence the stakeholder may have on the project. Stakeholder types are:

Stakeholder Type	Description	Area of Influence	Examples
1 User	Hands-on user of call center equipment	Usage, data entry, problem identification	■ Timely, clean data entry ■ Identifies system problems to appropriate resource ■ Actually uses system vs. prior or shadow system
2 Manager	Manages call center agents, users	User priorities and activities	■ Allows time for user to learn system and use it effectively ■ Establishes performance metrics
3 Developer	Participates in creating call center system	Use or withhold expertise	■ Controls how much creativity, energy, commitment they bring to ensuring timely system development

(continued)

Stakeholder Type	Description	Area of Influence	Examples
4 Process Owner	Significantly impacted by call center	Ensure overall system effectiveness	■ Monitors system implementation and performance ■ Ensures that problems affecting system are addressed
5 Executive	Senior level who controls resources and/or acceptance	Legitimacy, resources, priority	■ Legitimizes system, commits implementation resources, sets performance expectations for stakeholders within his domain
6 Informal leader	Can influence acceptance of system	Expertise, personal power	■ Advocates system usage

2. Level of Impact of the Changes on the Stakeholders

Understanding the degree of impact the changes will have on the stakeholder.

High—Significant changes to job
Medium—Moderate changes to job
Low—Few or small changes to job

3. Importance of Support

Understand how necessary the stakeholder's support is to the successful implementation and deployment of the changes

High—Imperative that the stakeholder supports the program
Medium—Important to have stakeholder's support, but not necessary
Low—Support is helpful but not needed

4. Stakeholder Commitment

Understand the stakeholder's level of commitment to project success.

High—Strong supporter; sees benefits of the change and is committed to project success
Medium—Somewhat supportive, but needs more information
Low—Does not really support the project as currently defined

SECTION 2:

Analytical CRM—Measuring People, Process, and Technology

Why Should You Measure Customer Service?

The primary purpose of any CRM strategy change is to improve customer satisfaction or customer-perceived value. What we found through our years of watching companies provide service is that they not only need to measure the customer service index but they also need to measure the elements that make up customer service, that is, their people, process, and technology solutions. Many times it is these precursors to the customer satisfaction index (people, process, or technology) that are not being done well and the end result is that the customer does not get the service they expected or wanted. In this section of the book we not only look at how to measure your customer satisfaction, but we also provide information, case studies, and formulas to measure how you are providing service via people, process, and technology.

What makes a customer service center world class? It all comes down to skilled people, well-executed processes, and reliable technology. More than anything else, customers say they want to have a satisfying sales and service experience. Skilled customer service center agents who know how to engage a customer and leverage the capabilities of today's technology can create a "branded" experience for their customers. Your customer service center can be a strategic asset, and a competitive differentiator, for your organization.

—Alan Chute, Ph. D., Director, CRM Institute, Avaya, Inc

In this section on analytical CRM we will look at:

- Understanding ROI
- Intelligent analytics
- How benchmarked measurement provides the data for change
- How to measure customer service agents
- How to provide feedback to customer service agents
- ROI for training customer service agents
- ROI for measuring customer dissatisfaction and making changes
- How to calculate customer lifetime value
- How to calculate market damage due to poor service
- How to measure, market, and manage the changes to service and ROI
- How to calculate the cost/benefit of a customer care center
- Case studies in benchmarking, measuring customer service agents, and ROI

By the examples we provide in this section, we want executives to see the customer interaction center as the source of data about customers so they will use the raw data from the call center to make analytically based business decisions. Again, the shift we want to evoke by providing a section on measurement is the thought that the call center is the brains to the data executive's need to predict the future and stay ahead of it.

Customer Lifetime Value

Everyone is talking about customer lifetime value (CLV), but does anyone really understand what it is or truly understand what it takes to achieve it? To begin to address CLV, the more sophisticated topics of calculating customer value, understanding customer loyalty, determining overall customer profitability, and ultimately achieving business growth based on the same needs to be understood. While companies are investing billions in operational CRM systems, very few companies have attempted to understand CRM effectiveness. Yet, shareholders are demanding financial accountability. And why shouldn't they? Technology is very expensive and it does not always give the results expected.

Until recently a heady economy could mask the failure of enterprise resource planning, CRM, supply chain management, and sales force automation and other big IT projects. With little to show for the years of undisciplined, often profligate IT spending many companies are demanding proof of payback at each junction of an IT project by CIOs. This requires CIOs to add financial expertise to their technical and business repertoires or to work very closely with their CFO. In *Internetweek*, July 16, 2001, the following quotes in David Lewis's article, "Top Execs Rein in CIOs" appeared showing the frustration of technology, its current lack of return on the investments, and the direction the executive community is going:

> If CIOs are at the executive table as a peer, then they develop an intuitive sense of how technology needs to be aligned with business goals and where technology can offer a competitive advantage.
>
> —Tom Mangan, Andersen Consulting's CIO Advisory Service

> We are now putting all technical projects through regular ROI analysis.
>
> —David Billings, CIO of Airborne Express

> Among the areas where CIOs can help their CEO, CFO, and other executive partners is to suggest ways technology can bring in more business from existing customers, support new channels of distribution and cut costs.
>
> —David Lewis, author of "Top Execs Rein in CIOs"

The trend towards the gold rush mentality of technology being a panacea that will fix everything seems to be coming to a close. With the realization that executives need to understand not only what the technology will actually do, they also want to know how it will truly impact the bottom line. Doing a detailed analysis can allow you to aggregate the benefits and align them with the corporate mission, as well as encourage measurements and tracking of results. Why measure? It seems there is no other choice and those that understand how to do this will end up being the ones that have successful and profitable CRM implementations. We hope to provide you with enough information to pique your interest in learning to measure and to get you started.

Defining Return on Investment (ROI)

Every chief executive officer has a fiduciary duty to maximize the return on every dollar of capital available to the company. Therefore, with a limited supply of capital for investments in process enhancements, every proposal for capital expenditure must be accompanied by a complete financial analysis demonstrating the possible return to the company of the proposed investment. Many times people tend to avoid trying to do these kinds of calculations because they know that the numbers they have to work with are estimates. For most C-level executives, a well thought out estimate is better than nothing. Most CFO projections are just that, so don't be afraid to venture into ROI land. We have included ways to measure what most people think of as "soft skills." So even that area is no longer out of reach.

Everything is measurable. It is really about putting a stake in the ground and starting, gathering as much information from as many experts surrounding you, and then presenting it with an open mind to get feedback. In introducing the ideas behind ROI, we will focus on a call center in the following section to help the ideas of ROI become grounded in reality so that you can use them.

There are classically two ways to approach an ROI endeavor, cost reduction and/or cost avoidance.

Direct costs are those expense items that can be directly attached to a product or service offered by the company, and also can be easily tracked by the company's accounting system. Indirect costs are those less tangible costs not as easily tracked by the accounting system, and therefore often lumped as overhead.

Focusing on direct costs is the most common approach to ROI calculation, and, in our case of call center information/telecommunication technology investments. Some common direct cost savings are:

- Increased productivity allowing fewer agents to do more in less time

- Implementing information technology that replaces the agent's function altogether

- Reduced telephone costs due to less time in the wait queue

ROI calculations of this type are common, straightforward, and will not be discussed here, even though we strongly recommend that they be used in conjunction with the ROI calculation techniques discussed below.

1. *Profits from new revenues generated.*

   This approach works well for some call center investments and focuses on the simple concept that certain enhancements in customer service will result in retaining more customers, and that retained customers will continue to purchase from you and produce profits. Our example below will focus only on this approach, since it is more subtle and less often taught in MBA or other business education programs.

   Prepare yourself for some resistance and criticism in this category of cost/benefit analysis, because some financial professionals find this approach more difficult to accept, less tangible, more difficult to measure, or hard to tie directly into the project being considered.

2. *A combination of savings and earnings.*

The combination of savings and earnings is nice, but one important design rule in calculating ROIs is "keep it simple" for the audience to understand and to believe.

By assisting your colleagues in presenting a credible and well documented ROI, you are substantially increasing the probability that the company you are working with will actually implement your suggested call center enhancements. Ultimately, "hard dollar" ROI arguments are what sell new technology investments. The approach that we are doing good things for our customers, also known as "soft money," frequently does not convince top management to take action.

REVENUE ELEMENTS TO BE CONSIDERED

From our call center baseline survey research, we will have determined the process where the company's performance is low and where the impact on customer satisfaction is high. The model that we need to develop for the company is "If we invest in and improve the selected process, what will the increase in customer loyalty and repurchase be worth in dollars and cents?" The data we need to determine added income value from this customer is:

1. The average number of purchases made each year, and the profit margin per purchase

2. The average number of years that a customer remains loyal to the company

COST ELEMENTS TO BE CONSIDERED

The cost elements are determined by:

1. A bill of materials with costs of all the pieces of the proposed information technology

2. A cost estimate of the labor charges to install, train, and maintain the information technology investment

3. The cost of capital over the lifetime of the information technology to be implemented

COMPUTING A REALISTIC ROI

The computed ROI is simply the total income divided by the total cost times 100 to state it in terms of a percentage. ROI for customer service investments of 50 percent to 200 percent are quite common.

In addition, when technology or process has been changed or updated, there is a tendency of management to discount the need for budgeting money for training employees in the new systems. There is a sample calculation on computing the ROI for training employees. This is a simple calculation, which should help executives understand that if they don't train people to use the new system, they won't use it, and the money spent on new technology and changes to process will virtually be wasted.

MEASURING ALL THE ELEMENTS IN A CRM SYSTEM

In designing a CRM system it is important to be able to measure and learn from the data output of the CRM whole system—the various parts and also as an integrated system. That integratedCRM data across all multiple e-touch cutomer points (including the Web, ATM, POS, call center, kiosk, direct sales, mobile devices and so on) is what will provide the key to where changes or improvements need to be made in order to ensure true customers satisfaction.

Taken together, both operational and e-business systems create enormous, granular data sources in open formats, which need to be combined, analyzed, and measured, that is, for this volume of data to elicit any meaning, the CRM metrics must be augmented with financial data to arrive at such critical indicators as revenue, profitability, and ROI. CRM Analysis needs to be intelligent enough and integrative enough to enable customers, to measure revenues, profits, and customer satisfaction—not just clicks.

This integrative type of measuring capacity helps organizations to:

- Speed decision making

- Enhance legacy implementations (that is, leverage ERP or CRM analytics)

- Improve margins

- Maximize ROI

The issue really comes down to analysis. The fact is that no one out there has the "single" answer, since this is a multiple data source, multiple function, multiple system, multiple business process problem. It takes in-depth analysis, in conjunction with the operational CRM and business process systems, to really understand and affect customer lifetime value. Companies need to analyze more than just the customer service database. They need a tool to bring in the other customer service systems (ACD, IVR, eCare, etc.), the financial, the on- and off-line transactions, the prospecting and affiliating communications. In addition other factors affecting the real measurement are understanding:

- Service level agreements

- The interaction center's responsiveness and management of the interaction life cycle

- What is takes to "certify" an interaction center, (which requires deep customer service benchmarking of the service delivered to customers)

Focus on Analytics

The following case studies in Chapters 8, 9, and 10 are directly from customers who used analytics to measure customer service satisfaction. From the examples, you will be able to see the needs and requirements the customers are pushing for and the functions and benefits they want.

ANALYSIS VS. REPORTING

While many CRM technologies claim that they provide business analytics, in fact, they are merely providing simple metrics reporting. The trouble is, stark data points don't provide enough meaningful context or rich, textured knowledge that can be effectively leveraged by sales, marketing, and service channels to measure results and target appropriate changes to key business processes.

Straight Reporting Mean Dumb Data Points and Results in One-Time Usage

Straight reporting tells *what* happened. It only provides:

—Single data sources

—Basic top-level data points such as: number of e-mails sent, bounced-back e-mails

—Simple counts

—Segmentation

Intelligent Analysis Means Smart, Meaningful, and Manageable Information and Results in Repurposing

Analysis that demonstrates what happened, why, when, where, and how, providing panoramic customer perspective, so next steps/action items are easily identified and leveraged across business channels is important if you want to change the right things in your business process. Analysis explains how the *total* customer-facing business is functioning, that is:

—Multiple data sources

—Sophisticated reporting

—In-depth, contextualized knowledge

INTELLIGENT ANALYTICS

The key is that a company needs CRM analysis that drills down to deliver the what, where, why, when, and how—the granular yet contextualized details needed to fully understand the efficiency and effectiveness of today's e-businesses. The measurements need to go far beyond raw data/metrics reporting by mining, measuring, and managing real-time customer interactions/indicators such as Web logs, automatic call distribution systems, and e-commerce transactions to enable business leaders to plan, manage, and execute strategies and processes based on in-depth analysis and understanding of the customer relationship. In addition, a CRM measurement application needs to do more than merely run reports that analyze the efficiency of a discrete operation, but rather illuminates the effectiveness of an entire customer-facing business.

By illuminating the complete business picture, the CRM analytics need to not only reveal the overall context, but also reveal critical details like customer retention and profitability, strategic effectiveness, and workforce optimization.

The solution needs to allows companies to:

- Track trends and study historical patterns

- Analyze strategies and implementations

- Forecast future usage

And then be able to answer questions such as:

- How call volume is affecting customer service

- Which products are having the greatest impact

- What aspects of products are generating inquiries, and/or positive and negative service levels

Customer Lifetime Value Calculations

The main purpose of a customer satisfaction surveying program is to measure the company's performance with respect to elements important to customers. In *Listening to the Voice of the Customer*, by Dr. Anton, very detailed information is provided to design customer satisfaction surveys. In this book we provide a process to calculate a customer's lifetime value to your bottom line. By the end of this chapter you will see how valuable customers are and will want to make sure you are doing everything you can to keep them happy. Then in the following chapters we will show case studies where measuring other parts of the business will help to make sure that you are able to keep your customers.

As we saw in the stats in Chapter 1 on customer retention, gaining a new customer costs 5 or 6 times more that taking care of an existing one. So we are suggesting that you have a strategy on who are the customers that you want to have for a lifetime and then a plan on how to take care of them. Dr. Anton is a great example of a cash cow type customer. He flies on United Airlines and with over 150,000 miles logged, he is a 100K frequent flyer traveler now. "Benefits are great and so is the service so I keep coming back!" Those are the kinds of customers you want to keep coming back for more. Figure 7.1 provides a visual way to differentiate between types of customers.

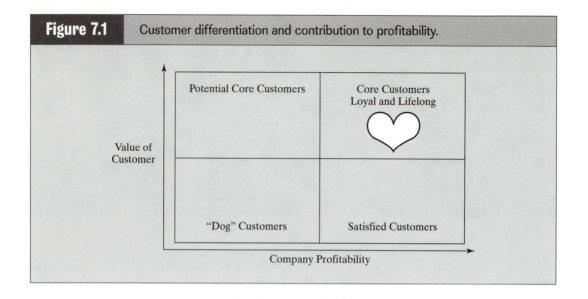

Figure 7.1   Customer differentiation and contribution to profitability.

The figure has two axes, based on the two fundamental goals of the company: x = company profitability and y = value of the customer.

Following the Pareto principle, the core group of customers in the upper left hand side constitutes 20 percent of all customers, but 80 percent of the company's sales volume and profits. So the place to focus your marketing budget is on the customers who add the most value. A company can use its expertise and technology applications, quality, and people to nurture this group to create customers for life.

Another analogy to differentiate a customer base is shown in Figure 7.2. Some of the services and products provided for each group may not be valued by some of the other customer groups, thus driving up costs with no tangible benefit. In the same vein of reviewing products and services, you'll want to examine how you are designing your CRM system so that it meets the needs of whoever your target group of customers is. The various parts of the customer segments provide differing profit margins. Table 7.1.

> *You may think you make products, but what you make is loyal customers.*
> —Mark Hana and Peter Karp, in *Beyond Customer Satisfaction*
> *to Customer Loyalty* by Keki R. Bhote

The primary form of payback or return on a customer satisfaction surveying program comes from retaining customers by allowing a company to better engineer the customer's experience to increase the frequency of "great" experiences, thus leading the customer to the preferred company of choice.

The connection between a customer satisfaction surveying program and the bottom line is the value of customers "saved" from leaving the company. In order to convert the number of saved customers to a bottom-line dollar

TABLE 7.1—VARIATIONS ON CUSTOMERS AND HOW PROFITABLE EACH SECTOR IS TO YOUR BOTTOM LINE.

Type of Customers	Percentage of Customer Base	Percentage of Profit
Platinum	10	25
Gold	15	25
Silver	35	45
Bronze	20	5
Tin	20	−15

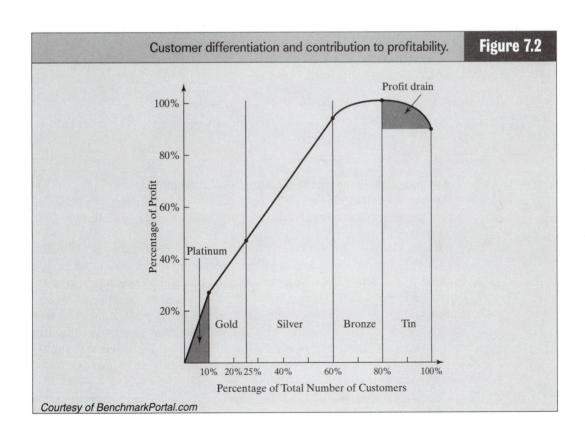

Customer differentiation and contribution to profitability.   **Figure 7.2**

Courtesy of BenchmarkPortal.com

amount, the managers need to calculate the customer lifetime value (CLV) of the target customers.

Many customers change vendors frequently; others stay for years with the same firm. When a customer is gained or saved through customer service, it is not only the revenue generated in one month or one year that constitutes the value of that customer. It is the present value of the future revenue stream generated from that customer for as long as the customer remains with the company. This is the only valid measure of the worth of a customer. The means to compute the CLV are available by borrowing financial concepts and models.

For the sake of illustration we will demonstrate a customer lifetime value calculation assuming that:

1. The stream of revenues from the customer is level across time at $25 per month or $300 per year

2. The interest rate (opportunity cost) is the bank rate paid on the money for which no other specific use is made and will be assumed to be 9 percent

3. The time a typical customer stays with a company is 3 years

The calculation is then:

$$\text{CLTV} = R\left[\frac{1 - \dfrac{1}{(1 + i)^N}}{i}\right]$$

R = annual revenue received from a loyal customer
i = the relevant interest rate or opportunity cost of money per period
N = the number of periods in which a customer makes purchases

In our example, the lifetime value of our typical customer is $759.39.

Calculating the value of a saved customer is identical to calculating the lifetime value. Why? Because a customer saved can be expected to stay another lifetime—everything else being equal. This argues for substantial latitude to be given to a customer contact person to do what it takes to save the customer for the company. This is especially true given the difficulty and expense of recruiting new customers. Even if the customer is simply wrong, it can be more profitable to keep that customer than to be "right" and lose the customer.

We have found two of the most effective strategies for maximizing the value of a relationship to be:

1. Developing targeted offers to stimulate incremental sales

2. Launching a preferred-customer program for a company's best customers as airlines do with their frequent flyer programs

To sustain the relationship, marketers need to monitor customer needs, measure satisfaction levels, and respond to customer life cycle changes.

Employing customer satisfaction programs as an integral part of continuous quality improvement is crucial to an understanding of its payback. Like internal quality initiatives, the customer satisfaction surveying program impacts profits several ways, by:

■ Identifying the process(s) for change that will maximize the impact on customer satisfaction

■ Preventing erosion of the customer base

■ Minimizing negative word of mouth (WOM)

■ Understanding better what the customer perceives to be a value-added experience, worth a premium price

For more information on customer satisfaction surveying programs look at *Listening To The Voice Of The Customer: 16 Steps To A Customer Satisfaction Surveying Program*, by Dr. Anton.

In the next section we provide some easy-to-follow formulas to calculate

■ Impact of negative word of mouth

■ Impact of poor service

■ Impact of improving the service

■ Net value of complaint handling

■ Prevention of problems

■ Value of better accessibility of your service

Customer Lifetime Value Calculations

Average customer lifetime =	9
Initial cost =	$900
Price of initial purchase =	$5,000
Expected yearly additional revenue =	$500
Interest rate	9%
Customer lifetime value =	$7,098

(continued)

Increasing Customer Lifetime Value Calculation:

Price of initial purchase of second product	$300
Expected yearly additional revenue =	$300
Increased customer lifetime value =	$2,099
Total customer lifetime value =	$9,196

Market Damage Approximations

Total customer lifetime value =	$9,196
Word-of-mouth factor =	15
Influence rate =	100
Lost profits per lost customer =	$10,576
Number of complaints =	100
Percent complaining =	11%
Customers experience the problem =	909
Complaints resolved satisfactorily =	65%
Market damage =	$9,984,353

What if?

More people learn of the problem?

Word-of-mouth factor =	15

More people complain?

Percent complaining =	11%

More complaints resolved satisfactorily?

Complaints resolved satisfactorily =	65%

Customers as corporate assets:

Percent of customers that score 5 =	14%
Approximate total number of customers =	100000
Total customer lifetime value =	$9,196
Customer asset =	$128,747k

If you would like to get a copy of the customer lifetime value spreadsheet to use in your company please log on to:

www.benchmarkportal.com/store/search_by_cat.taf?media_type=&_
function=detail&Inventory_uid1=82

You will be asked to input some information in order to best direct your request and then it will go directly to the customer lifetime value spreadsheet.

Benchmarking Your CRM Center

A BANK CASE STUDY IN PEER BENCHMARKING

We will start with measuring how a company can benchmark a CRM center. With that baseline, you can begin to understand what in the CRM process might need further attention. We'll provide a case study for benchmarking a call center so that we are not talking in theory, but giving you real-life scenerio so that you can see how someone else used benchmarking to change the way they are providing service. We will then look at case studies and tools to measure employee performance (the people who are providing the customer service and managing the customer relationship) and also technology that helps to garner why customers are not happy, and with that information, how major business decisions are made that change profitability.

Now that top executives in both the public sector, or government, and the private sector, or industry, are convinced that the customer service center is a strategic weapon for getting customers, keeping customers, and growing profitable customers, the importance of performance benchmarking has become mission critical. Peer benchmarking is a structured, analytical method of comparing the performance of two or more customer service centers in order to determine best practice goals and to ensure competitive customer relationship management functionality leading to market dominance. It is the best way to determine if the money you are spending in the call center is returning on your investment and providing the customer service functions you want it to.

Most companies don't think to benchmark this part of their business, but when they understand that obtaining a new customer is six times as expensive as retaining an existing one, they begin to realize the value that the call center can bring. To get out of the cost containment rut, a customer service center needs to assess the gaps in its current performance so that it can then become a profit center.

Peer benchmarking of a mission-critical company process, such as accounting, manufacturing, and shipping has been around for years. The process is well documented and is a popular way to answer the question "how good is good enough" when it comes to the performance of a department or process within an organization. Benchmarking is a structured gap analysis of performance metrics for organizations with similar characteristics. That is, it is logical to compare banks with banks, insurance companies with insurance companies, and the like. In order to most easily understand a peer benchmark and its value, we will use an actual case study.

Establishing a Peer Group

Most customer service center benchmark research has the following issues or problems for making sound management decisions:

- They do not have sufficient participation of other customer service centers to make any real statistical comparisons that have a significance level worthy of management's time. In other words, there are simply too few customer service centers in their database. If a benchmark study has less than 400 customer service centers, the data comparisons probably do not represent the performance of customer service centers in your space.

- They compare your customer service center performance to others in your industry, that is, banks to banks, insurance companies to insurance companies. In our experience, this is not a valid comparison since in our database alone, banks range from customer service centers with 100 agents to those with 1,000 agents, from those handling one million calls per year to 20 million calls per year. These banks do not have the same challenges and are therefore not a valid benchmark comparison.

For a valid comparison, the characteristics of a customer service center need to be defined. For example, let's assume that your customer service center had the following characteristics:

- Call volume is at least 80 percent inbound calls
- Calls are at least 60 percent business-to-business
- At least 500 agents handle more than five million calls per year

For the comparison to yield meaningful data, your center would have to be compared with other customer service centers with the same characteristics so it would result in an "apples to apples" comparison of performance.

Selecting and Defining Performance Metrics

The next section addresses which customer service center metrics to manage in the discovery process of comparing a customer service center to your peer group of customer service centers. The Purdue University Benchmark Research Web site at www.BenchmarkPortal.com provides a simple and cost effective way to create a peer benchmark report.

The metrics most important in the peer group benchmarking investigation are described below in two categories, those metrics that impact efficiency, and those that impact effectiveness. A very general benchmark goal is suggested for each metric; however, in the actual performance comparisons, this should be done directly with your self-defined peer group. These metrics are described and defined briefly.

SPECIFIC EFFECTIVENESS METRICS

Effectiveness metrics are those that address the caller's issues, thereby achieving the strategic goals of the customer service center: getting, growing and keeping loyal profitable customers.

1. Caller Satisfaction

    Most customer service centers have some method of asking callers how satisfied they were with the calling experience. Suggested measures are what percentage of callers are willing to give you a perfect score, that is, a 5 out of 5, a 7 out of 7, or a 10 out of 10 points. This is not easy to achieve and a reasonable benchmark goal is 50 percent.

2. First Customer Service Resolution

    Callers want their issue resolved with only one customer service call to your company (also called "first time final" or "once and done" calls). This means no transfers and no callbacks. A good benchmark target for this metric is 85 percent.

3. Percentage of Calls Blocked

    This is a measure of caller accessibility. By dividing the volume of calls handled by the calls offered, the percentage of calls blocked is determined. A target goal for this metric should be under 4 percent.

4. Average Speed of Answer (ASA)

    Average speed of answer (ASA) is also a measurement of customer accessibility when managed to an hour or half-hour increment. ASA is determined by dividing the total queue time by the total calls handled for the measurement period. A good benchmark is 18 seconds, managed to the half-hour period.

5. Service Level (SL)

   As with ASA, service level (SL) is also a measurement of caller accessibility. Service level is computed by determining the percentage of calls that are answered within X number of seconds in a distinct period of time. Also, as with ASA, it is critical to manage SL to an hour or half-hour period, which ties the measurement to the customer experience. A common benchmark target is 80 percent answered in 20 seconds managed to the half-hour period.

6. Percentage of Calls Leading to an Up-Sell or a Cross-Sell

   As customer service centers move from cost centers to profit centers, a measure of effectiveness is the ability to detect opportunities for making sales, shifting the focus from productivity to profitability. A benchmark for this metric is an excess of 20 percent of calls should result in an opportunity to at least do an "up-sell" to the caller.

SPECIFIC EFFICIENCY METRICS

Efficiency metrics focus on achieving the call center's effectiveness goals as inexpensively as possible. Some of the important efficiency metrics are as follows:

1. Calls Handled per Shift

   This metric will vary widely depending on the industry studied. If we study all respondents in our benchmark database, the average is 43 calls per shift.

2. Percentage of Callers that Abandon

   If a caller accesses the customer service center ACD, Automatic Call Distributor, is then placed into a queue, and is not handled by an agent within an acceptable time, he or she will hang up, or abandon from queue. The percentage of abandons is a good measure of how efficiently the center is managed. The benchmark is less than 4 percent for abandoned calls.

3. Average Talk Time (ATT)

   Average talk time (ATT) represents the amount of time an agent is engaged with a caller. The metric usually includes conversation time and hold time (when the agent puts the caller on hold to ask a question, access reference material, etc.) It does not include queue time. ATT varies considerably with the industry segment and purpose of the call. An all-industry benchmark would be less than 5 minutes.

4. After Call Work Time (ACW)

   After call work time (ACW) is the time an agent spends completing a transaction precipitated by a phone call after the call is released. The benchmark goal should be less than 3 minutes.

5. Percentage Occupancy

   The formula for occupancy is average talk time (ATT) plus after call work time (ACW) divided by average talk time (ATT) plus after call work time (ACW) plus time waiting for calls. The target for this metric should be at 90 percent.

6. Cost per Call

Cost per call is a figure that most customer service centers are able to compute. It is determined by dividing the operating budget by the number of calls handled by the center. Although it varies widely, the fully-loaded average for all industries is about $7 per call.

7. Percentage Calls Handled by Self Service

The percentage of all calls that are handled by the interactive voice response (IVR) unit is an indication of efficiency. The target benchmark for this metric should be 20 percent or more.

8. Percentage Schedule Adherence

Schedule adherence ties directly to the management of the forecasting and scheduling process. Once a schedule is created that determines when each agent should be at his or her position and available to take calls, this metric monitors how well the agents adhere to that schedule. Most companies set a 95 percent target, meaning that each agent is logged onto or off of the system, within the leeway of 1 to 3 minutes, 95 percent of the time.

9. Annual Turnover Percentage

Turnover is normal, and should be expected in any company. However, an excessive rate of turnover can hurt a company financially. The benchmark is less than 10 percent turnover per year (leaving the company). This does not include movement to other areas of the company or promotions.

The Case Study Organizational Profile

This case study describes the benchmarking experience of a customer service center in a banking and financial services organization in North America. This company, with $3 billion in assets, operated 22 customer service centers and employed 325 telephone service representatives who annually handled 4,524,000 calls. The primary functions of these representatives were customer service and handling complaints. Ninety percent of the calls they handled were inbound. The other 10 percent were follow-up outbound calls.

This bank participated in the Purdue benchmark research and has given its permission to use the data without revealing the identity of the bank. The Purdue benchmarking team selected a peer group, that is, a group of customer service centers with a similar profile to this bank's call center. The profile delimiters used were industry segment (that is, banking and financial services), number of inbound calls handled (in this case, 2 million to 5 million calls), number of telephone service representatives (200 to 400), type of calls handled, and many more.

The next sections of this case study will:

- Give examples of the reports the bank's benchmark team used to change performance
- Explain the initiatives selected by the benchmarking team
- Report on the final actual improvements in performance that resulted six months later

Selecting Improvement Initiatives

Once you have put in the benchmark data, via this online process, you get a profile of the call center. In the profile are several reports that can help a company to determine the improvement initiatives to begin with. Those are:

1. Peer Group Performance Matrix

2. Inbound Performance Comparison Report

3. Performance Ranking Report

4. Group versus Solution Optimizer Report

PEER GROUP PERFORMANCE MATRIX

The first report shows the peer group performance matrix, Figure 8.1.

This report uses an efficiency index. An efficiency index is a combination of 10 performance metrics that are related to productivity. Examples

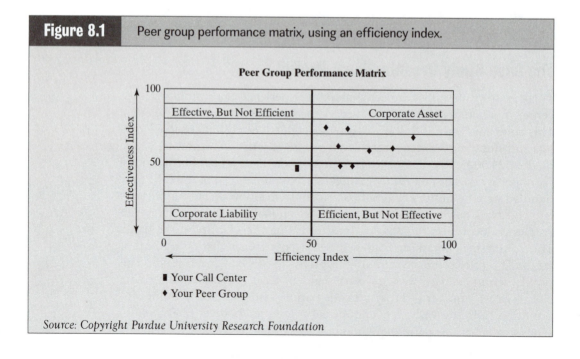

Figure 8.1   Peer group performance matrix, using an efficiency index.

Source: Copyright Purdue University Research Foundation

would be average talk time, average after call work time, and calls per telephone service representative per shift.

To create this matrix, the efficiency index is plotted on the x axis, and the effectiveness index is plotted on the y axis. Customer service centers that are very inefficient at doing a very ineffective job for their companies are considered a corporate liability, whereas customer service centers that are very efficient and doing a very effective job for their companies are considered a corporate asset.

The performance matrix shows that the case study bank's customer service center is performing at the level of a corporate liability while six of its peer group customer service centers achieved the status of a corporate asset. Two of the peer group customer service centers are in the efficient but not effective quadrant. It is immediately obvious to the benchmarking team that they must drill down to determine what factors are causing this less-than-acceptable performance.

Though the peer group performance matrix is not an actionable report, it is a high-level and accurate litmus test of the call center's ability to provide the customer-relationship-management best-practice standards of peer group customer service centers with the same business challenges. So, the next step is to find one or more of the possible root causes of the low performance.

INBOUND PERFORMANCE COMPARISON REPORT

The first drill-down report is called the inbound performance comparison report. Figure 8.2 shows a partial listing from this report. The peer group best is the top 10 percent of a peer group.

Excerpt from the inbound performance comparison report.	**Figure 8.2**

Inbound Performance Comparisons

Metric Description	Your Center Response	Peer Group Median	Peer Group Average	Peer Group Best Median	Peer Group Best Average	All Participants Median	All Participants Average
Average Speed of Answer (seconds)	35.0	20.0	32.2	12.5	17.1	25.0	33.3
Average Talk Time (minutes)	4.2	3.0	7.2	3.0	3.4	4.0	10.2
Average After Call Work Time (minutes)	3.0	1.0	5.3	1.0	1.1	2.0	6.8
Average Calls Abandoned (%)	7.0	3.0	5.0	2.0	2.8	4.7	5.5
Average Time in Queue (seconds)	54.0	35.0	44.3	16.0	18.4	34.0	43.2
Average First/Final Calls (%)	65.0	79.0	77.3	85.0	86.1	79.0	68.1
Average TSR Occupancy (%)	76.0	80.0	79.4	87.0	89.1	79.0	74.8
Average Adherence to Schedule (%)	81.0	89.0	87.8	92.0	95.3	84.1	88.0
Average Calls/Shift/TSR (calls)	58.0	70.0	83.2	85.0	86.5	70.0	69.2
Average Attendance (%)	75.0	90.0	88.7	85.0	87.7	88.3	88.8

Source: Copyright Purdue University Research Foundation

This report shows the following:

- Customer service center performance metrics descriptions in the first column

- A column with the actual customer service center performance metrics (noted as "Your Center")

- The peer group medians and averages

- The best in peer group medians and averages

- The average for all participants

For brevity purposes, this excerpt shows only 10 customer service center performance metrics that highlight management opportunities. It immediately became clear to the benchmarking team that the customer service center is underperforming on the following metrics:

- Average speed of answer

- Average calls abandoned

- Average time in queue

- Average first/final calls

- Average telephone service representative occupancy

- Average adherence to schedule

- Average calls per shift per telephone representative

At this stage of the research by the benchmarking team, it was already becoming clear which metric may be having the biggest impact on performance and customer service. The most important caller satisfaction driver is the ability of a customer service center to answers callers' questions on the first call with no transfers and no callbacks. In Figure 8.2, this metric is called the "average first/final calls" (also sometimes called "average once and done calls"). The bank's score is 65 percent, compared with the score of 77.3 percent for the peer groups of banks. The difference of 12.3 percent may appear small, but when the cost of this lack of performance is calculated for this bank, it totals over $2 million each year. That expense makes it worth launching an improvement initiative.

PERFORMANCE RANKING REPORT

The second drill-down report is called the peer group ranking report. Figure 8.3 gives a partial listing of this report.

This report gives the benchmarking team an even more granular look at how the bank compares, metric for metric, with its peer group of banks. For instance, when it comes to blocked calls, the case study bank is actually

	Excerpt from the peer group ranking report.					**Figure 8.3**	

Peer Group Ranking Report

	Blocked Calls	Adherence	ASA	ATT	Abandoned	Queue Time	Occupancy
Metrics →							
Your Percentile →	95.7%	26%	87%	22%	52.1%	74.0%	18%
	.04%	95%	5	2.2	0%	10	91
	1.85%	94%	7	3.6	2%	11	88
	2.81%	92%	10	3.7	2%	13	86
	3.05%	91%	15	4.2	2%	15	85
	3.17%	90%	22	4.9	3%	16	82
Rank	4.84%	90%	25	5.1	4%	20	77
	5.80%	89%	31	5.3	5%	32	73
	5.82%	88%	31	6.6	6%	36	71
	6.45%	86%	50	7.3	7%	39	68
	7.78%	82%	60	8.5	7%	42	63
	8.44%	77%	68	9.1	9%	45	60

Source: Copyright Purdue University Research Foundation

doing rather well, performing in the 95.7 percentile and ranking second. However, in the important performance metric of telephone representative occupancy, the bank is only ranked 11th, and only in the 18th percentile.

The team wanted to select the one metric that may be causing the most damage to performance—that is, finding the lowest hanging fruit—so management can direct a focused budget for an improvement initiative. (Again we want to point out that CRM is about change, about changing the way service is being provided. And this is why we spent so much time in the first section of the book on understanding the nature of change. Measurement can tell you what to change, but not how to go about making the changes so that they are accepted and not sabotaged.) Not shown in Figure 8.3 is that the bank ranks at the bottom, having had the absolute worst performance, on the metric of "average first/final calls." That initiative became the focus of the bank's benchmarking team.

GAP VERSUS SOLUTION OPTIMIZER REPORT

The final report is called the gap versus solution optimizer report. A partial listing of this report appears in Figure 8.4.

This reports gives the benchmark team a listing of all gaps in excess of 20 percent, that is, the major ones. For each gap it provides a list of potentially applicable solutions to reduce that gap. The figure lists only one such gap—"percent of once and done calls"—although there were a total of eight major gaps in performance at the bank's customer service center that would have their own list of optimized solutions.

Figure 8.4	Excerpt from the gap versus solution optimizer report.

Gap vs Solution Optimizer

	Solution	Cost Per Seat ($)	Implement Time (days)	Risk Factor (0-100)	Gap Impact (%)	ROI (%)	Optimal Decision
	Applicant Testing	100	30	40	20	374	6.49
	Skill Based Routing	400	50	50	75	315	4.51
GAP:	Applicant Screening	250	40	30	30	184	2.18
"Once	CT Integration	900	120	75	90	137	1.91
&	Value Based Routing	400	60	60	55	128	1.49
Done	Monitoring/Coaching	300	60	40	65	118	1.33
Calls"	Product Training	600	90	65	35	91	1.01
	Expert Systems	1500	180	95	55	89	.94
	Contact Tracking	3000	120	85	50	64	.85
	Performance Comp	300	30	10	15	64	.65
	CB Training	600	90	35	35	53	.61

Source: Copyright Purdue University Research Foundation

From the previous reports, the benchmarking team decided that the biggest negative gap in performance seems to be the average first/final calls, or "once and done calls." The gap versus solution optimizer report then became a management aid to select that one solution that may produce the best results with the minimum corporate resources.

This report lists 11 solutions that could be implemented in the order of most desirable on the basis of the optimal decision index. This index is calculated by statistically averaging the most important issues that managers should consider when selecting any improvement initiative:

- **Cost per seat:** Many solutions are priced on the basis of cost per seat. Knowing this factor allows the manager to quickly determine if there is enough money in the budget to even consider the initiative.

- **Implementation time:** This is an estimate of the average implementation time to complete the installation of the solution. Most managers prefer to select initiatives that can be implemented within approximately six months.

- **Risk factor:** Most managers are risk averse. The risk factor has been developed over time by discussing solutions with those that have already implemented a solution. Sometimes high-risk solutions are worth undertaking, but only in light of the other decision factors.

- **Gap impact factor:** This factor gives an indication of the percent of the gap that will be reduced by the successful implementation of a particular solution.

- **Return on investment (ROI):** This is the standard ROI equation that decision makers use most often in selecting one solution over another.

From the gap versus solution optimizer report it becomes clear that applicant testing and skill-based routing are high on the list of potential improvement initiatives. In this particular example, the bank's benchmarking team received management's approval to pursue both initiatives. Specifications were prepared, a request for proposal (also called RFP) was issued, vendors were selected, and the initiatives were launched and successfully completed.

Monitoring Improvement Processes

It is important to not only make the changes, but also to monitor the changes over time to make sure they are getting the results needed. In this case, six months after the successful installation and implementation of the two improvement initiatives, the bank benchmarked again and found:

- The percent of first/final calls improved by 11.6 percent
- The average time in queue was reduced by 2.8 percent
- The average TSR occupancy was improved by just over 6 percent
- Calls per TSRs per shift were increased by 9.4 percent
- Caller satisfaction rose by almost 7 percent

The bank spent approximately $600,000 for the two improvement initiatives, including the selection process, the cost of the software and hardware products, the training costs of the TSRs, and the installation services costs from a third-party integrator. When the improved metrics were converted to new revenue, reduced operating cost, and customer satisfaction, the estimated ROI was in excess of 100 percent in 16 months of operation.

Benchmarking cannot guarantee the success of any improvement initiative. However, this case study does prove that by scientifically selecting initiatives based on hard facts, not just personal intuition, or gut feel, management can effectively target improvements that have the maximum impact on the company's bottom-line profits.

Measuring People Who Provide Service

In the bank case study, one of the issues was employee performance. Sometimes poor employee performance is related to complicated case management systems or unclear processes and procedures and sometimes it is related to limiting technical issues, like being able to bring two screens up at once. In order to understand what is affecting the performance of the employees who are providing service, it makes sense to measure the service they are providing and begin to pinpoint exactly what needs to be changed. Sometimes it is behavior related: training specifically directed to that can make all the difference in the world. Our experience with call center employees is that if you give them feedback in a meaningful and concrete manner, they are happy to change the way they are doing things. Just the mere fact that they might be measured is a motivation to provide better customer service. As the old saying goes, "You get what you measure!"

MEASURING CUSTOMER SERVICE EMPLOYEES FOR MAXIMUM PERFORMANCE

Staffing is by far the highest cost in any customer service center. In fact, Purdue University research found that the average cost to replace a CSR is $6,350. Improving the efficiency of your human resources can result in substantial productivity and profitability gains. To do this a company needs trend analysis and performance measurement capabilities. This enables customer service center management to increase the efficiency of its systems and the effectiveness of its people, realizing rapid return on investment and increasing profits to new levels.

Technology has played a growing role in modern customer service centers for the past several decades. And with each new technological development the profitability bar gets raised yet again. Although each individual piece of customer service center technology, for example, ACD, IVR, predictive dialer, and so on, adds to the growth of the customer service center, the disparate nature of these technologies does not allow for an integrated approach to boosting efficiency, productivity, and profitability in the customer service center. What we have found is that a system is necessary to:

- Measure service levels in the call centers or the e-commerce enabled universal customer service centers

- Motivate agents with goal setting

- Measure performance objectively and automatically

- Maximize agent productivity

- Improve service levels by providing agents with concrete feedback and the opportunity to learn and grow

Technology related to human performance needs to provide information for:

- Front-line managers a simple, predefined agent performance evaluation or report card based on selected performance indicators.

- Business managers/analysts to have direct access to detailed performance data for intricate analysis. Powerful ad hoc tools allow complex "what if" scenarios.

- Executive managers to review customer service center analysis reports, or operations performance status of the customer service center and perform simple drill down analysis of key data.

Figure 9.1 gives a process that can be followed to enhance performance. In addition, if the software can track specific performance indicators that have been specified by management to measure success (revenue per agent-hour, right party connect time, agent schedule adherence, etc.), then goals can be set and results tracked with a series of measurements. If these results can be viewed across time by day, week, month, or year then they give great insight for the performance evaluation process because they provide a concrete, historical look at performance. Being able to view them across personnel to track the effect of staff changes or new training techniques, and

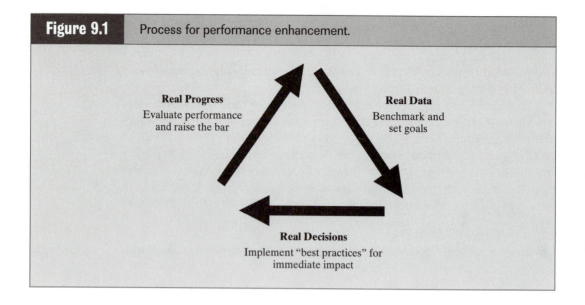

| Figure 9.1 | Process for performance enhancement. |

Real Progress
Evaluate performance
and raise the bar

Real Data
Benchmark and
set goals

Real Decisions
Implement "best practices" for
immediate impact

across work groups allows managers to compare teams and campaigns. It also allows them to target training and motivational programs.

Performance Measurement That Improves Customer Service

Let's take a look at a case study for measuring human performance and examine the capability to have technology enable human performance. We wanted to provide this as an example so that when you are deciding what technologies you want to include in your CRM practice you will have at least one example of technology that can *enable people.* This is a relatively new thought in leadership. This will help you to determine what you want technology to provide you and help to justify why you are buying it. First we will look at what the technology does and then see the ROI calculations.

This particular software takes information from various aspects of the technology, and as shown in Figure 9.2, then feeds it into a process with various forms of outputs. In order to get those outputs, information needs to be input. This includes performance indicators and goals. Just the mere fact that management is sitting down to figure out what these inputs for success are is heading the customer service center in the right direction. This process of figuring success indicators and goals begins the focused attempt to create excellent CRM.

A key performance indicator (KPI) is a predefined set of one or more of the results that are being tracked. For example, the KPI availability tracks the time an agent spends working the phones, taking breaks, training on skills, and calculates the percentage of when an agent is actually working

Figure 9.2

This figure depicts the process of taking data from customer care centers and translating it into usable data to evaluate agent performance with outputs being in the form of e-mail, print, faxes, etc.

CENTERFORCE ANALYZER

ACD
Predictive Dialers
VRU
CTI
Enterprise Apps
Internet

Web Browser
E-mail
Print
Fax
Excel/Word
PC Client

the phones. The next step is to set goals for each key performance indicator. For example, a key performance indicator can be dollars collected per hour for a collections customer service center and the goal could be $200 per hour for a junior-level agent and $300 per hour for a senior-level agent. You will want to analyze where your value levers are to provide the best return on your center, Figure 9.3.

Figure 9.4 is an example of goals that might be set by the customer service center management. Goals are set by skill level according to the definitions set by the customer. In this example we have defined New Hire, Sophomore, Junior, and Lead as the skill levels. The actual performance of

Figure 9.3

Your value levers determine what to measure and provide the best return on your center.

Where are your value levers?
Measuring Your Return

Outbound & Blend
- Right party customer services
- Handle times
- Wrap up times

Inbound
- Handle time
- Service levels
- After call work
- Web transactions per agent

Enterprise
- Dollars collected per hour
- Sales per hour
- Customer service calls handled per hour
- Service levels
- Orders processed

| **Figure 9.4** | Key performance indicators for various levels of customer service agents. |

Courtesy of Centerforce Technologies

the agents, supervisors, etc. will be compared against goals to give the management team an evaluation for each performance indicator. Following is a partial list of typical KPI measurements (see Figure 9.5):

- Percent Promises-to-Pay vs. Right Party Handle Time

- Working Phone Percentages

- Dollars Collected per Hour per Agent

- Agent Time Distribution by Customer Service Center

- Working Phones Times Distribution by Customer Service Center

- Wrong Party Wrap Up Time by Agent

- Right Party Wrap Up Time by Agent

- Call Attempt Distribution

- Customer Service Distribution as a Function of Connects

- Right Party Connect Distribution

- Hourly Connect Rate

- Connect and Promise Rate per Day of the Week

- Agent Handle Time per Connect

- Station Utilization Rate

When the customer service center's organizational changes and assignments of agents to supervisors change, one can still have a historical view of each agent's performance. In addition, when managers can review the performance of a supervisor over time, even though agents may be reassigned

Key performance indicators for various customer service agents. This shows how Performance Indicators (PIs) can be changed based on what your center needs to measure.	**Figure 9.5**

Courtesy of Centerforce Technologies

to different supervisors, they also can understand the dynamics that go into making that manager successful.

Another important feature is being able to cut the data in different ways. Figure 9.6 shows that the various dimensions can be rolled up into a broader category, for instance, January, February, and March can be rolled up into Quarter 1. In reverse, a broad level can also be drilled down to analyze a narrower level; for example, March can be drilled down to analyze the days within March. The work group dimension can be any work-related dimension. For example, different buckets for collection can be tracked, or results from different client companies can be kept separate for service bureaus.

Various ways data can be shown to give many views of the information depending on the audience.	**Figure 9.6**

Dimension	Roll Up/Drill Down Detail
Time	Year, quarter, month, day, review period, date range, day of week
Personnel	Company, customer service center site, manager, supervisor, agent
Work Group	Group level 1, group level 2, group level 3
Evaluation Data	Operation Performance Status, ReportCard, Performance Indicators
System	Customer service center application: ACD, IVR, CTI, predictive dialer, enterprise application, internet

The data can be viewed to see one customer service center or many. A supervisor can look at several agents at one time, Figure 9.7.

The goals of an individual agent can also be seen, Figure 9.8.

When performance measurements are compared to the goals, it becomes clear the areas for specific improvement. For example, Figure 9.9 is a chart of performance measurement that indicates percentages of:

- Right Party Talk Time

- Right Party Wrap Up Time

- Wrong Party Talk Time

- Wrong Party Wrap Up Time

- Idle Time, etc.

This chart shows that this agent spent 47 percent of his or her time on "Inbound Talk Time." With a simple point-and-click, you can drill down to analyze these results by level of the organization or drill across to view different time frames or work groups. Additionally, you can choose whether to view the data in graph (Figure 9.9) or chart form (Figure 9.10).

When managers want to benchmark an agent's performance against other agents, it is great to have a tool that will show this graphically, as in Figure 9.11. This kind of information can help define your center's

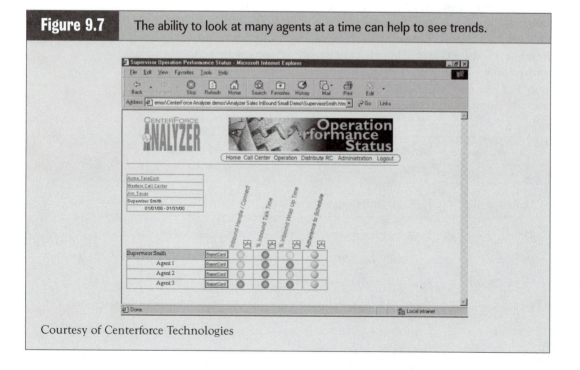

Figure 9.7   The ability to look at many agents at a time can help to see trends.

Courtesy of Centerforce Technologies

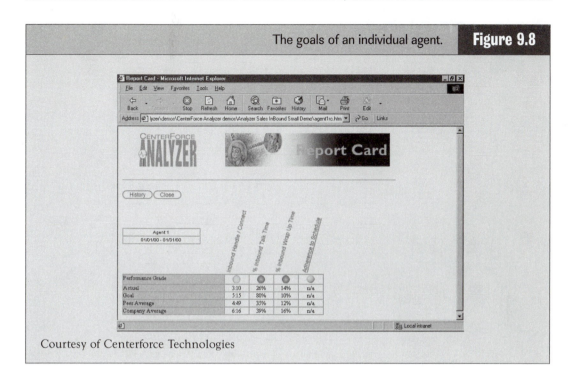

Figure 9.8 — The goals of an individual agent.

Courtesy of Centerforce Technologies

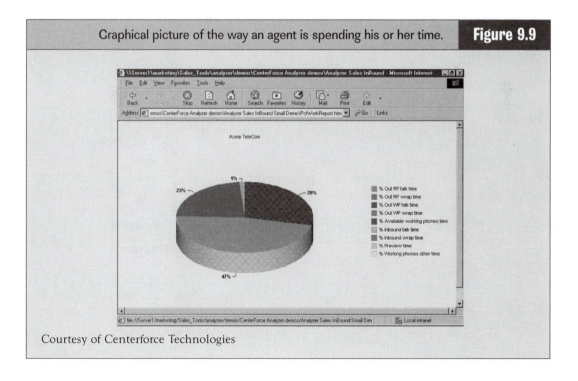

Figure 9.9 — Graphical picture of the way an agent is spending his or her time.

Courtesy of Centerforce Technologies

Figure 9.10 Graph of average talk time and wrap up time that shows potential opportunities for development.

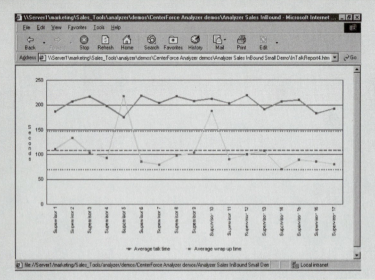

Courtesy of Centerforce Technologies

Figure 9.11 Graphical representation of the ability to drill down across multiple dimensions.

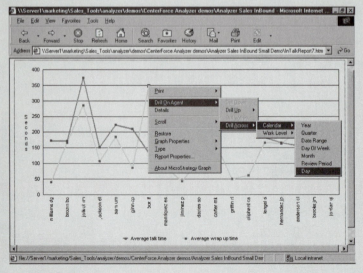

Courtesy of Centerforce Technologies

current results and will serve as a baseline for setting attainable goals. In the comparison of the RPC time to promises for all agents the manager can get "what if" answers in minutes, Figure 9.12.

Another important item would be to be able to allow customer service center managers to get a quick view of the performance of their organization by showing a comparison of the goals set to the actual values for each performance indicator. In Figure 9.13, these kinds of results are coded for easy, at-a-glance deciphering by the busy customer service center management team.

Your computer screen shows:

■ A red value means the goal has been missed by a large margin

■ A yellow value means the result was within 30 percent of the goal

■ A green value means the goal has been met or exceeded

By drilling down, a manager can get the same view of each supervisor's agents. By drilling up, a similar view is available of an entire organization and each of its customer service centers. Clicking a History button offers a view to see those same performance indicators across time. By simply clicking on anything blue and underlined, a manager can data surf anywhere in the defined dimensions. By clicking on ReportCard, managers get a more

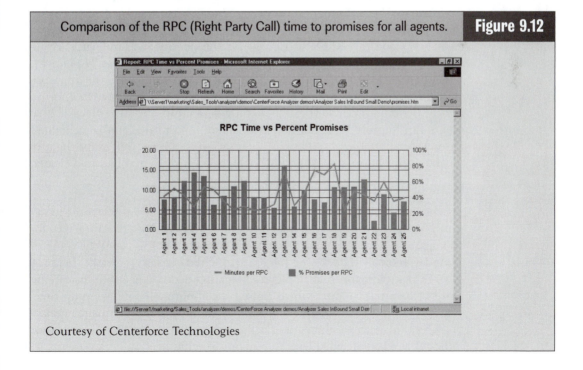

Comparison of the RPC (Right Party Call) time to promises for all agents.   **Figure 9.12**

Courtesy of Centerforce Technologies

Figure 9.13	Operation performance status report.

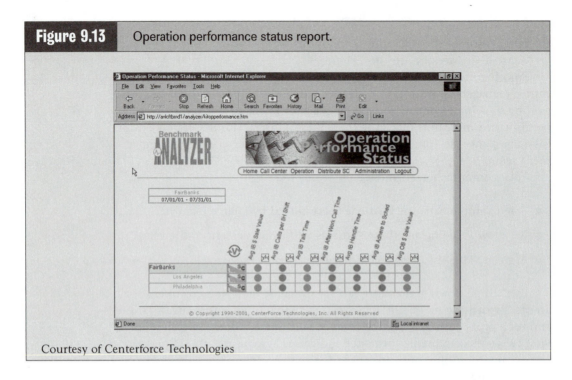

Courtesy of Centerforce Technologies

detailed analysis of the corresponding individual. An example of a typical re-port card is shown in Figure 9.14. For example, a performance grade of RED was given for the performance indicator "Wrong Party Wrap Up Time" because the actual value, 35 percent, was far greater than the goal of 8 percent. A per-formance grade of GREEN was given for the performance indicator "Avail-ability" because the goal of 80 percent was exceeded (actual was 74 percent).

When a supervisor can print out a report card along with the appropri-ate performance indicators and goals this can be a very effective tool to use during periodic reviews. These tools provide a clear, objective view of how agents can improve their performance. When report cards can be generated for each personnel level of the customer service center, as well as for the cen-ter and organization, then the whole operation's effectiveness becomes clearer.

MEASUREMENT EXAMPLE: WRONG PARTY WRAP UP TIME

This performance measurement, Figure 9.15, shows that Agent 9 is consistently much higher than the average for the customer service center and the goal for "Wrong Party Wrap Up Time." It also demonstrates that this is not the result of a one-day anomaly that skewed the data (i.e., child got sick, car broke down, or other things that happen to employees that affect performance), but instead the result of habitual conduct which caused the abnormally long wrap up time. This long-term view is an excellent tool for training and performance evalua-tions. Performance measurements like these allow you to view each performance indicator at a very detailed level to pinpoint specific areas of improvements.

A report card provides supervisors with an effective tool for evaluating and reviewing agents.   **Figure 9.14**

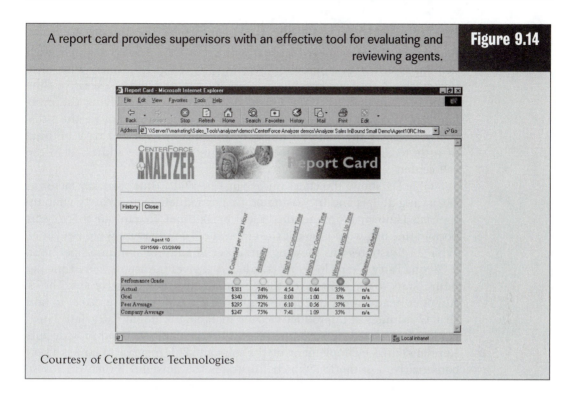

Courtesy of Centerforce Technologies

Graph of wrong party wrap up time for Agent 9.   **Figure 9.15**

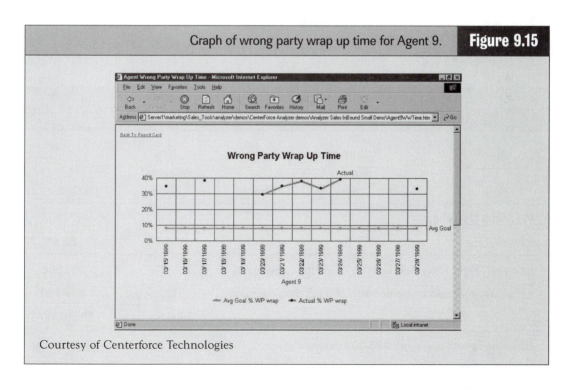

Courtesy of Centerforce Technologies

MEASUREMENT EXAMPLE: PRODUCTIVITY IMPROVEMENT

Rapid ROI can be achieved in many different ways. In this example we'll demonstrate ROI by improving "Wrong Party Wrap Up Time." With technology this company was able to pinpoint the problem of excessive time spent in "Wrong Party Wrap Up Mode." Only after identifying the problem can your call center managers employ strategies to improve the situation. Otherwise the manager might be making changes that have nothing or little to do with the real root causes that need to be addressed in the call center.

Table 9.1 shows the effect on "Right Party Talk Time" (the key factor in generating dollars and increasing profits) by reducing wrong party wrap up time (also known as unscheduled agent break time). To translate this to your bottom line one would look at the amount of "Wrong Party Wrap Up Time." Table 9.1 illustrates this showing a result of 12 additional minutes per hour. If "Wrong Party Wrap Up Time" is reduced, it gives the agents more time per hour to talk to the right party, thereby increasing their effectiveness. The assumption made in the calculation is that if the call center were able to take that 12 minutes of unproductive time in Table 9.1, "Right Party Talk Time" could be increased by 20% (the second line in Table 9.1) and provide substantial savings by implementing the software. This increase to 20% is a very conservative assumption which illustrates the powerful return on investment opportunity. The savings are calculated as follows:

$$20\% \times (\$25,000) \text{ salary per agent} = \$5,000 \text{ per agent}$$
$$100 \text{ agents} \times \$5,000/\text{agent} = \$500,000 \text{ savings}$$

TABLE 9.1—EFFECT OF INCREASING RIGHT PARTY TALK TIME (BY DECREASING WRONG PARTY WRAP UP TIME)				
	Current Minutes/ Hour	Change	New Minutes/ Hour	% Change
WP Wrap Up Time	12	−8	4	−70%
RP Talk Time	15	3	18	20%*
Increase "Right Party Talk Time" by 20% for a savings of				$5,000
For a customer service center with 100 full-time agents				× 100
			Total Savings	$500,000
*full-time agents averaging $25,000 per year.				

MEASUREMENT EXAMPLE: ADHERENCE TO SCHEDULE

In this example, Figure 9.16, the performance measurement for "Adherence to Schedule" shows the percentage of time an agent adheres to his or her set schedule. For this agent, only 65 of the scheduled 85 hours were actually worked, resulting in 76 percent of this performance indicator's goal.

A more detailed analysis is available by comparing the agent's anticipated schedule (the first bar on the left) with the actual times of day the agent worked (the second bar). The percentage of time adhering to schedule is calculated and compared to the goal to evaluate how well the agent adhered to schedule. The chart in Figure 9.16 graphically displays in red on the computer screen all the time when the schedule was not adhered to.

S: Schedule for Agent 1

A: Actual time usage for Agent 1

Blue: time spent working phones

Yellow: time on breaks

Green: time spent for training

Red: time NOT adhering to schedule

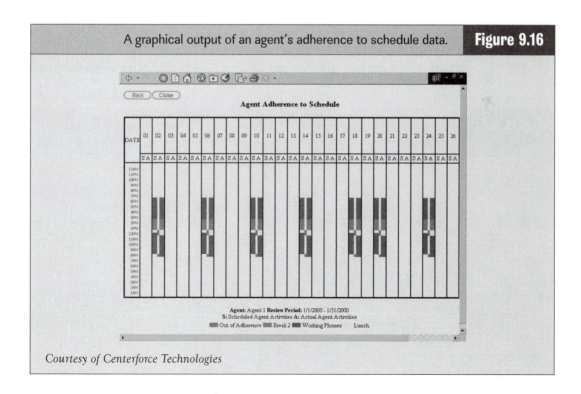

A graphical output of an agent's adherence to schedule data. **Figure 9.16**

Courtesy of Centerforce Technologies

MEASUREMENT EXAMPLE: WRONG PARTY WRAP-UP AND GOAL SETTING

We are going to show an example where "Wrong Party Wrap Up Time" can improve outbound call performance. The KPIs we are going to look at include:

- Right Party Talk Time
- Wrong Party Talk Time
- Right Party Wrap Time
- Wrong Party Wrap Time.

In the analysis of this financial institution called Fairbanks, it was found that the Wrap Up Time per Wrong Party Contact (WPC) was a great opportunity for improvement. Figure 9.17 shows agents were taking a long time to wrap up calls. The opportunity for savings is illustrated in Figure 9.18. This customer used a 3-step process to make changes similar to that in Figure 9.1. They began with Step 1 (Figure 9.18) by benchmarking their center to baseline their existing performance. They then introduced CenterForce Optimizer "Best Time to Call" software which increased their right party contact. The second initiative (Step 2) was to implement Centerforce Analyzer to measure agent schedule adherence. This resulted in reduced wrap up and idle time, which gave them more productive minutes. They were then able to increase their call list (portfolio) without significantly increasing staff headcount. By continuing to benchmark and raise the performance bar, after 1 year (Figure 9.18) Step 3 shows a range of improvements, including an increased list size of +300%, wrap up time −42%, and other improvements.

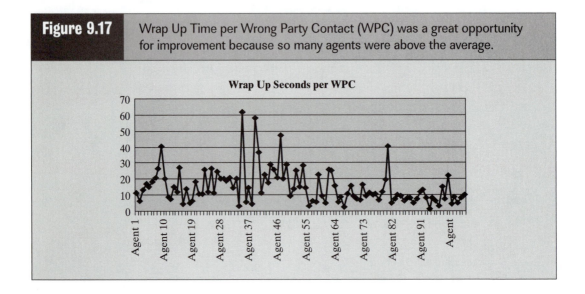

Figure 9.17 Wrap Up Time per Wrong Party Contact (WPC) was a great opportunity for improvement because so many agents were above the average.

MEASUREMENT EXAMPLE: WRONG PARTY WRAP-UP AND GOAL SETTING

It's easy to see why one of the most powerful return on investment elements for this Fairbanks financial institution is their ability to recognize and adjust "Handle Times" and "Wrong Party Wrap Up Times." No matter how diligent the supervisors are, this tends to be unscheduled agent break time that eats away at productivity. "Reducing wrap up time gave us more minutes of talk time to schedule calls into. With only a 10 percent increase,

The three steps in Figure 9.1 used in a real situation to increase CRM.	**Figure 9.18**

Step 1   Initial success with CenterForce Optimizer

	Change
Dials:	−34.6%
Connects:	−2.63%
Right party contacts:	+11.86%

Step 2   Set goals to raise the bar

- Reduce wrap time
- Reduce idle time
- Increase portfolio

Step 3   Build on success with CenterForce Analyzer

(Results after one year)	Change
List size	+300%
Wrap up time	−42%
Idle time	−26%
Connects	+253%
Right party contacts	+53%
Delinquency	−66%

Summary

- Fairbanks Capital increased right party contacts with CenterForce Optimizer
- CenterForce Analyzer showed them where they had room for improvement: wrap up time and idle time
- Setting goals and implementing training and incentive strategies for these metrics improved performance and gave them more productive minutes in each hour
- Fairbanks used this productivity to increase their portfolio. CenterForce Optimizer now puts even more RPCs into each hour

the system paid for itself within a year. We actually think we can double that!" declared Bart J. Bailey, collections technology manager at Fairbanks Capital.

The technology for call center goal setting and report card applications measured agent, team and call center performance against user-defined goals, providing immediate access to accurate, well-organized performance results. This particular technology was able to consolidate and process data from predictive dialers, ACDs, CTI systems, and enterprise applications. It runs on open standard hardware in a Windows NT server environment. The program uses a standard browser interface using either Internet Explorer 3.0 or higher, or Netscape 3.0 or higher, and requires no additional user hardware installation.

"Before we added the technology we had no mechanism in place to give a collector accurate reporting of how they're doing. We generated system reports from other software and from our host system, but had no way to combine the data and show the agents their results. We had no way of calculating "Right Party Talk Time" versus "Wrong Party Talk Time" or translating that into lost revenue. This new technology gives us the culmination of the data in one report. Now we are able to monitor how the agents and supervisors are doing, all the way up to the performance of the entire call center," explained Bailey.

The system uses goal setting software for different personnel levels within the organization. Now that they can correlate data from different sources within their center, they use performance indicators to generate a report card for each employee and for the entire call center. They use the colorful performance measurements to analyze their results and set future training and agent motivation strategies.

"Now that we're able to see long-term result trends versus goals set, we're able to demonstrate definite performance indicators of the agents and give them new goals to reach. We're raising the bar across the whole center. It's also a coaching tool for supervisors in different departments. The technology enables us to identify our lowest and highest performers so we can target where to put our training dollars and energies," commented Bailey.

Fairbanks has also changed how they do performance reviews. Prior to installing the technology, agents were given monthly reviews on results that supervisors couldn't back up with data. These monthly performance reviews were their only feedback. "Now we've got access to reliable data to show a progression throughout the month. And we can use the report cards to compare agents to their peer group with objective data. They're trained and given feedback throughout the month now," Bailey continued.

Fairbanks also makes use of schedule adherence software to ensure agents are logged onto the dialer when they should be. "If we've scheduled agents to make outbound calls at their best time to make a right party contact, our agents had better be on the dialer to make those calls. If they're not, it's pure lost productivity. Before we had no way to manage that; now the technology shows us if our agents have a trend of not working the hours they're scheduled."

Bart Bailey describes Fairbanks's future plans to use this kind of human performance technology in their inbound customer service department: "We want to have one centrally located report card for the whole company. If upper management wants to see what one division is doing they can drill down to see the details. For customer service we want to monitor performance on how many calls are handled per agent, how much time is spent on each call, schedule adherence and overall performance of the individual departments and the whole company."

The Purdue University Industry Database contains call center performance metrics from thousands of member centers. When the CenterForce Analyzer is combined with the BenchmarkPortal.com datamart, it provides Web-based enterprise benchmarking services. Multi-tiered membership services enable automatic data collection and Web analysis tools for peer group benchmark comparisons. On-site Benchmark Analyzer installations provide agent level scorecards and customer service center performance measurement plus benchmarking services. This provides integrated benchmarking. See Figure 9.19 for an example.

Since the technology they purchased is an e-commerce enabled CRM tool, Fairbanks plans to track whether service levels change with the advent of e-commerce. This assessment will help determine if they are driving more or less activity using the Internet on the payment process, and to see if inbound call volumes change as a result. In the next section we will look at

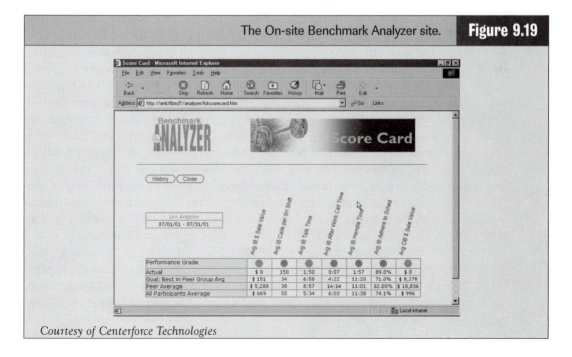

The On-site Benchmark Analyzer site. **Figure 9.19**

Courtesy of Centerforce Technologies

the value of integrating a performance feedback tool to drive employee development and job satisfaction as well as integrating CRM data tools within the operations of your organization.

Performance Feedback Evaluations

Once companies have collected organized data from one of the technology application tools discussed in the previous section, they will need a practical approach to provide the performance feedback to the customer service agents. This is a great example of how technology and people need to interface to get the highest return for an operation. If the performance information is gathered and compiled, but never delivered to the customer service agent via interaction with their supervisor, then the technology serves no real purpose. This case study is about an employee development process. This is separate from disciplinary action process or the promotion/raise process in this company and with very good evidence to support that strategy.

Some of the following information is excerpted from a chapter by Tanya Koons and Jonetta Pettway in *Recruiting, Training and Evaluating Call Center Employees, ASTD Case Study Series, 2001*[1] where Edcor's evaluation process for customer service agents are discussed. Tanya is the general manager and a member of the executive management team. With over 10 years' experience in call centers, operations, and employee incentive and development, Tanya manages the shared services group of human resources. Her responsibilities include recruiting, training, quality, HR policy, and incentives as well as facilities. Edcor obtained its ISO 9000 registration under Tanya's leadership. Tanya is also a certified lead auditor and heads up the ISO steering committee, where policy is driven and corrective and preventive actions are monitored for the entire company.

For more than 20 years, Edcor has been an industry leader in providing integrated technology and single-source, outsourced services for corporate education and training, tuition assistance, and customer relationship management solutions. Edcor currently employs more than 400 persons, including more than 200 call center agents, more than 40 systems and programming professionals, 55 client relationship managers, and executive and administrative staff. Edcor invests in talented people who believe in creating a valued customer experience. Edcor has had explosive growth and part of that growth is attributed to how Tanya directs the development and nurturing of employees to make the changes necessary to deliver the next level of expertise to support the growing needs of the business. This development process is a "win-win-win" situation for Edcor, their employees, and their customers.

Edcor's global customers include such companies as General Motors, DaimlerChrysler, AT&T, Microsoft, Cisco, and UPS, with all customers benefiting from sophisticated, best-practice targeted recruiting, assessment, training, and retention processes, required to meet the demands of their diverse

---

[1] Used with permission of Tanya Koons, Edcor

customers and a fast-paced, dynamic industry. With Edcor's excellent customer service, companies experience the advantages of having outsourced
these functions with increased service levels resulting in consistent program
administration throughout all assigned locations, accurate reporting, enhanced response time, historical record keeping capable of supporting U.S.
government agency requirements such as OSHA, the FDA, or international
trade requirements like ISO 9000. The service Edcor offers provides companies with the time and ability to focus on core competencies and to focus
their energies to strategically manage their human capital resources.

Edcor currently maintains call center support hours from 7 A.M. to
9 P.M. Eastern time Monday through Friday to support client-employees
located internationally. The call center conforms to the clients' holiday
schedules to ensure that the customer service center is aligned with the
service needs of the employees. In addition to the customer service support
hours, Edcor operates its computer network 24 hours each day, seven days
per week. This around-the-clock operation allows customers to obtain both
general and personal account information through interactive voice response (IVR) systems and the World Wide Web, as well as other multi-
media channels, like e-mail.

Most companies do not see performance evaluations as a way to build
the culture. However, at Edcor, by applying a specific performance evaluation methodology, Tanya has been able to develop an internal culture that
builds teamwork and overall employee job satisfaction. She uses the performance evaluations to enforce behavior the company wants repeated. The
evaluation methodology also supports the ability to maintain longevity of
key personnel through a hands-on approach in building their skills and development, thereby reducing attrition. The case study details the performance feedback tool designed to keep communication flowing, build
employees' skill sets, and shows standard operating expectations and guidelines to ensure high-quality services. It also contains the processes value in
retaining employees who are already fully functional in their positions. We
recommend reading it in its entirety, but offer some of the highlights in
this book.

Most department managers and leaders within the organization dread
the whole process of evaluations, in part because it is time consuming and
may involve coworkers' sensitivities. The process requires spending time
assessing the individual's performance (output) verses the company's performance standards in measurable descriptions or examples whenever possible. Tanya feels that the time required to do evaluations is not only necessary
but essential to manage the human capital asset. Many managers balk at the
amount of time required to do a great job, but without spending that kind
of time, the company loses in attrition costs, which are about $6,350 to re-
place one agent. When someone in a leadership position is hired at Edcor,
they are introduced to the performance evaluation process early on as a way
to introduce them to the company culture and environment.

Especially difficult are those evaluations where critical feedback is needed to change a behavior or improve a much-needed skill set. The goal is to offer feedback and make specific suggestions for change in such a way that the evaluation promotes a behavior or mindset change and does not discourage or upset the individual. The approach the evaluator takes should support positive changes and not cause the person being evaluated to walk away disappointed in the review of his or her performance.

An understanding of the issues that evaluators struggle with makes it is easier to design an evaluation process, forms, and procedures that help overcome their fears and develop their ability to feel good about doing evaluations. The following paragraphs describe Tanya's methodology and specific tools. It is advisable to develop a full-performance evaluation package with tools because it simplifies and speeds implementation, provides consistency, and makes it easy to manage with little or no involvement from HR. Managers like a tool kit approach because there is no guesswork.

Building the Foundation

If you want the performance process to be consistently utilized, accepted, and also drive a positive outcome, then you must first take the time to establish the foundation. What is it that you want to offer feedback on? In Edcor's environment it is a combination of skill-based objectives and quantifiable outputs. Determine what 10 or 12 areas best represent your call center organization's performance needs (KPIs) and then establish standards or descriptions for each of those categories. Develop a standard form or tool to capture and deliver this information and determine the appropriate frequency in which to review the information with each employee. In many organizations, the evaluation process often helps the trainers in identifying common areas where performance is lacking, so they can adjust their programs accordingly to better support the needs of the organization.

To help you identify what types of tools establish a solid foundation, take a moment to review one of many competency descriptions Edcor uses for their call center agents. An example of telephone etiquette is given in Table 9.2. Creating a standard for telephone etiquette helps provide the right kind of feedback to the employee and ensures that all leaders are consistently scoring employees and supporting the program objectives as well as the company objectives. This is a great example where skill and statistical performance are both evaluated. The following rating standards are what Edcor uses to evaluate staff: needs improvement, meets expectations, and exceeds expectations.

Developing these standards assists the evaluator to stay objective and not be swayed by personal opinion. Using the standard for telephone etiquette above, if a person has a hard time maintaining a monthly phone monitoring score of 3.50 or better, then the evaluator must choose "needs improvement." If an employee disagrees with a particular ranking, the evaluator can point to the standard as a reference at how they arrived at their

TABLE 9.2—TELEPHONE ETIQUETTE

Exceeds expectations: This person displays a high level of energy and treats every call as if it were the first. Their phone statistics consistently exceed the standard percentage required to maintain program objectives. This person receives feedback (written and verbal) and acknowledgment for exhibiting great customer service skills from clients, customers, and employees. This person consistently maintains a monthly average score of 4.50 on the observer checklist in all categories.

Meets: This person consistently meets the telephone statistic standards established within the program. They practice good customer service skills and regularly use job aids and policy books to reference solutions or answers for callers' questions. They are receptive to feedback and coaching on alternate approaches to service oriented situations. They have a pleasant disposition on the phone and are able to work with a diverse caller base. This person is able to incorporate standard observer checklist guidelines into everyday phone calls and maintains a monthly average score of 3.50-4.49 on scored calls.

Needs improvement: This person struggles with controlling difficult customers. They often allow an upset caller to alter their tone and control the conversation. They do not consistently obtain the minimum phone statistics needed to meet program requirements for individual performance on a monthly basis. They can often meet program guidelines, but cannot maintain the average over time. This person also does not regularly follow the observer checklist guidelines and is inconsistent with the speaking skill sets. In addition, this person is unable to maintain the monthly average score of 3.50 or better which is the desired score for this level of position.

conclusion. The most important aspect of developing the competency standards is that the employee has a clear description of what specifically their leader expects. They know what it will take to be seen as an employee who "exceeds expectations." This also helps when an employee does fall into the "needs improvement" area. If it is clear in the beginning what behavior or action will lead an evaluator to a mark in this category, then the employees are usually more accepting of the feedback.

Writing the Evaluation

Once the foundation has been established, you can start the actual evaluation process. The two basic ingredients for writing an evaluation are knowledge of the person to be evaluated and knowledge of how to write an evaluation. First, an evaluator should be sure he or she knows about the person. It is important to review the person's entire contribution and performance record for the period being evaluated. In Edcor's environment, performance logs are used to track positive accomplishments, learning experiences, and areas that a person has struggled with. By keeping this record as a working document, it is easy for the evaluator to recall all the events, dates, and examples with a quick review of the log. It is also a great tool if agents move from more than one supervisor in a given year, as a way to understand historical performance and where they are in terms of coaching and development. Second, it is important that the evaluator be familiar with the evaluation form and with the standards and rankings.

One of the most difficult parts of the process for many evaluators is translating their knowledge of the employee into appropriate language on the form. The goal is to have an evaluation that will be most helpful to the person being evaluated, so the language must be clear, honest, and unambiguous. Tanya recommends that organizations give their staff a two-hour evaluation-training refresher course just before evaluation time each year. Not included here, but in the ASTD book's chapter are practical tools to guide the manager in the evaluation process:

- A list of suggested adjectives that support each category rating (i.e., exceeds expectations = above and beyond, exceptional, consistently exceeds, leader overall etc.)

- Sample competency skill descriptions (i.e., telephone etiquette)

- A list of adjectives and verbs to describe performance

- A list of phrases to describe key skills

- A sample review form

- Defined descriptions of evaluation scale (i.e., meets expectations = good or very good)

Presenting the Evaluation

The written assessment is only one part of the process. How an evaluator presents the evaluation is just as important as what is written. (Remembering that verbal communication is only seven percent words, this is very important.) Because the written assessment and presentation are so closely entwined, it is necessary to include things like reviewing the evaluation scale, defining each rating, and the standards that support each category.

Edcor leaders clearly communicate to the employees that a "meets" means good or very good performance. An employee who does not understand that terminology could feel he or she is just "ordinary" or "adequate," and nobody who works hard wants to feel that is all they are valued as. You want to set the tone in such a way to represent that the overall feedback of the review is very positive, but there are also some areas where they are still progressing or areas that need some extra attention to achieve a higher score. By doing this, the agent will be less likely to be alarmed when they see the "needs improvement" box checked in any one category on the form. People by nature see the check marks before they see the words behind it. If the person being evaluated has negative first impressions, it would be hard to turn that around and have a meaningful and non-defensive discussion with them. This goes back to what we learned about how humans react to information that may feel threatening (Chapters 3 and 4). It is important to give feedback to enhance the performance without discouraging the employee or making them defensive.

Tanya also feels that an evaluation is not the appropriate place to reprimand an employee or write up a disciplinary action form, even if the employee is getting critical feedback. (Disciplinary action is done in a separate meeting and occurs at the time of the incident—not once a year in the performance appraisal meeting.) The performance evaluation feedback should provide the evaluator with an opportunity to drive the employee toward a change in behavior or in a skill set. It can be determined later and in another format if an employee's issues are so severe that the person should start down the disciplinary process.

Similarly, Tanya's experience has shown that an evaluation is not the appropriate situation in which to offer promotions. In many companies evaluation, development, and promotion are all part of the same process. This is part of what distinguishes the employee development process at Edcor. Also, the company does not promote someone because of the time of year, but rather when that person has developed the skills and experience needed to take on the new role. Once they have obtained the appropriate skills and experience, they now have the opportunity to apply or be considered for a new role if one becomes available. The evaluation process helps identify areas to work on to allow time for that skill to be developed, so they can be ready for the next available opportunity when it arises.

The wording in an evaluation should reflect the philosophy that promotions are separate from reviews. For example, Edcor managers do not name or promise a position when writing a review. Naming a specific title could put the company in a compromising situation. This could lead to a situation where the person never accomplishes the skills, but points back to the review as a commitment to put him or her in that role. In addition, if the focus is on skill set versus title, the employee has an opportunity to develop for more than one future position.

If an employee has false expectations about his or her performance or about the likelihood of receiving a raise or promotion, Tanya asks her managers to evaluate themselves with the following questions:

- Is this management's fault?

- Did we give appropriate feedback during the year to assist the employee in being successful to meet his or her job objectives?

- Were we able to be honest about the employee's performance?

- Did we give concrete examples of what was good or excellent and what would be better if the employee took another action?

Once the evaluator has completed the rough draft, Tanya teaches her managers that it is crucial to read it aloud as if you are the person receiving the review. By doing this, you can catch errors or awkward phrases that you didn't realize were there. She also reminds them that their management team may read the review to get an impression of their skill and ability to offer appropriate feedback. Tanya emphasizes that the managers should think of their role not only as the evaluator, but as if they were under review. This helps the reviewer bring more humanity, honesty, simplicity, and kindness into the review process, thereby encouraging the employee to grow further. This growth by the employee adds to the human capital asset and the company's brain trust and bottom line.

The ROI of Training that Impacts the Bottom Line

FOCUS ON ANALYTICS

CRM analysis can deliver the ability to examine business operations and customer interactions from multiple angles with the right technology. In the following case studies we want to show examples of how technology can deliver information not only about the services being provided but lead to the discovery of new information, that, if missing, could demoralize employees or cause major customer attrition. In this first case study, we will look at the value of training employees and in the second how understanding customers' complaints and responding to them can make or break a company's profit and loss statement.

The Issue

The issue in this case study was to see how quickly the bank customer care employee could close a case with a customer. In some cases it was taking some agents longer than others and the bank wanted to figure out why.

THE UNKNOWN DANGER

If they did not know why it took some agents longer than others, they would not know how to target their training to get the highest performance from the customer service agents. In addition, they were concerned that they would have customers feel that they were not being taken care of properly. Understanding that an unhappy customer generally leaves your bank, and takes their money with them, the bank wanted to make sure they provided the best service possible.

THE CALL TO ACTION OPPORTUNITY

The employees at the bank that were interested in the information from the call center are shown in Table 10.1. The first data the team looked at was the average length of time in days it took representatives to close a case. Figure 10.1, shows that Iris, on average, takes the longest to close a case. An impulse decision at this point, without more in-depth call center data, would be to say that Iris was not performing compared to her peers. However, this team knew the power of the call center data and kept exploring to uncover the real issues.

The next cut of the data looked at the average length of time in days it took representatives to close a case for complaints requiring follow-up versus the type of complaint, which included incorrect payoff, incorrect type of check, or an ATM card problem. What they found was that the ATM card problems seemed to be taking the longest time to close (Figure 10.2).

> *Give a man a fish and you feed him for a day; teach him how to fish and you feed him for a lifetime.*
>
> —Lao-Tzu

TABLE 10.1—DEPARTMENTS INTERESTED IN THIS CALL CENTER DATA	
Report Types	**Audience(s)**
Trend	Executives
Drill Down	Call Center Manager
Diagnostic	Training
Data Mining	Sales

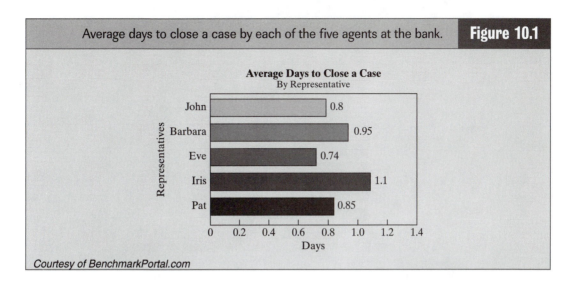

Average days to close a case by each of the five agents at the bank.   **Figure 10.1**

Courtesy of BenchmarkPortal.com

Sleuths that they were, they kept exploring. When they looked at how quickly the various agents were at closing the ATM card issues (Figure 10.3), they found a very interesting and surprising result. Iris, who had the longest overall time to close cases, had the shortest time to close the most difficult type of case. So they realized that Iris was handling the most difficult calls in the shortest amount of time. And had they called Iris on the carpet for what seemed like poor average performance with respect to her peers (Figure 10.1), they might have taken the employee who handled their most difficult problem, the best and demotivated her. Then they looked at caller satisfaction rating for each representative (Figure 10.4). They found that Iris

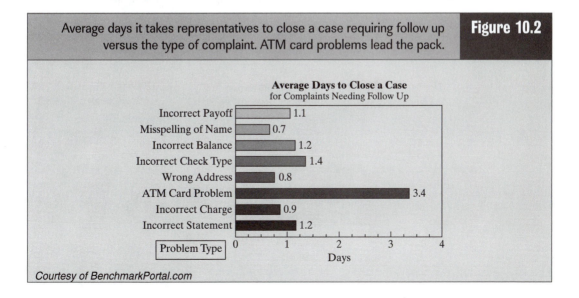

Average days it takes representatives to close a case requiring follow up versus the type of complaint. ATM card problems lead the pack.   **Figure 10.2**

Courtesy of BenchmarkPortal.com

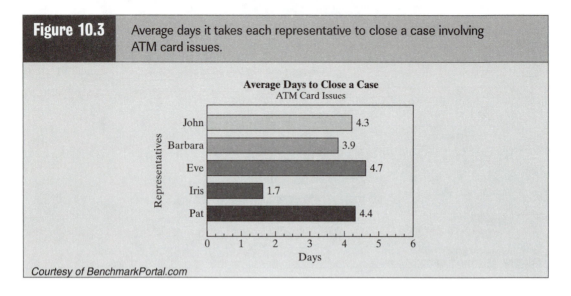

Figure 10.3   Average days it takes each representative to close a case involving ATM card issues.

Courtesy of BenchmarkPortal.com

had scored the highest at 91 percent for ATM issues. When they talked to Iris, they found that Iris had worked in the ATM department at the bank before coming to the call center. Iris intimately knew all about the ATM aspects of the bank and was incredibly knowledgeable in this area.

What the management decided was that they wanted Iris to transfer her knowledge about the ATM issues to her colleagues, which made her feel empowered, respected, and acknowledged for her excellence in a particular area. They began routing the ATM calls to her while bringing the other call representatives up to speed. In addition, they asked the other agents to share their knowledge on other types of calls with Iris. This really helped Iris, because it was valuable experience for her for job advancement and obviously

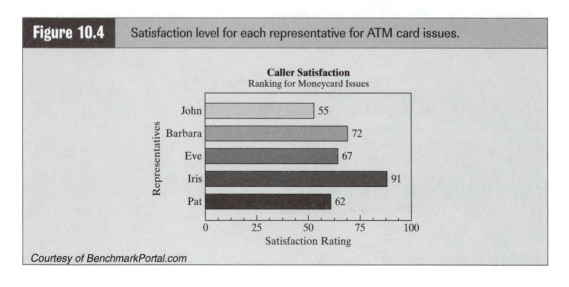

Figure 10.4   Satisfaction level for each representative for ATM card issues.

Courtesy of BenchmarkPortal.com

improved cross-training quality for peers. It made Iris feel that her management really cared about her success and was on her side to help her succeed and grow as an employee. One of the most frequently stated reasons listed on employee exit interviews for why a person left a company? "My manager did not care about me or my development."

> Every day 250 million people wake up in America and most unfortunately plod out of bed, yawn and figure, "Oh hell, I've got to make it through another day at work." How can you improve anything with attitudes like that? You've got to make your workforce feel like they personally make a difference, everyday.
>
> —Lee Iacocca, former chairman of Chrysler Corporation

THE BUSINESS IMPACT IS SEVERAL-FOLD:

- Keeping customers

- Keeping customer satisfaction high

- Targeted training for individual skill gaps

- Empowering employees and reducing attrition.

ROI

The return on investment for this case has several factors, the ROI of:

- Targeted agent training

- Potential attrition and agent turnover

- Measuring customer satisfaction

We will look at customer lifetime values in the next chapter.

We'll now look at the ROI for training or the investment in increasing the human potential. In the past, decision makers and managers may not have understood that there is a connection between human potential and a company's profit. And even if leaders have a sense that there is a connection, they don't know what to do about it. There are tools and processes that can help everyone from the executive to the call center manager understand the connection between developing their people and the bottom line. The core of that is the effectiveness of the selection, recruiting, training, development program, and, "If you have no people, you have no business." This can be fully understood when executives and managers understand the impact people have on the business. To understand this, ask yourself, "Do the machines run by themselves? Can the process remember how to follow itself?"

The reality is: the link (and many times the bottleneck) to process and technology is still people. With the understanding of the importance of people and the tools available to guide human performance, managers have a creative edge on their competitors. It is also important to fully understand how and when to use the tools for human performance, what they do and how they work to gain the full advantage. These tools and processes create a new management theory, Human Potential Management (HPM), that provides the foundation for connecting the bottom line to the human potential value of corporations. The benefits of implementing these tools and training are:

- Reduction of turnover

- Increased customer service

- Increased profits and sales

The return on investment of selection and training can be in the thousand percent range when well implemented.

Relating to Traditional Accounting Measures

Business has traditionally measured the bottom line in one of two ways: the quantity of gross profits and the quantity of net profit. New measurement systems to measure the true value are becoming recognized. As little as one-third to one-half of most companies' stock market value is accounted for these days by hard assets such as property, plant, and equipment. The growing share of measurement lies in intellectual property or what has been coined "soft skills" or "invisible" assets, which are related to the people part of the business. Part of this new theory is to erase the notion that those things that have been coined with "less than" terms are not bottom-line affecters, and replace that with the fact that these are assets. These bottom-line assets include things like customer satisfaction, internal business processes, an organization's ability to learn and grow, and the effectiveness of the corporate culture.

Part of the reason the financial reporting process has not shifted is that it is anchored to an accounting principle developed centuries ago. Today this archaic process is highly standardized and governed by a set of generally accepted accounting principles, or GAAP, which are widely recognized by lenders, investors, regulators, and others. GAAP standards tell companies how and when to deduct expenses in the current fiscal year or to amortize them over several years. They describe how to assign other costs, such as legal, consulting, and overhead, to each widget coming off an assembly line.

The keys in this current GAAP system are objectivity, exactness, and comparability. Inherent in financial accounting is the language of traditional business—concrete, pragmatic and measurable. In the transition from the HPVs (human potential values) to the visible context, embracing the language of traditional business assists companies to shift to this new paradigm in accounting and management. This is a guideline to changing current accounting principles to take into account all the variables that make a business successful over the long haul.

One of the reasons that training does not impact the bottom line is that it is not designed to do that. It is designed to inform, make aware and educate. However, while those traditional values and goals of trainers are good, trainers have to make the jump to designing training that focuses on impacting the business results like productivity and setting up measurement systems to track the results all the way to the bottom line. That is the new goal of training in organizations and is a huge paradigm shift for the training world. Experts in this area are the Frankly Covey Institute for Return On Investment group lead by Jack Phillips and Ron Stone. We've referenced their body of work in this field, upon which many of the ideas in this next section are based.

Business Strategy and Human Capital Assessments

Dr. Petouhoff's simple ROI of training can transform the way you feel about training, whether you can get the funding for it and the value it can bring to a company as well as who you choose as your training partner. Because Dr. Petouhoff came from the management side of the house and was later asked to development training as part of a reengineering project, she knew too well how irritating it is for line managers to have their people go to training and then have next to nothing about the employee's work change. Training seemed to be a vacation day for employees—a day off from their usual grind. She was flabbergasted when she realized that there wasn't any way to measure the before and after effects of a training session on how the employees change in work performance affected the bottom-line. There were many influences on Dr. Petouhoff's view on human capital asset management. Among them were Paul S. Adler, Mark A. Hueslid, Peter M. Senge, David Ulrich, Daniel Goleman, Sally Helgelsen, Richard Barrett, Jack Phillips, and Ron Stone.

As she began to develop the training for the reengineering project, she designed the training so that it would impact business; to her, training was a business tool. The differentiating line between most company's training is that the training programs only measure employee reaction to level 1 or 2 measurement standards (Table 10.2). And since 99 percent of all training is still designed like that, that is why most managers and executives are disappointed when they send people to training—nothing really changes about the employee's performance.

> Change happens. The winners will be able to adapt, learn, and act quickly. The losers will spend time trying to control and master the change. The new HR has a responsibility to build the organization's capacity to increase marketplace skills and embrace the pace of change.
>
> —David Ulrich, "A New Mandate for Human Resources,"
> *Harvard Business Review*, Jan-Feb 1998

What we have found is that training programs that surpass the competition are usually designed by groups of people, including trainers, line managers, HR, and employees who understand the gaps in performance and know what information they would need to change the way the employees are doing their jobs. Whether HR can transform from the traditional mind-set of "training as learning" to "training as changing job performance" greatly depends on how and whether they are integrated into the everyday work life of customer service agents. Unless they sit in the chair of an agent and know what the agent goes through (yelling customers, not the right information on the screen at the right time, complicated computer systems) they can't design training that will impact business. We encourage all of HR and anyone else designing training to live in the shoes of the person you are going train for a week or two before even putting fingers to the keyboard to get a dose of reality.

Training that is designed to impact business is designed to a Level 5 measurement (Table 10.2), which includes changes to how employees do their job, the impact of how those changes in employees doing their job better affects the business, and the ROI of the training. ROI is the comparison of the cost of the training versus the increase in productivity, sales, etc., that the training created.

ROI Training Example: Training to Increase ATM Skills/Capabilities

To properly set the stage for the value of calculating the ROI of training employees, we wanted to provide a real life example of how training, for instance, can have a great impact on the business. In this example, we will look at the return on investment for training a call center representative to have better ATM card issue knowledge when dealing with their customers.

The formula for calculating Return on Investment (ROI) is:

$$ROI = \frac{\text{Net Program Benefits}}{\text{Program Costs}}$$

In this example, we have two call center reps, Eve and Iris. Eve has skill gaps in knowing how to close the ATM cases. It takes Eve about 6 hours a day to resolve ATM cases whereas Iris has ATM skills and only needs to spend

TABLE 10.2—LEVELS OF MEASUREMENT FOR TRAINING
Level 1—Smile sheet—did employees like the training? or the trainer?
Level 2—Did employees learn something?
Level 3—Did employees apply it on the job?
Level 4—Did that change in job performance affect the bottom line?
Level 5—ROI—comparison of the cost of training versus the effect on the bottom line.

about 2 hours a day resolving the same kinds of issues. Both salaries are the same, $20 per hour or about $40,000 per year.

The first thing we can evaluate is a productivity calculation, which shows where the employee's time and energy are being spent. This concretely tells upper management whether they are getting the most out of their employee.

Productivity Calculation

Eve— $2/8$ hours $= .25 \times 100 = 25\%$ Productive

Iris— $6/8$ hours $= .75 \times 100 = 75\%$ Productive

Since Iris spends less time resolving the ATM issues (2 out of 8 hours on ATM issues which leaves another 6 for other productive work), Iris is 75 percent productive. However, since Eve does not have this same depth of knowledge, she is only productive 25 percent of the time. From the calculations below, we can see that we are paying Eve $30,000 to have a skill gap that we have not addressed because we do not believe training pays off.

Productive Work	Dollars Paid for Skill Gap
Eve— $.25 \times \$40,000 = \$10K$	$.75 \times \$40,000 = \$30K$

What is more impressive is to look at the next level of calculation: comparing the cost of a training solution as corrective action versus the cost that her lack of ATM knowledge is costing the company.

Now let's consider the cost of a training solution. An average training course can be estimated to be about $2,000 for a day. Many times that training day can include other call center reps, so the return amortized over a group of 20 agents can be even higher because the cost/agent is lower. In this case we will just look at the impact of changing Eve's skill.

The benefit of the solution is the increase in Eve's productivity from not having a skill gap of about $30,000. The cost of the solution is the cost of the day of training, or $2,000. The ROI is 1,400 percent, where the cost of training Eve is well worth the investment.

$$\text{ROI} = \frac{\text{Benefit of Solution} - \text{Cost of Solution}}{\text{Cost of Solution}} \times 100$$

$$\text{ROI} = \frac{\$30,000 - \$2,000}{\$2,000} \times 100$$

$$\text{ROI} = \frac{\$28,000}{\$2,000} \times 100$$

$$\text{ROI} = 14 \times 100$$

$$\text{ROI} = 1,400\%$$

This means that for every dollar spent on training fourteen dollars returns to the company.

With this kind of simple yet direct calculation, it can be made clear to executives and managers the value of using the tools available to increase the human potential of their organizations.

Attrition Calculations—Cost of Replacing People

CUSTOMER SERVICE AGENTS

The cost of attrition can be calculated by looking at the replacement cost of hiring a new employee and the number of employees that leave every month or year. Call center representatives fall into the category of clerical/administrative salary range (Table 10.3). That means that the average annual turnover cost per employee is 50 to 80 percent of their base salary.

TABLE 10.3—TURNOVER COST SUMMARY FROM THE JACK PHILLIPS INSTITUTE ON ROI. TURNOVER COSTS SUMMARY	
JOB TYPE/CATEGORY TURNOVER COST RANGES AS A % OF ANNUAL WAGE/SALARY	
Entry level-Hourly, nonskilled (e.g., fast food worker)	30–50%
Service/Production workers–Hourly (e.g., courier)	40–70%
Skilled hourly (e.g., machinist)	75–100%
Clerical/Administrative (e.g., scheduler)	50–80%
Professional (e.g., sales representative, nurse, accountant)	75–125%
Technical (e.g., computer technician)	100–150%
Engineers (e.g., chemical engineer)	200–300%
Specialists (e.g., computer software designer)	200–400%
Supervisors/Team leaders (e.g., section supervisor)	100–150%
Middle Managers (e.g., department manager)	125–200%

Notes:

1. Percents are rounded to reflect the general range of costs from studies.

2. Costs are fully loaded to include all of the costs of replacing an employee and bringing him/her to the level of productivity and efficiency of the former employee. The turnover included in studies is usually unexpected and unwanted. The following cost categories are usually included:

Exit cost of previous employee	Lost productivity
Recruiting cost	Quality problems
Employee cost	Customer dissatisfaction
Orientation cost	Loss of expertise/knowledge
Training cost	Supervisor's time for turnover
Wages and salaries while training	Temporary replacement costs

TABLE 10.3   (CONTINUED)

3. Turnover costs are usually calculated when excessive turnover is an issue and turnover costs are high. The actual cost of turnover for a specific job in an organization may vary considerably. The above ranges are intended to reflect what has been generally reported in the literature when turnover costs are analyzed.

Sources of Data

The sources of data for these studies follow three general categories:

1. Industry and trade magazines have reported the cost of turnover for a specific job within an industry.

2. Publications in general management (academic and practitioner), human resources management, human resources development training, and performance improvement often reflect ROI cost studies because of the importance of turnover to senior managers and human resources managers.

3. Independent studies have been conducted by organizations and not reported in the literature. Some of these studies have been provided privately to performance resources organizations. In addition, performance resources organization has conducted several turnover cost studies, and these results are included in these analyses.

For instance, if you have a 100-seat call center and you lose 20 percent per year, that is 20 people. And let's say their average salary is $40,000 per year. Attrition, though you probably don't have it in your line item budget, is costing you:

On the low side: 20 people leaving/year × .5 (40,000) = $400,000

On the high side: 20 people leaving/year × .8 (40,000) = $640,000

With these figures you can start to look at the human potential value in your organization and determine if you are spending your money wisely or letting it leak out in ways that you never realized were making a difference.

ENGINEERS

When looking at the cost of replacing engineers or managers, the cost of attrition is even higher. For a technical person who makes $50,000 per year, the replacement cost is about $150,000 for someone who has been there five years. You have spent on attrition, if in a year, you have:

20 people leave = $6 million

100 people leave = $15 million

EXECUTIVES

When looking at executives' salaries of $150,000 or more, the cost of attrition becomes even more substantial. Replacement cost of an executive is two to four times the cost of their salary, so taken at an average of three times, the cost is:

one executive leaving = $450,000

five executives leaving = $2.25 million

ten executives leaving = $4.5 million

This, of course, does not take into consideration stock options and other perks afforded to executives.

Using Technology the Smart Way: ROI of Improved Customer Service by an Airline

ONE COMPANY'S STORY

The Customer Service Issue

What would make your customers loyal: Having them file a class action suit against you or you providing a grandfather clause? The call center manager at a major airline noticed a little spike in calls from passengers in weeks 9 to 13 of a 21-week overview of call volume.

TABLE 11.1—DEPARTMENTS INTERESTED IN THE CALL CENTER DATA	
Report Types	**Possible Audience(s)**
Trending	Executive Level
Diagnostic	Marketing
Frequency	Sales
Drill Down	Public Relations
Event Driven	Call Center

The Unknown Danger

What was causing this spike and what impact might it have on retaining customers and increasing revenues?

The Call to Action Opportunity

In this case study there are a number of departments that could use this information as shown in Table 11.1. The list of audiences is given and the types of reports for each audience is provided. In general, each type of report takes the information collected in the call center and puts the data in an easy-to-read format providing the missing pieces of the puzzle.

The first graph (Figure 11.1) of the call center data is a classic chart of airline passenger call volume (number of calls/day). The call center manager no-

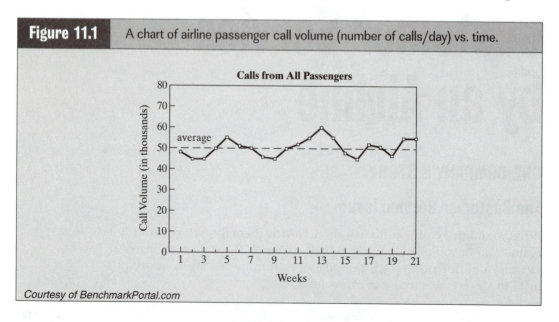

Figure 11.1 A chart of airline passenger call volume (number of calls/day) vs. time.

Courtesy of BenchmarkPortal.com

ticed the increase in calls in weeks 9 to 13. While the increase was not way above the average (the dotted line in the graph), the call center manager realized from having looked at these kinds of plots that something might be up.

The call center manager then looked at the call volume from 100K-mile frequent flyer passengers (Figure 11.2). For this particular customer segment of extremely valuable customers, the call volume had risen substantially above the average calls. The next step was to isolate why the callers were calling so much more. Figure 11.3 shows how the data was isolated just to that period from weeks 9 to 13, which we will refer to as period 2, in comparison to the time period before that, period 1.

In Figure 11.4, the reasons for calls during periods 1 and 2 are given and include flight plan, schedules, frequent flyer mileage, etc. What can be garnered by comparing these two graphs is that the complaints are very similar. This still does not account for the spike in Figure 11.1. So the next step was to look at how frequently a complaint type was made in the two periods. Figure 11.5 shows that lost mileage in period 1 was about half of what it had grown to in period 2. Now this was getting down to the issue!

We tend to meet any new situation by reorganizing, and a wonderful method that can be for creating the illusion of progress while producing inefficiency and demoralization.

—Petronium, Greek philosopher, 210 B.C.

What the information in Figure 11.5 shows is that the passengers were upset about the mileage they had lost. When this was investigated further in the call logs, it was found that the 100K-mileage customers felt it was

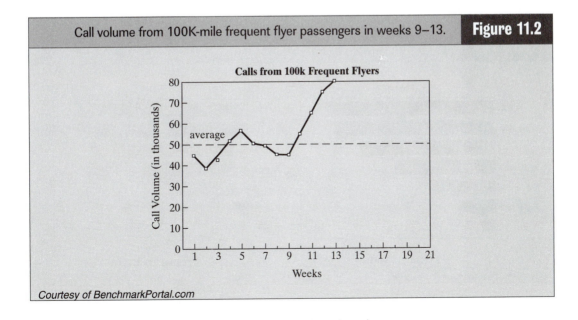

Call volume from 100K-mile frequent flyer passengers in weeks 9–13.   **Figure 11.2**

Courtesy of BenchmarkPortal.com

Figure 11.3	Close-up on call volume spike in 100K-mile frequent flyer complaints during period 2.

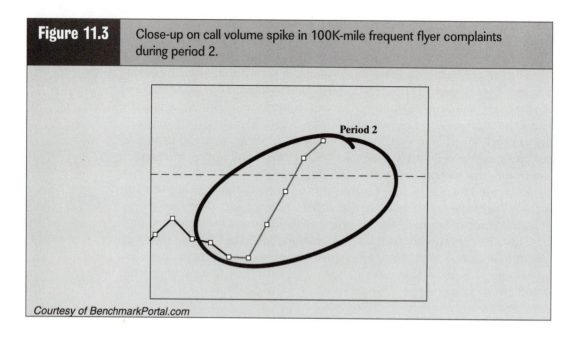

Courtesy of BenchmarkPortal.com

unfair that the airline industry had decided to change the policy on accumulated frequent flyer miles when they had been promised something else. When the program had first been introduced, there wasn't any time limit on use of the frequent flyer miles. The change in policy was telling the passengers that they now had to use the miles within a certain time period or lose them. This, of course, infuriated the 100K-mileage passengers who saw themselves as loyal customers. They had responded to the incentive to be loyal, and expected the airline to honor its word.

Figure 11.4	Reasons for complaint calls during Period 1 and Period 2.

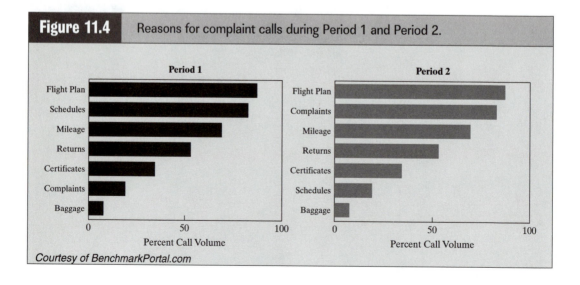

Courtesy of BenchmarkPortal.com

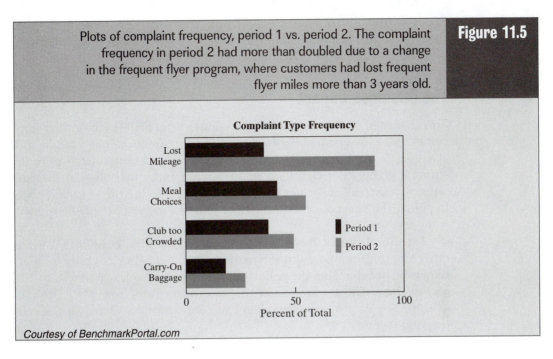

Plots of complaint frequency, period 1 vs. period 2. The complaint frequency in period 2 had more than doubled due to a change in the frequent flyer program, where customers had lost frequent flyer miles more than 3 years old.

Figure 11.5

Courtesy of BenchmarkPortal.com

When the data was plotted without the 100K-mile frequent flyer passengers' complaints, the curve fell very close to a normal period of complaints (Figure 11.6). This is when the call center manager and the executives knew they had isolated the main issue and needed to make a different business decision. The executives decided to create a change in policy on the

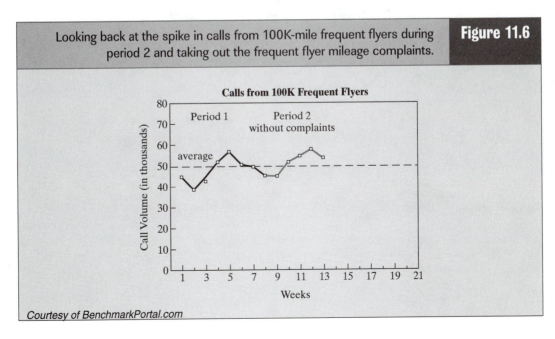

Looking back at the spike in calls from 100K-mile frequent flyers during period 2 and taking out the frequent flyer mileage complaints.

Figure 11.6

Courtesy of BenchmarkPortal.com

frequent flyer miles. After the 100K-mile frequent flyers were given back their frequent flyer miles, complaints from the 100K-mile frequent flyers dropped dramatically during period 3 (Figure 11.7).

The Business Impact

This change in policy was causing the same issue in many of the airline companies, but only one had Forward Intelligence™ from their call center and acted on it. The business decision based on this call center data was to institute a grandfather clause on frequent flyer miles that allowed the passengers to keep all the miles they had earned up to the time of the change in policy; the new policy with the time limits of use would only be applied going forward.

For this airline, it meant saving thousands of loyal customers. For another large airline that did not have the action data, they not only lost customers by not changing the policy but they also had a class action suit filed against them. The average cost of this lawsuit was very expensive. The cost of using the data from a well-oiled call center that has done peer benchmarking is much less.

Figure 11.7 After the 100K-mile frequent flyers are given back their frequent flyer miles, calls from this group drop dramatically during period 3.

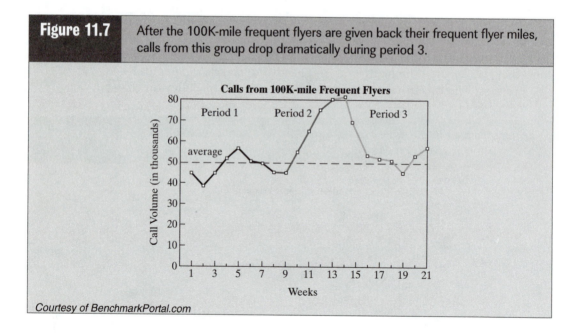

Courtesy of BenchmarkPortal.com

Measuring Process: Promises, Promises— Service Level Letdowns versus SP3M™

So you want to set up the best CRM program in your industry and you have already:

- Benchmarked your customer service center
- Benchmarked and measured your employees
- Mapped out all your processes
- Removed extra steps by business process reengineering
- Bought technology that enables your people and processes

After all the benchmarking, planning, and changing, what happens if along the way a department manager or a call center agent doesn't do what they said they would? You can have all the pieces of CRM in place, but without a solid agreement on who is going to manage what, by when, with specific measurements, the chances of having and maintaining a successful CRM implementation decrease dramatically with each passing day. Producing exceptional quality customer management and service remains an unattainable goal, not a reality to your staff. Your competitive edge becomes status quo. Your company becomes one of the pack. Your level of service looks no different from your competitors. And, as a result, the return on your investment for technology is far less than you expected.

Thus far you have a good handle on calculating customer lifetime value (Chapter 7). You know the value of providing consistent and exceptional service to your customers. This was the foundation of your CRM investment. Yet the magic is still missing. You have not reached a breakeven point on your technology implementation. Your company is still in the red, no nearer to recouping your investment. Without practicing the art of consistent measuring, marketing, and managing, CRM results are reduced to a collection of data with superficial meaning.

CRM is a favorite marketing buzzword and is often overused. And the "management" part of C-R-M is overlooked! What happens when a company wants to use CRM? What exactly does that mean? Exactly how is that going to work beyond buying and installing expensive technology? How is the relationship with the customer going to be managed? Who is held accountable for outcomes of the results produced?

> Today, when people say "implement" CRM, they often think about technology; the reality is that you can only enable CRM with technology. There is a pattern in the marketplace where some big technology is introduced and everyone gets excited about tracking customer information with it. But CRM is more than that. You need three things: a means to track the information, the ability to evaluate customer performance with metrics, and the means to make change happen. To make change happen, we evaluate the infrastructure and process capability of a company to learn and do better next time. Most of them don't have a practical solution to manage the change. And when they measure customer service they rarely include employee performance.
>
> —Heidi Wisbach, manager of CRM analytics, Cap Gemini Ernst and Young from *Marketing News*, May 7, 2001

CRM and Service Levels ARE Business Critical!

Does the Egyptian plover (a rare bird) have service levels? The key job of this bird is to pick the teeth of crocodiles. That bird had better get it right. A misdirected peck into a decaying molar can mean the difference between getting dinner and being dinner! Business critical indeed.

> —Mike Pettit, IT partner, Taylor Walton Solicitors

For CRM suppliers (internal and external), ASPs, code supporters, and others in the IT world who exist on promises of efficiency, reliability, and specialist knowledge, the financial price of failure can be every bit as terminal as for the croc's hygienist. Whether the people you depend on are internal or external suppliers, the game is the same, "Do what you said you would do." However, even though the promises were made, it just does not seem to work like that in real life.

With external suppliers it can be somewhat easier to set up a system where, when service is not delivered, the supplier can be docked payment, or worse, dropped as a supplier. Qualifying a new supplier is oftentimes even worse in that you don't know what their warts are going to be. Sometimes better the devil you know than the devil you don't. Internal suppliers tend to be more difficult to assess penalties against. Unless there is some sort of chargeback system, there are no real penalties for missing the service mark. In either case, clients historically tend to roll their eyes at the mention of service level agreements (SLAs) in facilitating customer relationship management.

Percentage of North American companies that outsource development and maintenance of their CRM apps: 60 percent.
—Harte-Hanks, *Jupiter Media Metrix,* July 2001

With 60 percent of CRM applications being outsourced, SLAs are very important and even harder to control when they are outside your organization. When we asked why service level agreements got a negative response, we were told that many times these documents were never referenced again after first being written. Staff who did the actual fulfillment of SLAs were typically not included in the level setting nor reminded of the metrics or changes made to service levels. Another client said that unless the whole enterprise is involved and committed to using the service agreements, then all it takes is one weak link in the chain to bring down a service level percentage. There is nothing to be gained from advertising your inability to meet service levels. And then finger pointing begins. There is no accountability. It turns into a "They promised and did not deliver . . ." mud slinging match. Traditionally the answer has been to write the service level metrics into performance appraisals to be used as criteria for raises and bonuses. This is a management option but too often is not done because the nature of some fast moving customer service centers may be based on hitting daily targets as opposed to quarterly goals. Keeping written performance appraisals up-to-date in these environments is not practical unless it is made part of the culture as exemplified by Tanya Koons at Edcor (Chapter 9).

Another important issue with service levels that came up in talking to clients was accountability. When we found service level agreements that did work, they were in organizations that had people dedicated full time to making sure the service levels were managed. When companies did not have at least two people (depending on the size of the organization and the number of interrelated departments working on fulfillment of the agreements)—a director level and support staff—mostly dedicated to this process, the responsibility of engaging in service level discussions at the staff level often fell through the cracks. This was because, on top of someone's regular job, they were assigned extra duty to capture data and manage the reporting needed to maintain service level agreements. What some management did not understand was that it is a full-time job to have someone manage the quality process of managing service levels.

In some cases service level agreements are so important that the courts have examined limitation clauses in them over the past decade. The need for providers of key services to adopt service levels can literally save millions of dollars. The ability for a company to enforce a clause is dependent upon

- Are losses excluded if they arose before a contract was signed?

- Is there a vast gulf between the limitation level and the insurance coverage?

- Will a restriction above the maximum service credits be considered reasonable?

- Has the provider accepted a general obligation to use its endeavors to put things right?

- Has the limitation been expressly negotiated and acknowledged as a price factor?

One of the issues can be with suppliers that are trying to provide products and services to larger companies. Many times companies have internal struggles and politics that interfere with the supplier's ability to build relationships and provide good service. Companies see a supplier as an expendable commodity, that is, if you won't do it, Lear, Magna, Visteon, or whomever can.

> In the Automotive Industry it has been hard to create relationships because the OEM's apply pressure to the Tier 1 suppliers. That pressure then gets applied to the Tier 2 suppliers to reduce costs. The reduction in costs can sometimes cause a decrease in quality. The result can become that the customer pays more and gets less. We pride ourselves on creating partnerships with our backbone engineers to become bartering units within their organizations. This ensures that costs are reduced without a negative impact on quality or the integrity of the product.
>
> —Nick Petouhoff, Engineering Manager, Automotive Systems,
> Johnson Controls, Inc.

A major automobile manufacturer in Detroit recently demanded overnight that all its suppliers drop their prices by 5 percent. Actually, it was less a demand and more that they just issued new purchase orders for 5 percent less. Suppliers actually stopped shipping to the automobile manufacturer for two days until they backed off. Concrete service levels with a process that makes success or failure public tend to help force people to do the right thing.

Managing the Quality Process of Customer Service: The Schwartz-Petouhoff Measure, Market, and Manage Service Model (SP3M™)

We are introducing in this book a new methodology called the SP3M Service Model, to measure, market, and manage. The SP3M Service Model is a step-by-step process that can be followed by those chartered within your organization to ensure that your CRM data warehouse becomes your company's gold mine.

The model introduces, from tactical and practical experience, a three-part process that has produced exceptional service and produced measurable positive improvements to the bottom line in companies that have followed it. SP3M is one of the most comprehensive approaches to effectively implementing service level agreements in the market today. The SP3M process clears the way for mutually understood expectations between the various suppliers to your company and your service level delivery agreements with your customers. SP3M narrows the gap between perceived and actual levels of service. SP3M is opportunistic in nature, capturing, examining, and ensuring usage of critical data from CRM systems and other applications that direct your organization in focusing on what's most important to your company's profitability.

Some of the benefits of implementing the SP3M model are:

- Greater awareness of operations involving vendors, suppliers, outsourced, and in-house functions

- Targeting areas of improvement that improve profitability first

- Increased interest on the part of staff to exceed service levels

- A method to justify capital outlay of funds

- Continuous and consistent objective performance feedback

- Assurance that all parties understand expectations and metrics

- Maximized control over internal and outsourced functions

BACKGROUND ON THE CREATION OF THE SP3M SERVICE MODEL

In their consulting experience, Lisa M. Schwartz and Dr. Natalie L. Petouhoff recognized a general malaise in organizations attempting to monitor and measure for service level metrics. The mere mention of maintaining service levels brought a hush of silence from middle management in the front of the conference room and moans and groans from staff positioned in the back of the room.

Conversely, in her experience, Schwartz had seen fantastic results produced by managing with service level agreements. She had participated in several successful implementations; managing 24/7 critical care environments, managing outsourced service providers, furthering CRM activities and goals at clients such as Arthur Andersen, Andersen Consulting, Geffen Records, and Cedars-Sinai Medical Center. During Schwartz's operational direction at Geffen Records, the company was selected by Computerworld as being one of the top 25 most innovative networking companies in the world. And again under the leadership and operational direction of Schwartz, Cedars-Sinai's data center and call center achieved the best in class rating from the Gartner Group. Her execution entailed detailed project plans, complete with negotiated service levels and associated revenue generation, revenue recovery, customer acquisition, and customer retention models. She brings over 20 years of consulting to the areas of technology implementation, call center design and management, quality and change management program implementation, risk assessment, and business development.

> Revenue recovery by measuring results is the foundation to reducing operational costs. By identifying reoccurring problems, designing and implementing change management and service management programs, valuable budget dollars can be saved.
>
> —Lisa Schwartz, a partner of LMR Associates

Schwartz and Petouhoff decided to examine different service level environments for common success quotients and come up with a model that could communicate their collective experiences. They defined the successful use of service levels as being

> *Organizations whose stakeholders are currently directing and motivating their divisions and staff daily, focusing on exceeding predefined metrics of service, and targeting specific areas most critical to the bottom line and to the customer.*

Naturally, in most organizations, measuring every area of service would be a daunting task. And not every area is as critical as the next. By using the 80/20 rule and practical experience, Schwartz and Petouhoff could examine the service areas which brought the most immediate payback.

WHAT DOES A SUCCESSFUL SP3M SERVICE MODEL IMPLEMENTATION LOOK LIKE?

1) Measure

Stakeholder Support—Communicate importance to staff, set the scope, determine priorities, capture baseline data, determine measuring/marketing ROI, negotiate service metrics, define the tools, communicate to staff, implement measuring tools

In all successful cases, stakeholders and management identified the most critical operations paramount to the company and then the most important functions critical to acquiring customers and building customer loyalty. Each of these distinct areas was set out in order of importance. Then it was determined if these areas could be effectively measured with the current technology in place. Existing baseline data was captured, if available. If the service area was considered critical, then a decision was made to invest in monitoring, measuring, and reporting tools in the most critical areas first.

In all successful cases, service metrics had been previously negotiated with customers. With the customer's metrics and the company's metrics in hand, meetings with outsourced service providers, product suppliers, and all upstream providers that impacted delivering service to the customer were held (Figure 12.1). Through negotiations involving all parties, agreements were documented on which vendors, suppliers, and outsourcers were responsible for which service, end to end. Specific uptimes and service delivery metrics were documented. In some cases, customer responsibilities and escalation policies were described as well.

Most importantly during the agreement negotiation, several presentations were made to staff to solicit their feedback and to announce the importance of their role in driving the SP3M process to produce exceptional results. As a parallel step, measuring tools and technology were chosen and implemented to capture and report on critical functions within the companies. Upstream service level providers, outsourced resources and product suppliers also chose measuring tools that would produce compatible inputs for regular service reports used in the SP3M market step.

2) Market

Internal Marketing: Stakeholder Support—Communicate importance to staff, regular presentation and executive summary report on results to execs, detailed report presented to staff/provider, acknowledge successes/motivate provider/staff awards, identify opportunities for improvement, solicit staff/provider solutions for improvement

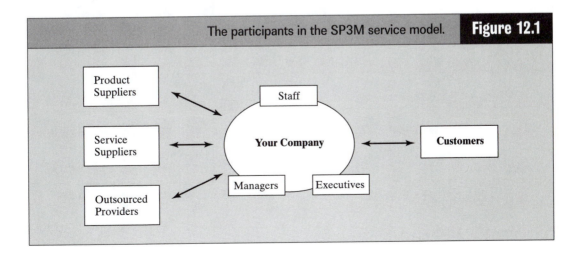

The participants in the SP3M service model.   **Figure 12.1**

External Marketing: Stakeholder Support—Communicate importance to customer, view regular presentations and reports on results to customer, acknowledge successes/communicate performance gap, present staff/provider solutions to customer and barriers to success, get customer's buy-in on solution and expected time frame for improvement, solicit customer feedback

In the most successful cases, Schwartz and Petouhoff found that the reports and outputs from the service level measuring tools were used as a means to inform *all* (with emphasis on the *all*) internal company staff, management, stakeholders, executives, service providers, suppliers, vendors, and others about the monthly good and the bad in an executive summary format (Figure 12.2). This is the most important step in the SP3M model: the market step.

What usually happens is that benchmarked data and service level results are captured in three-ring binders distributed as hard copy or e-mailed to a few interested parties. In these instances, the report rarely got read, left buried in the "to be read" pile with no actions taken to improve upon service or CRM data. These cases are classic examples of organizations that are not actually driven by producing consistent concrete measurable results. The return on investment for CRM technology is minimal under these implementations. The lack of company-wide *effective* marketing of service level and CRM data is the "kiss of death" for any service driven organization.

Figure 12.2	Executive Summary Scorecard for CRM and SP3M that allows a team to understand where the team stands on meeting their collective and individual goals with respect to service levels and at the same time provide targeted focus for the team to take action on.

	Jan	Feb	Mar	Apr	May	Jun	Jul	Aug	Sep	Oct	Nov	Dec
Call Center	R	R	R	G	R	R	G	R	G	R	R	R
RM	G	R	R	R	R	R	G	G	G	G	G	G
Marketing	R	G	G	G	G	G	G	G	G	G	G	G
Billing	R	R	R	R	R	G	G	R	R	G	R	R
Field Service	G	G	G	G	G	G	G	G	G	G	G	G
Sales	G	G	G	G	G	G	G	G	G	G	G	G

Source: Used with permission of LMR Associates

The view Lisa and Natalie, implementers of successful service levels and CRM, was if you have invested money in customer relationship management technology and you are measuring your customer service data, you must equally market the outputs with importance and even a sense of urgency because providing excellent service is everything to the bottom line.

Marketing the findings internally to establish new service goals, acknowledge successes, and redirecting staff, management, and providers for the next month's important areas of focus is critical. This activity aligns your organization for the final step in the SP3M model, the manage step.

Externally, when appropriate, CRM data was also used as a method to market to customers. The company's current objectives and how these objectives were addressing customers current needs were highlighted. This indeed is value-added marketing—internal and external customers love to know what you have done for them lately. An easy-to-read service report (Figure 12.2) in front of the right audience, with a bird's-eye view of before and after measurements, shows the customer that you care and you have actually done something about it with measurable results. Company-wide, empowering communication and marketing is the essence of the SP3M market step.

3) Manage

All changes to service metrics are approved by customer and/or execs only. Seek provider's agreement to proposed change, create master implementation plan, create plan for HW/SW process changes and baseline service measuring tools, impact to service levels, add/change/delete from report, communicate change to stakeholders/staff/providers, coordinate change process, hold team progress meetings, escalate roadblocks of critical nature, team implements solution, communicate outcome of implementation to stakeholders/customer/providers/staff

In all successful cases, the manage step of the SP3M model was executed by having the manager and a director with the right behavioral characteristics (see Chapter 4 on SPP) for leading the CRM and service level charge. Schwartz and Petouhoff found that in all cases the individuals that were selected to ensure fulfillment of the manage and market steps had great people skills, great presentation skills, were skilled in the art of motivating people, and were the tenacious "pit bulls" in getting the details of each project completed on time. They also had creative problem solving and innate leadership ability. These individuals were identified using the assessments as high Is with a secondary or tertiary C or D on the CRM SPP DISC profile. By identifying these qualities in a service level director or manager, the necessary natural and strong communication skills inherent in these types shined through and ensured success in the market and manage requirements of the SP3M model.

In all successful cases, proposed changes to service level metrics were submitted for approval at the highest levels only. The service level manager or director would submit all changes up the ladder so that no ad hoc changes to metrics could be made by anyone unless approved at the highest level.

As a result, staff were always focused on the right metrics and the objectives. When approved, any changes in the metrics were marketed to the staff, management, executives, and providers, communicating the new goals and the estimated timeframe for implementation.

In fact, all major changes and new projects were included as announcements and marketed to all levels. This ensured the awareness needed to fulfill the new objectives and also ferreted out any colliding schedules that would make fulfillment impossible.

When proposing changes or new projects, as part of the approval process, a recalculation on the return of investment was done to ensure that these changes made sense financially (Figure 12.3).

It was important to note that organizations that followed SP3M service model understood the importance of motivating and including all levels of staff and management during the measure, market, and manage stages. It was observed that even with all the self-service applications and automated monitoring tools, most of the customer service was still provided by people—either directly interfacing with the customer or by building the infrastructure to create customer relationship processes and run technology. When staff buy-in was gained, the structure of the SP3M service model, if followed, guaranteed consistency and even produced better results than the established metrics. The old adage, you get what you focus on, fits here. In the end, it came down to people (employees) not technology providing service to people (internal or external customers).

In this context, service management can be defined as conformance to internal and external customer requirements and needs. The SP3M process, regardless of how and where applied, consists of two principal components. They are:

- The service management process

- The problem-solving process

The service management process is an ongoing proactive and focused approach that drives toward positive results in meeting customer requirements (Figure 12.4). On the other hand, at times, the problem-solving

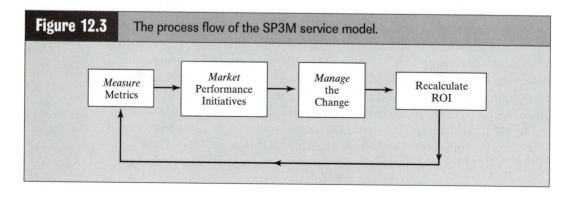

Figure 12.3   The process flow of the SP3M service model.

	Comparison of traditional and SP3M views of service management process.	**Figure 12.4**
	Traditional View	**SP3M View**
Definition of Service	Goodness	Identify Critical ROI Metrics—*Measure*
System for Achieving Greater Quality	Inspection	Proactive Efforts—*Market* the Results
Performance Standards	Allowable Levels	Improve on Outcomes—*Manage*
Measurement	Statistics/Indices	Recalculate ROI Metrics

Source: Used with permission of LMR Associates

process is employed as a reactive consequence, as needed, to identify and solve problems, as well as to discover and fix errors. You'll see distinct examples as we step through the SP3M process.

PROCESS AND CHANGE

Let's say that we have the results from a customer satisfaction survey or other data collected on a process. The results are substandard to our normal operation. The question then becomes, what do we do with the data? How do we transform that data into action that produces meaningful change that can impact the bottom line? Things got measured, but no actions were performed after the measurement. Direction and focus had gone missing (Table 12.1).

The SP3M process connects business service goals to bottom-line company goals. Table 12.2 shows the various levels of measurement and the value of each of these steps in the SP3M process. Unless all steps are taken,

TABLE 12.1—TRADITIONAL WAY OF MEASURING AND MANAGING SERVICE.

Levels of Measurement

Measure, but without direction

No accountability

No responsibility

No action

No real change in service

TABLE 12.2—LEVELS OF MEASUREMENT AND VALUE TO THE COMPANY WITH THE SP3M SERVICE MODEL.	
Levels of Measurement	**Value to the Company**
Level 1—Measure—get the data	Identify critical operation metrics, customer acquisition and retention metrics
Level 2—Measure—analyze the gaps and plot it	Use data to identify service satisfaction gaps
Level 3—Market—make the info public	Change the way service is provided
Level 4—Manage the changes to service	Change in service impacts business
Level 5—ROI	Measure before and after and calculate ROI
Source: Used with permission of LMR Associates	

the reality of realizing a return on investment (ROI) for CRM cannot be achieved. Without following a proven process, using CRM to improve customer service can turn into being lip service.

The equation below can be used to calculate the ROI.

$$\frac{\text{Cost of Loss of Customer} - \text{Cost of Fix}}{\text{Cost of Fix}} \times 100 = \text{ROI}$$

REALIZING THE VALUE OF SPM3 INITIATIVE

In general, SP3M involves a comprehensive approach to improving service management and maximizing performance of expensive technology that is intended to help achieve profitability by:

- Creating a customer-focused and quality-driven internal environment, led by senior executive management with a commitment from all levels of the organization

- Identifying *in a systematic way* the essential and critical processes leading to the outcomes customers need and expect

- Describing, measuring, and continuously improving the effectiveness of those key processes, using reliable methods of measure

- Involving all staff, as well as suppliers and internal and external customers of the organization in the process

Companies that adopt this approach stress that these service efforts must apply to everyone in the organization and to all operational aspects of the company. Significant time and resources are invested in continuing education to support this practice. This service-seeking approach reflects an underlying belief that the cause of a quality problem may be some component of the process of providing service. The process must be analyzed and constructively changed. Employee involvement in the work teams, as well as customer participation, is essential in quests for greater success. The steps in the SP3M model are given in detail in Figure 12.5. We will go through the steps with some practical thoughts in each step to help demonstrate how this is done and the impact it can have.

MEASURE

Setting Expectations—Determining the Scope of the Project

Meaningful service level agreements happen from excellent planning. However, in many organizations time spent thoroughly understanding the service requirements in advance can be deemed an activity for shrinking violets. Especially in IT teams, preparation is not always fashionable. Technology people tend to be focused on the technology and not on the process of providing service and definitely not on the people part of the process. However, experience shows that only partially thought-out service levels have desperate results. Part of the planning process is understanding the results of the service and how people, process, and technology can provide that. Many times service levels are written for the technology only. However, we suggest that every touch point is important and that includes the people providing the service.

A robust service level agreement reflects common sense project discussions and seeks a balance of interests. The impossible is neither offered nor required. The salesman's promise of "always available, always the best" service must be coldly examined against actual ability and expectation. Remember that commitments entered into in the heat of a sales success are usually viewed very differently later. Those commitments must be agreed upon and managed.

Another issue can be how realistic the agreement is. The current vogue, but misleading, service description of "24/7 availability" is an example of something that is not realistic. This type of slogan ignores the difference between marketing hype and IT reality. Truly successful service level agreements are based on achieving a realistic service target. Phrases like "99.8 percent achievement" or "24/7 availability" as measured at the server over a period of 3 months makes more sense for both service provider and company. If one is going to test the servers, for instance, that means there is a period of time they will not be available. It is this balance between an objective "24/7" and

| **Figure 12.5** | Steps in implementing the SP3M service model process. |

Measure

The steps for *measure* are:

- Set expectations—determine the scope of the project
- Analyze the process of providing service
- Communicate the service plan and expectations
- Capture the data
    - Benchmark your baseline
    - Determine differences over time
- Analyze the data
    - Determine what is important to providing service
    - Identify areas of opportunity
        What is measurable/costs associated with it
        What are the priorities
            What changes will make a difference quickly
            What changes are longer term initiatives

Market

The steps for *market* are:

- Report on findings
    - Acknowledge work done or successes
    - Good news and the opportunities
- Create a plan to make changes to take advantage of the opportunities
    - Get staff buy-in and agreement (internal service and product providers)
    - Provide direction and top management support
    - Get external service providers' and product providers' buy-ins and agreement

Manage

The steps for *manage* are:

- Create an integrated master plan and schedule, action items, due dates, and point persons and their team members
- Create a plan for software/hardware/process changes
- Communicate the change plan to stakeholders so they know it is changing

(Continued)	**Figure 12.5**

- Hold regular team leader meetings to review change plan, report progress, roadblocks, and solutions

- Hold regular team meetings to create the change plan, review and report progress, road-blocks, and solutions

- Team leaders and members implement solution

Then the process begins again with the measuring step where the changes are captured, benchmarked and analyzed, marketed, and managed. The team repeats the process. Service generally improves or remains stable because it is continuously being monitored. However, there are times when service can be negatively impacted by a crisis, by the implementation of an untested change, or by an event of unpredictable nature.

Source: Used with permission of LMR Associates

achieving "99.8 percent" that differentiates the mature service provider from the zealous salesperson.

When working with the health care industry, Schwartz and Petouhoff found that key to this step is identifying service goals. Examples are:

- Do you want to measure the entire hospital, certain departments, the data center, or the call center?

- Do you want to do a pilot measurement program in one area first?

- Are you willing to calculate the ROI for the process of actually measuring service in all these areas (i.e., staff to track stats, automated tools for measuring, software and associated hardware for measurement of service levels, and reporting regularly)?

- Do you have existing baseline measurements to help determine realistic starting points for service metrics in your environment?

Using a hospital as an example, one needs to consider all the areas that could be measured and which ones will be included. A hospital could measure the nerve center of technology, including the data center operations, network infrastructure, processing cycles, call center data, secure access to patient data, power generator operation, backup systems, physical security levels, etc.

An example in the data center is the tracking of the disk storage capacity; for processing there would be the CPU availability, the network monitoring traffic levels, and segmentation. Secure remote access to patient data could be everything from monitoring fetal heart rates so that doctors could see them to nurses being alerted if a wheelchair had gone missing (patient tracking). Patient data might include labs (blood work and x-rays), billables (every aspirin, Q-tip, and towel used), to accounts receivable tracking. Another interesting application is the process of distributing medication. The centralized pharmacy function loads the carts (similar to airline beverage carts) with the daily drug doses for admitted patients. Essentially, it is an itemized pill distribution plan. As the nurse approaches a room, they log in their code and the door to the pill unlocks and the patient gets the pill.

Other things that determine whether a patient gets good customer service are all sorts of administrative trivia, accounting, budgeting, time tracking, and scheduling of hospital employees and inventory. In one hospital even body parts were tracked via an application in the data center. The tracking involved shipment of the transplant organ, where it was stored, and who it was to be delivered to, with estimated time of arrival. So the scope really comes down to understanding the department you want to measure, what it needs to provide, and what can be measured. Whether it is ER, surgery, after patient care, or the cancer ward, each one has very different metrics that are considered critical.

In many cases, many of these types of functions are managed from a central nerve center, with some of them being outsourced to vendors. In some cases the systems were interdependent, and when there were times when something did not go right it had to be determined which vendor had the hiccup in service. That's where service levels come in handy. Department heads and service management know exactly who to call when the hiccups occur. In a hospital there are many applications that are used to provide service, hundreds in some cases. The point of detailing this is to help you think about what it is in your organization that would constitute something that would make or break a customer's experience with your company, or in the case of a hospital, the patient's experience of receiving care. Service in a hospital can be a matter of life and death.

ANALYZE THE PROCESS OF PROVIDING SERVICE

Within the framework of the SP3M model's emphasis on planning, organizing, and monitoring for high quality service, one of the best examples of this in action is the monitoring of established service level agreements, with customers creating an agreed-to standard measure of service which serves as a comparative benchmark. In doing this you can ask yourself and the customer:

- To what areas do we want to assign measurable metrics? Why?

- What do you want the metrics to tell you?

- Are there automated tools in place to measure?

- How will those particular metrics tell you if a customer is satisfied?

- What is the turnaround time if something does fail?

- What are the fixed charges for failure to comply?

- Who is accountable for the budget and overruns?

- What is the process of updating a system? (without upgrading every-thing at the same time)

- Who is the point of contact to manage the change requests?

- Do the programmers understand they have to hand in their change project plans?

- Who has to be notified? (Sometimes the sales department promises something and then there are not enough resources and the system crashes!)

STAFFING FOR CHANGE

The next step is deciding who is the point of contact or team leader in each of the areas you are measuring. You'll want to determine how to tell if they are really participating or not and lay out the consequences of not being committed to the process of providing service. An important distinction here is to not make this an executive mandate. Those turn off employees faster than anything else. Rather, to pull off customer service you will need a leader who is the "glue." Here glue connotes a person who can entice, market, enroll, and ensure that the things that need to get done are done. Typically this person is a very high I (refer to Chapters 3 and 4 on behavior analysis).

You'll also want to provide that person with the resources to implement the customer service process, which includes FTEs, technology, office space, etc. So it is not only the leader but also the staff and suppliers who need to be proactive thinkers. Remember in the Operational CRM part of the book where we looked at people and change? It is important to go back and really understand the issues surrounding selecting the best people for the most critical objectives in your company, especially when you implement the SP3M process. That person will also need to talk to management proactively to get resources and money to get the job done. This may even mean a few full-time employees to manage the SP3M process. If management is willing to spend money on personnel for the SP3M process, this is a very good sign they are truly committed to exceptional service being a company reality. This justification can be done by comparing the loaded or burdened salaries of those employees with the cost of losing customers (gaining new ones cost 5–6 times what retaining them does) or the cost of not providing service.

Percentage of companies with no employees dedicated to CRM: 35 percent
Percentage of companies with 1 to 4 employees dedicated to CRM: 42 percent
—Harte-Hanks, *Jupiter Media Metrix,* July 2001

Then once you have decided what you want to accomplish and have the measurement process organized and documented, you'll want all stakeholders who have contributed to it to sign it. It then should go straight to the CEO as should any changes. That's where the accountability shows up.

COMMUNICATE THE SERVICE PLAN AND EXPECTATIONS

Once the team has put a stake in the ground and made a service plan, it is time to communicate that plan to anyone who might have a stake in it. Since you have been talking to many of the stakeholders to get their input in creating the service levels, they will not be shocked by the news. In fact, they will accept it more when they have been a part of creating it. We now know this to be true from what we learned in the chapters covering people and change. When people are included, their Reptile Talk™ is less.

This step is to manage expectations to get business results. You've probably heard of the expression, "Frustration is when reality does not meet your expectations." We have found that providing service is really a matter of managing expectations. If the expectations are higher than reality, the level of frustation will be too; if the reality is greater than what is expected, then, all things being equal, it is a break even point.

$$\text{Expectation} - \text{Reality} = \text{Level of Frustration}$$
$$10 - 100 = -90 \quad \text{low}$$
$$100 - 10 = \quad 90 \quad \text{high}$$
$$100 - 100 = \quad 0 \quad \text{break even}$$

What we want in the communication step is to show everyone involved how what they do contributes to the big picture and that if one part of the process breaks, then the overall big picture of providing great customer service begins to fall apart. Making a chart as in Figure 12.6 helps everyone to picture their part in the success supply chain.

CAPTURE THE DATA

In capturing the data, you'll want to determine a way to benchmark your baseline. A good source for benchmarking information is www.Benchmark Portal.com. You'll then want to determine which of the metrics are suspect, which will provide the most gain and have the most potential of realizing your customer service goals. The next part is to look at the gaps. With the profile provided by benchmarking against best practices (at a benchmarking center like www.BenchmarkPortal.com) or what you want the service levels to be, you then want to look at what you have obtained (the "as is" state and the "could be" state). You'll also want to look at differences over time, so you'll need a way to graph the information to present to the group. It is best to start thinking about the presentation of the material early in

| Mapping each department's goals into the big picture. | **Figure 12.6** |

Big Picture Goal: Company to provide great customer service			
Department 1	Task to provide service	Measurement of task	Gap in Department 1 in providing service
Department 2	Task to provide service	Measurement of task	Gap in Department 2 in providing service
Department 3	Task to provide service	Measurement of task	Gap in Department 3 in providing service
Department 4	Task to provide service	Measurement of task	Gap in Department 4 in providing service

the process. It can affect what you measure and how you measure when you know you are going to present it to a whole group with a lot at stake.

Having the right tools to measure is very important. You'll want to think in terms of proactive measurements and reactive measurements. Proactive tools provide you a way to monitor things so that you can prevent a problem from turning into a disaster. Reactive tools may need to be employed when there is a crisis, but eventually you will want to get all the crisis situations handled via root cause solutions and then shift to using proactive tools and mindset. Also you'll want to look for tools that can help automate capturing the data, otherwise it can be very labor intensive and take a long time to analyze. Equally important is finding a tool that will present the information in a comparative fashion over time.

ANALYZE THE DATA—NETWORK MANAGEMENT CASE STUDY

Once you get the data, you'll want to determine what is important to providing service. You can begin by asking questions like, "Why would a network begin to slow down?" You may find that the issue is not as clear or as obvious as you would like, nor is the solution. But that does not mean a solution does not exist. It just takes a bit of detective work. In one case study, Schwartz and Petouhoff looked at a LAN/WAN network setup in a Los Angeles office. The network was a larger replica of one that was functioning perfectly in Atlanta. Atlanta was the main office and that's where all network configurations originated for all worldwide installations. The Los Angeles network manager baselined the network measurements with a network analyzer and found that the slowdown was occurring mostly at a particular time of day. The network manager consulted with experts outside of the company in network analysis. The manager explained that the system kept going down, but when he reported to Atlanta, they seemed to think it should be fine. The reason for going to outside expertise is to learn the state of the art in the field of how others are solving the issues, as well as to think outside the everyday thinking that was going on in this situation.

One company in particular was very helpful. This was a fast Ethernet switch company. When the network manager told Lisa and Dr. Nat he had eight floors of people logging into the network during peak periods they told him that amount of activity would max-out a nonsegmented 10MB Ethernet LAN. Being new there and not wanting to step on any toes, with Dr. Nat and Lisa's guidance he went back to the manager at the Atlanta office to inquire about the amount of traffic on the network there. That office only had 100 people logging in concurrently. Conversely, the Los Angeles office not only had over 1,000 people but also eight remote locations and over 30 pilot servers in-house. The network manager knew that to make the best argument for change he had to document his findings and the proposed solution.

In talking to the Ethernet switch vendor manufacturer, he found they offered a product that he could test on the network to see if the problem was resolved. He measured outages frequency and network traffic before and after installing the product in consistent conditions so that he was comparing apples to apples. A few years ago, it was one of the first implementations of a fast Ethernet switch (which are common today), so the idea of using it was not common knowledge and not something known to the Atlanta office because their traffic was one-tenth of the Los Angeles office and the average size office was under 100 users. He then compared the stats for outage/downtime with the cost of the switch.

It became clear very quickly that the cost of the outages far outweighed the $16K for the switch. But the network manager knew that if he had not done his baselining before and after the change, documented the change in traffic measurements and improvements in response, and calculated the ROI of the change, he would never have gotten his boss in Los Angeles or the Atlanta office to agree to spending $16,000 on unproven technology. In the end, the switch segmented the network which solved the slowdowns and server crashes and was happily purchased by the firm and resulted in no more system crashes!

You can see by this example how the network manager:

- Identified areas of opportunity

- Measured and baselined the activity before and after

- Determined the measurable costs associated with it

- Marketed the findings to management and Atlanta

- Established that it was a priority for change

- Fixed the problem

Another important thing to consider in this step is to measure at peak times. A network can function perfectly for a long time without outages and then all of a sudden fail. The reason correlated to seasonal changes in one case study where (150 to 300 page) corporate tax returns were being produced for a very large Hollywood production company. Network and system slowdowns could be prevented if that peak usage time had been predicted months in advance. One good system outage could have caused return deadlines to be missed.

The lesson learned is to understand your service process—what is mission critical, what times of the year are peak times, and plan for them. As a result of monitoring, suppliers can make recommendations to companies so that they can streamline their business operations. This is SP3M service management operating at its best—communicating critical measures, jointly improving systems and processes, thereby creating a closer partnership between the suppliers and the company.

MARKET

Visibility is everything. And that is the goal of this step. If you have information about the levels of service, good or bad, but it stays in three-ring binders or is sent to people with too much to read, you know it will end up continuously being shuffled to the bottom of the "to read later" pile. Of course the intention is there to read it; no one would ever really mean to shelve a report they asked for, but the truth is that in the fast-paced world of business, in our fire-fighting modes, most of us don't even have time to open up all of our e-mails much less read details of some large report, even if the report is about an important entity: the customer.

And that is why, if there is an organized meeting where the information is collected and analyzed by the full-time quality service manager and that information is reported on a regular basis, the information will be heard and can be acted upon. The key words there, of course, are *acted upon*. The action part means that people will be motivated because of the publicness of the report, that is, there is no escaping the service chart, especially when senior management is present. We suggest that senior management show up for at least the scorecard part of the meeting. They don't need to stay through the discussion/solution part of the meeting, but it is essential for them to show they care about whether service is being provided or not. If senior management does not show up to review meetings, then employees think initiatives aren't important.

All measures of service have some degree of subjectivity, but your company can strive to evaluate service in a very objective way. The SP3M service reporting mechanisms used to monitor performance mutually benefit the company and the internal and outsourced (external) suppliers because they are easy-to-read reports and can be used to quickly identify areas that may need adjustments in valued resources. These resources may be material in nature, or consist of personnel shifts in assignments or projects. Inside of this commitment, if a company has designated employees whose primary focus is following the SP3M monitoring system and producing reports with executive summaries, then these reports can drive staff meetings and determine opportunities for improvement. Monitoring service levels and publishing data play a key operational role in making strategic decisions, as well as substantiating actions and costs associated with the improvements.

The executive summaries (Figure 12.2) used in SP3M reporting, designate service levels with a traffic signal type indicator where the colors would denote:

Orange (O) = Exceeded

Green (G) = Met

Yellow (Y) = Under Review

Red (R) = Did Not Meet

The number of items met is compared with the total possible to meet and the result creates a monthly performance measure percentage. Quarterly and annual trends are also presented and are important in understanding where overall quality performance is heading over time. Example areas of the reports can include:

- Executive summary by critical area (historical accounting of service)
- Number of calls received
- Average response time to service calls
- Abandon call rates
- Average answer time
- On-line system availability

When an area is shown in red (Figure 12.2) meaning it does not meet agreed upon service levels, it becomes clear very quickly that this is an area to examine immediately for improvement. In presenting this information to all the staff, the staff understands clearly what the area of focus is this month. What we found in implementing the marketing stage of SP3M, a very skilled, facilitative leader was most often at the helm directing the presentations and meetings to ensure the meetings did not deteriorate into "let's point out who is doing something wrong."

The team dynamics became very solution oriented. In other words, when one area was red, they all put their heads together to determine how they could fix this. And much of the fix-it part of the meeting was done in the smaller groups even before they came to the larger town hall meeting, so that solutions would be presented alongside the red, yellow, and green charts. It was the group brainstorm and energy that solidified the final course of action. The teams would proceed, with very clear direction on their part to change that red to green or even orange!

Call Center Case Study

One month, a call center received a red on the executive summary service management report. One hundred dollars was offered to every agent if they produced a green for the next month on the call center report. This would require teamwork, as there were a number of measurements that were rolled up into the call center summary. Each day a team huddle was held in the morning and afternoon. The team organized themselves such that they ensured they had adequate coverage when fellow agents were out or late. They kept track of their stats daily. In the evening they reviewed the stats to see how they did and planned for the next day's activity. Being motivated to produce the result, the call center agents began to manage themselves. Because they were asked by the director to give reports daily, they knew their management was interested in their work. There was no one in the company that did not know what they needed to do. Their goals and objectives were very clear. Responsibility and accountability were covered.

When you measure people, many times they feel uncomfortable or think measurement is a personal reflection of their work. How the measurement process is presented by management greatly affects how employees react to it. We generally like to coach management before they present so that it doesn't backfire. We have seen cases where because management was so unaware of how they presented things that even in trying to do the right thing they alienated their employees. Managing change is an acquired art. In this case the SP3M model was used to measure, market, manage. A successful market stage resulted in the staff feeling comfortable with the measurement and also accountable for producing the result. The red moved to a green within a month. The agents got their money and the satisfaction of being acknowledged for a job well done at the next monthly staff meeting. The executive summary report remained green from then on.

The end result was a motivated staff who felt special and acknowledged. Consequently, with happy call center agents, the customers were receiving a very high level of service.

MANAGE

In the manage step it is important to:

- Plan the work

- Work to the plan

This involves creating an integrated master plan and schedule, action items, due dates, and point person(s) with the buy-in from each of the team members. This plan would include software/hardware/process changes. And before the change is going to affect a stakeholder, they need to be notified. As the changes are taking place, it is important to monitor the change process, review the plan, update it, and report progress or roadblocks of plan and solutions.

It is absolutely paramount that service level agreement metrics are not changed on the fly. These changes should only be approved by key stakeholders in the process. This ensures that there is no confusion at the staff levels as to who sets the metrics. A change to a metric can be made with good justification, but again it must be approved at the highest level and documented. Most importantly, the change must be well communicated to all management, providers, and staff so all have new awareness of the level of service expected.

Technology that Optimizes CRM

THE TECHNOLOGY QUESTION

In the previous chapters we have looked at the people and process part of CRM. We saw technology that:

Enables People

- Centerforce
- Behavioral Assessments, LMR Associates.com

Enables Process

- BenchmarkPortal.com
- SLAs via SP3M, LMR Associates.com
- Edcor
- Centerforce

Now we will take a look at technology. John P. Robertson, a vice president of CRM at Edcor, was at a recent ICCM conference and he saw the change in the mood of the buyers of technology. "*Last year everyone was buying the latest thing, this year there was a malaised glaze over everyone. The technology boom went bust,*" he observed.

Robertson, with over 15 years' experience in consulting, technology, development, and operations, helps to lead Edcor's Customer Experience Management (CEM) Business Unit. Under his leadership, Edcor's clients have achieved ongoing strategic and operational results through the ever-changing CRM arena. Through Robertson's consultation and diagnostic reviews, Edcor's clientele have experienced flexible system design and integration, business process enhancement, software and Web application hosting, and have entrusted Edcor to oversee all customer service activities as a completely outsourced CRM program. Examples of operational success include a 16 percent increase in positive cross-sell, and a 9 percent conversion increase in customer retention. Moreover, Robertson has been crucial in growing Edcor's CEM capabilities into the international arena, with successful client operations in Mexico and Europe. He shares a list of questions to ask yourself, when thinking about a technology purchase, as well as a good Tom Sawyer story.

Are You Asking the Right Questions?

It is the CFO's fiduciary duty to question any capital expenditure. The questions are fairly common but demand accurate and substantiated answers, questions such as:

- Should we lease or buy?

- What is the payback period?

- What is the vendor's performance guarantee?

- What are payment terms?

- Can we negotiate a lower price?

- In today's economy, will the vendor burn through their cash?

These and many other questions are asked and answered in what can be an exhausting process. Like many other processes within organizations, this questioning process guarantees that the due diligence has been done to ensure that all the facts are available to make a financially sound business decision.

What's missing? Often when faced with a technology expense we forget to ask, "Is this the right thing to do? Will this drive revenue and increase profitability? Will the company obtain and retain more customers?" The typical CRM investment is born of the internal operations and technology groups, suggesting that this is a business strategy decision on an equal par with decisions around acquisitions and development of new product lines. The research involved in the release of a new cereal or style of shoe is immense—the consumer tests, the marketing plans, etc. Has your company done a consumer test to determine if people want to interact with you via the Web or any of the other multi-media channels of CRM? Or are you just assuming that because everyone else is doing so, it must be true and the thing to do? If they do want to interact via the Web, what do they want? How would they like to be supported? What other types of service do they need? Where is the strategy around relationship management and how does it support your business objectives? The implementation of CRM begins with a customer strategy (Chapter 1). Once your customer relationship strategy has been defined, then utilize technology to achieve your goals.

Marketing 101

"Say Tom, what ya' doin'?"

"I'm painting this here fence!"

"Too bad, we goin' swimming."

"Swimming? Why would I want to do that when I could be paintin' this here fence? This is the most fun I've had all summer."

"Really? Can we try?"

"I don't think so, only a special kinda' boy can do the right kinda' job paintin' a fence."

"Please? I'll give ya' my apple."

"Well awright, but only for a few seconds."

Tom Sawyer was the master. He may not have realized it at the time, but he established a marketing model that technology vendors have been following for years. The reality is that today's technological advances in the CRM industry are outpacing the public's ability to utilize the channels ten to one. I had the opportunity to speak with one of the vendors that supplies Voice over Internet Protocol technology (VoIP) recently. When he had finished telling me about all of the capabilities of his product, I asked, "Do you utilize VoIP technology in your contact center?" I had not expected a yes, but he proudly proclaimed "Yes, in all of our technical support centers." I don't think he anticipated my next question, "What percentage of interactions utilize that particular channel?" His answer—less than ten percent. The vendor was trying to sell something I didn't need, just like Tom convincing those kids that they really wanted to paint a fence. I don't think I'll be painting any fences today.

TECHNOLOGY OVERVIEW: HOW TECHNOLOGY CAN EMPOWER TECHNOLOGY

Now that we have looked at technology strategy, we will look at technology that can assure the ability to measure how well that technology is serving the customer and supporting CRM. This is done via a *technology* quality assurance program. In creating a section on how technology can empower technology we wanted to start by reviewing some of the observations we have seen:

- Companies have identified that the quality of service of their call center can be a sustainable competitive advantage.

- Companies are implementing complex technologies to make the call center more productive and to encourage self-service.

- Although new technology often results in heightened efficiency and productivity, its complexity also encourages unanticipated downtime and system failures, often negatively impacting the quality of service.

- As a result of the demand for high quality telephone interactions by customers, many companies have implemented technology quality assurance programs in their call centers to continuously measure and monitor the quality of service.

- A professional quality assurance program always includes both active and passive key performance indicators. These performance indicators can best by monitored by an automatic system.

- Successful technology quality assurance programs for call centers address the following issues:
  - Provide continuous peer group benchmarking
  - Measure key performance indicators before, during, and after implementation of various software and hardware components
  - Test individual parts, as well as the integrated customer contact center
  - Create stress tests under real-world conditions of customer calling loads (peak hours and/or seasonal times)
  - Are scaleable to meet future increase in call volumes
  - Manual quality assurance programs are marginal at best
  - In addition, marginal quality assurance programs only measure key performance indicators after the call is distributed by the ACD to an IVR or to an agent
  - Most marginal quality assurance programs do not catch important quality of service issues prior to the call reaching the ACD, or misinterpret what the root cause of the problem really might be. As a result, the quality of service suffers, as many problems occur before the call even reaches the ACD.

In the last five years, the call center has moved from a back-office cost center to the front line of the corporate customer relationship management (CRM) strategy. In this migration to CRM, the importance of the telephone service representative (TSR) has gone from the need for individuals with minimum skills at minimum pay to the need for the sophisticated knowledge worker of today.

In parallel with this evolution, technology has opened many additional channels of communication between customer and companies. The two most popular with customers, in addition to the telephone, are e-mail and the corporate Web site. However, since customers thrive on access to company information, a long list of other channels is also being selected by the customer. These include all of the following: voice mail, fax-back, kiosk, Web chat, and wireless devices such as cell phones, pagers, PC wireless, WAP devices, to name only a few.

Management of customer relationships through these additional channels has added an "e" to CRM, namely electronic customer relationship management (e-CRM). With the additional management challenge of these new channels, the call center itself is in a transitory state as it moves more and more to becoming the e-business customer contact center of the future.

Driving the contact center development is the growing realization that managing customer relationships is a key driver of bottom-line profits. Today's customers greatly value timely accessibility to product-critical information. In fact, the common vision of the customer contact center of the future is to allow customers access to information:

- at any time

- from anywhere

- in any form

- for free

Now that top executives in both the public sector (i.e., government) and the private sector (i.e., industry) are convinced that the e-business contact center is a strategic weapon for: a) getting customers, b) keeping customers, and c) growing profitable customers, the importance of a service quality measurement system, including performance benchmarking has become mission-critical to business survival.

As the "lightning rod" for customer interactions, world-class customer contact centers are becoming the single point of contact for customers. According to research conducted at Purdue University, over 90 percent of customer interactions will occur through the contact center by the year 2004.

For many companies, global competition has reduced products to mere commodities that are difficult to differentiate through features, functions, or price. Having reached parity, where price and quality are the "table stakes" of doing business, the paradigm shift is definitely towards customer accessibility. In fact, accessibility to a company's information has become an essential "product feature" according to research by the authors.

For the above reasons, frequently benchmarking contact center performance against a peer group of similar centers is a mandatory step in being competitive.

In this chapter we describe in some detail the importance of constant measurement of service quality regarding accessibility to information. We see significant benefit and significant risk in the technology of accessibility. When properly installed, integrated, and automatically monitored, these accessibility risks can be mitigated and managed. One product, by Empirix, can be used to constantly monitor inbound access to a contact center on a proactive basis.

This section provides a comprehensive review of designing, implementing, and maintaining a level of service quality that gives executives and call center managers the competitive edge to attract and maintain customers.

The Customer Contact Center Technology

As already discussed, new CRM strategies, plus a plethora of multimedia access channels like the Internet, have forced the evolution of traditional agent-intensive inbound call centers into highly automated, technology-enabled, customer contact centers, see Figure 13.1. Many call center interactions that previously required agent intervention are now fully automated. Self-service Web applications, interactive voice response (IVR), and computer telephony integration (CTI) systems enable customers to connect to a contact center, access their account, and complete a transaction without speaking with a live agent.

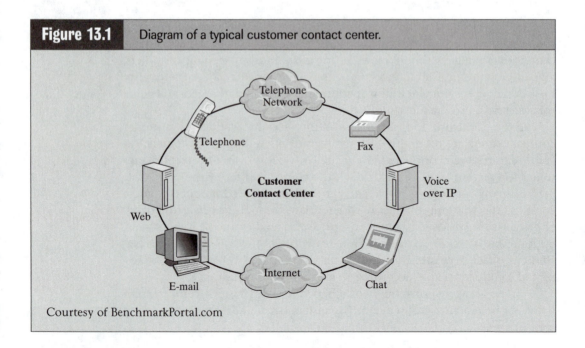

Figure 13.1   Diagram of a typical customer contact center.

Courtesy of BenchmarkPortal.com

HOW THE CUSTOMER GETS CONNECTED IN A TRADITIONAL CALL CENTER

A quick overview of how calls are routed through a traditional call center is provided to explain the possible operational risks involved in relying on the technology and current design of QA system strategies. Traditional call centers include an ACD, an IVR system, and sometimes a CTI system.

The ACD processes each call and routes it to the IVR, or queues it for distribution to an agent, see Figure 13.2. The IVR prompts callers with a series of menu choices. Working in tandem with the IVR and ACD, the CTI system accesses databases for caller account information and automatically processes the call without agent intervention. When a caller "zeroes out" to talk to a live agent, the CTI system provides caller account information to the agent's desktop in the form of a "screen pop" just as the call arrives at the agent's headset—a true integration of voice and data.

Importance of Customer Accessibility Technology

Recent studies have shown that the primary reason customers choose to stop doing business with a particular company is poor customer service. Companies competing for the attention of and loyalty from today's consumer must continue to improve the quality of the customer's experience with the contact center. Today, the customer's attention span is shorter than ever. Customers have more choices, easier access to information, and higher expectations of service and availability. Thus, as enterprises implement CRM

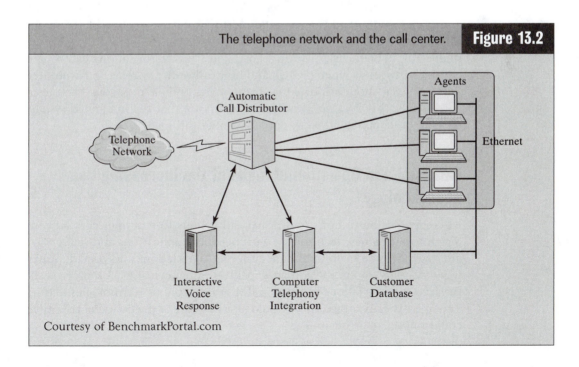

The telephone network and the call center. **Figure 13.2**

Courtesy of BenchmarkPortal.com

solutions to focus on customer service, retention, and acquisition, customer contact centers have increased in strategic importance.

Forward-looking executives have leveraged these contact centers with enabling technologies to provide additional services to customers. However, while trying to service the customer better and faster with technology, the complexity of that very innovative technology, coupled with the automation of customer interactions, can significantly decrease the customer's accessibility, if the system fails for even short periods of time. Contact centers can suddenly become inundated with calls. Wait times can skyrocket. Business is often lost, and resulting market damage is almost assured.

Unfortunately, failures in automated customer self-service systems are not always immediately apparent. Carrier and network routing problems may be intermittent. A handful of IVR ports may not be working properly. The wrong prompts may be playing. Customers may be getting disconnected. At one major computer manufacturer, their IVRs were answering customer calls but incorrectly taking customers to a prompt that played the message "All customer representatives are busy. Please call back later," and then "hanging up" on the caller. The call center manager wasn't even aware there was a problem—again, a very dangerous situation.

Because of the growing reliance on contact centers, senior executives should be aware of the impact of contact center accessibility failures and inefficiencies. We found that successful companies had implemented an effective risk-mitigation program which allowed customer accessibility to the contact center to be closely monitored through a rigorous QA system of automated testing. There is a large distinction between manual testing and automated testing and the importance of that will be explored later. In addition, many call center system and application failures will only show up under full, in-bound call loading. Load and stress testing allows call center developers to know where, when, and how call center systems and Web sites will fail. Even though individual component systems may pass stress tests successfully, this does not provide the assurance that the integrated system with all of its parts will work properly under full load.

Financial and Operational Risks of the Increasing Use of Technology

As companies move from traditional call centers to customer contact centers, integrating new technology, with network applications and self-service alternatives in order to automate customer transactions and provide seamless services is important and an expensive enhancement. As senior executives leverage the latest e-business, CRM, and telephony technologies to gain a competitive advantage, they should also be aware of the financial risks that could impact their businesses.

Service disruptions caused by contact center system failures or other operational issues significantly impact revenue. An audit of one high-tech manufacturing company revealed that each hour of interrupted telephone service could cost the company one million dollars in lost revenue. In some industries with low customer switching costs, such as the financial services industry or the travel industry, highly publicized, negative caller access events dilute brand equity and can cause significant customer churn. When adding up marketing and sales costs to acquire profitable new customers, the total cost of a single lost call or failed Web site transaction is considerable.

Although modern technology can have a major cost benefit for a contact center, it also increases the probability of operational failures and undiscovered customer service problems. Major operational risks in contact center operations include:

- Call handling errors or Web site errors

- Network performance/availability issues

- Implementation issues from inadequate application testing

- Outsourcing issues

A failure with one customer access channel often causes a chain reaction of failures with other access channels. For example, a recent brokerage Web site outage caused customers to inundate the company's contact center with phone calls. The customers who got through the busy signals experienced wait times exceeding ten minutes—not a happy situation.

There are several important factors in assessing operational issues related to customer contact centers. Those include testing:

- The system before deployment

- The individual components of the system

- The integrated call center and Web site systems

- The system under real-world loads

- Whether the tests are manual or automated

Maximizing the Customer Experience via Technology

A steady, lifetime customer revenue stream could hinge upon a single interaction that quickly changes a customer's perception and satisfaction with the business. The era of e-business decreases a customer's switching costs to a level where a competitor's product is just a "click away." The moment a contact center or Web site fails to deliver expected information or slows the transaction process, the customer may well look elsewhere.

Table 13.1 shows how a contact center can impact loyalty and repurchase. This study was conducted at Purdue University by the authors.

The key message in the research shown in Table 13.1 is that a company that hosts a well-designed customer contact center can actually garner 13 percent more customer loyalty than a company with an almost perfect product. The added 13 percent repurchase probability can easily pay for a world-class customer contact center. Also, an underlying principal is that more than 50 percent of all product problems are caused by the customer, and therefore, it is very, very unusual to have a product with almost no problems.

SELF-SERVICE TECHNOLOGY ALTERNATIVES—BENEFITS AND RISKS

Enabling self-service transactions provides economic benefits—it decreases agent costs and allows the most common transactions to be performed quickly and efficiently by the customer. Plus, studies conducted by the authors show that customers really appreciate self-service when it is easy to use, intuitive, and there is a reward for the time they spend helping themselves.

However, automation increases business risks by hiding problems customers may have accessing or using automated applications. Given the volume of calls in self-service applications, many organizations will not know if calls are being blocked, dropped, misrouted, or queued for an unacceptable period until it's too late. Organizations may not know until hours or days later that customers received busy signals or were routed incorrectly, or that the wrong prompts or applications were playing. Constant vigilance and benchmarking are critical.

Without supervisors and agents involved in the customer interaction with the contact center, the company may not have immediate visibility to operational issues and dissatisfied customers. Self-service applications remove the human control that provided companies with assurance over the quality of the customer's experience in the past.

TABLE 13.1—HOW A WELL-DESIGNED CUSTOMER CONTACT CENTER GARNERS LOYALTY.	
Product Situation	**Customer Repurchase Experience**
A product with almost no problems.	76% repurchase probability
A product with problems and an inferior customer contact center, namely a center with poor access to customer-critical information.	32% repurchase probability
A product with problems and a world class customer contact center, namely a center with seamless access to customer-critical information.	89% repurchase probability

THE IMPORTANCE OF QUALITY OF SERVICE MEASUREMENT PROGRAMS

A professional QA program should include both active and passive KPIs. Active KPIs are those metrics that are measured proactively, such as "secret shopping" a call center, or agent monitoring and scoring. Passive KPIs are those metrics taken directly by the ACD during and after the call. In addition, KPIs can be collected manually or via an automatic system. For this reason, QA programs consider the following:

1. Whether a QA program measures before, during, and/or after implementation of various software and hardware components

2. Whether the QA program is testing individual parts, or an integrated customer contact center

3. Whether the QA program tests under real-world conditions of customer calling loads (peak hours or seasonal times)

4. Whether the QA program is scaleable to meet those differing load volumes

Most QA programs only measure KPIs after the call is distributed by the ACD to an IVR or to an agent. This often means that the QA program will not catch important quality of service issues prior to the call reaching the ACD, or misinterpret what the root cause of the problem really might be. As a result, the quality of service will suffer, as many problems occur before the call even reaches the ACD. More will be covered on these issues in the next section.

Key Performance Indicators for Technology

DEFINITION OF A PASSIVE KEY PERFORMANCE INDICATOR

Key performance indicators (KPIs) are the critical measures that determine whether a system is delivering the best possible service typically related to an independent variable such as customer satisfaction. It is generally part of the QA program, including testing and ongoing monitoring. The term passive here is meant to convey that it is not proactive in measuring performance indicators, that is, it only measures after a call has been placed and distributed by the ACD to an agent or to an IVR.

LIST OF COMMON PASSIVE KEY PERFORMANCE INDICATORS

Examples of passive KPIs are all the measurements after the call has been placed by the ACD to an IVR or to a live agent. The following is a list of some common passive KPIs once a call has reached an agent. In the next section, we will look at passive KPIs of an IVR. These major types of errors illustrate the gamut of potential failures in automated telephony systems. Here are a few of the more common passive KPIs:

- Average Talk Time
  This is the total number of seconds the caller was connected to an agent. This data is available from the ACD.

- Average Speed of Answer
  This is the average time it takes for the call to be picked up by the call center's ACD. Often this is the number of rings before the ACD picks up the call and distributes it either to a live agent or to an IVR. This data is available from the ACD.

- Average Time in Queue
  This is equal to the total time in queue to reach an agent divided by the total number of calls answered. This data is available from the ACD.

- Calls Per Hour
  This is the average number of calls that an agent handles per hour. This data is available from the ACD.

- Hold Time
  This is the average number of seconds that a TSR places a customer on hold while trying to find the caller's answer. This data is available from the ACD.

- TSR Occupancy
  This is the average time that a TSR is in their seat, connected to the ACD, and ready to answer calls as a percent of the total time they are at work. This data is available from the ACD.

- Adherence to Schedule
  This is the average time the TSR is in their seat according to the work force management schedule.

MONITORING PASSIVE KEY PERFORMANCE INDICATORS

An example of a passive KPI is shown in Figure 13.3, where the flow and length of an IVR call is detailed. The time that each step takes for the caller to get to the information they need is a typical passive KPI. Based on the digits selected by the caller, the IVRs route calls through a preprogrammed call flow using conditional branching. As additional menus are added, the conditional branches become increasingly complex. For example, a typical banking customer might navigate through at least four menus and spend two minutes of the total call navigating the IVR. If each menu has six options, calls could be routed through any one of the 1,296 unique call flows that involves CTI and other telephony systems.

| | Elapsed time in an IVR menu prompt interaction. | **Figure 13.3** |

Elapsed Time

20 Seconds

PRESS
1 for ATM locator
2 to open an account
3 for account information
0 for a service rep

55 Seconds

Please enter social security no.
Please enter password

65 Seconds

PRESS
1 for savings information
2 for checking information
3 for line of credit information

80 Seconds

PRESS
1 for balance information
2 for checks paid and withdrawals
3 for deposits

120 Seconds

Listen to balance information

CALL TERMINATED

Courtesy of BenchmarkPortal.com

AN EXAMPLE OF A PASSIVE KPI FOR IVRS

As an example, we will use an IVR to show the problem of only measuring passive KPIs. The only way most companies know something is wrong with their IVR applications is if a customer calls to complain. However, many IVR transaction problems occur as a result of system or network slowdowns and failures outside of the IVR system itself. While most companies actively monitor their human call center agents to make sure customers are not encountering problems, most are not proactively monitoring their automated IVR transaction systems with active KPIs. This represents a significant potential business risk. We have found that IVR systems handle 70 to 80 percent of all customer inquiries in some companies. Undetected IVR transaction problems can quickly translate into lost customers and lost revenues. A single 20-minute outage or slowdown of IVR-based applications in larger call centers can impact thousands of calls at a potential cost in the tens of thousands of dollars.

What Can Go Wrong with an IVR

Most IVR application problems are not caused by a failure of the IVR system itself. They are the result of system and network problems external to the IVR. For example, a common problem occurs when mainframe database connections to the IVR slow down or fail completely. Mainframe slowdowns and outages impact IVR database lookups such as verifying account and PIN numbers, account balance inquiries, etc. Customers, thinking the IVR system isn't working, may try to "zero out" to a TSR. All of a sudden, queue times in the call center start shooting through the roof. Or, even worse, customers, faced with nonfunctioning systems, may simply hang up and call a competitor. Another common problem is when customers cannot get through because trunks are out of order or busy. At one large call center recently, an entire trunk group was out of order for 24 hours before the problem was discovered. It was estimated that over 20,000 customer calls were lost—forever.

Sometimes, undiscovered errors on IVR applications can cause customer calls to be mishandled or dropped entirely. For example, a large computer manufacturer using IVR for its customer service operations was unknowingly playing the wrong prompt. Callers to one of the company's many 800 numbers were greeted with "All of our representatives are busy. Please call back later." Callers were then "hung-up on." It wasn't until a customer called the company's main switchboard to complain that the call center became aware there was a problem. In another situation, a large bank had an undiscovered error in one of its IVR applications that caused calls received after 11:00 P.M. to go into an endless loop—very frustrating for the callers!

For smaller call centers, which do not staff 24/7 operations, IVR applications may be the only service available to customers for after-hours inquiries or transactions. If the IVR becomes unavailable over a weekend or holiday, it may take 48 hours or longer before the problem is even discovered.

How Often Do IVR Problems Occur?

Larger call centers with many IVR systems experience problems every day that impact their IVR applications and result in lost customer calls or calls overflowing to call center TSRs. When IVR problems occur, the resulting unexpected increase in call volume to TSRs out of the IVR systems can instantly generate lengthening queue times and reduced service levels, resulting in customers hanging up and/or recalling, or worse yet, going to the competition. One large call center estimated that it took nearly four hours for call center operations to return to normal after an IVR outage, and it was experiencing several of these outages every week. Customers, unable to use the IVR, would "zero out" to speak to a TSR, encounter excessive hold times, hang up, and try again later—obviously the problem was quickly out of control. This process starts a snowball effect as hundreds or thousands of callers repeat the same logical customer pattern.

Standard Monitoring Is Not Enough

In these situations, the IVR system itself may appear to be working normally to a network operations center when, in fact, customers are encountering problems. For example, if trunk groups are out of order, or call routing errors are occurring, traditional network and system management tools, like HP's Open View and/or Candle's solution, will not indicate that there is a problem. That is why conventional network-based system monitoring solutions should not be relied on as the only solution for detecting IVR transaction problems. Even after discovering the problem with one or more of the IVRs, finding exactly where the problem is and correcting it can pose a significant challenge. In an age of distributed call centers and distributed call routing, it can take hours just to identify the source and cause of an IVR problem if there are a large number of IVRs.

DEFINITION OF AN ACTIVE KEY PERFORMANCE INDICATOR

Active KPIs are those measurements that occur when we proactively do something to monitor quality. The KPIs resulting from agent monitoring are an example of active. Similarly, when we proactively "shoot calls" at an ACD and monitor its reaction and response time, we generate active KPIs.

LIST OF COMMON ACTIVE KEY PERFORMANCE INDICATORS

This is a list of common active KPIs resulting from bombarding an ACD with calls:

- Blocked Calls
  A common call handling error is blocked calls. Busy or out-of-order telephone trunks block calls when customers try to dial an inbound toll-free number. Unless trunks are actively monitored, managers may not be aware that calls cannot reach their contact centers.

- Dropped Calls

  Calls can also be accidentally dropped due to system failures when the call reaches the contact center's ACD. A financial services caller may spend several minutes navigating four IVR menus for an automated banking system. After selecting the correct digits to determine his/her checking account balance, a customer may hear silence and have the call dropped because the CTI or IVR application failed to connect to the mainframe database.

- Misdirected Calls

  A similar situation occurs when calls are misdirected. A customer may call an airline reservation hotline and navigate IVR menus to reach a domestic travel agent. Because of programming errors in the IVR call flow, the customer is connected to the automated flight departures and arrivals menu and is not allowed to "zero out" to reach an agent—very frustrating.

- Database Access

  A common call handling error that causes network congestion and customers to disconnect their calls is lengthy access times to account information. Fast access to mainframe databases is critical in CTI and IVR applications. Customers encountering longer than average wait times for balance inquiry information, or other automated transactions, may "zero out" to talk with an agent causing unnecessary live agent traffic.

MONITORING ACTIVE KEY PERFORMANCE INDICATORS

To achieve a new level of reliability in a call center's telecommunications systems and applications, one needs to identify the performance bottlenecks and call handling errors before new or modified systems and applications are deployed. If this is done, the costs of detecting and correcting problems will be significantly reduced. In addition, the risk of lost customer calls caused by unidentified problems can be substantially reduced.

The new paradigm shift in call center monitoring is that it is not just the traditional call monitoring, as most of us know it. In a recent survey of call center managers, 44 percent said that they had experienced a serious outage in their call center within the past 12 months. A whopping 32 percent had experienced a serious failure within the last six months. Perhaps these statistics shouldn't be surprising, given the complexity of today's integrated call center operating environment. Many of these outages could have been prevented by the use of automated test systems as part of a comprehensive QA process, including in-service testing of call center network connections, systems, and applications.

It is surprising that so many call centers, given the relatively high potential of experiencing a serious failure, take few if any preventative measures. Most call centers today perform only minimal testing of new or modified applications and systems prior to live deployment. Most testing that is done is manual, including testing of IVRs and CTI systems. Manual testing typically consists of a handful of people dialing in and trying to find problems—not very scientific or effective.

Manual testing, in most instances, simply cannot replicate the conditions that cause call center systems and applications to fail. This is because many network, system, or application failures only show up under load, that is, normal operating conditions, or under stress, or extreme operating conditions. Manual testing cannot replicate the call volumes or variability in call type and duration that cause systems and applications to fail. Manual testing also suffers from a lack of consistency and repeatability, two critical requirements for effective QA test plans. As a result, it is the customers who are finding most of the bugs and problems in call centers today, unfortunately.

AN IVR ACTIVE KPI EXAMPLE

The benefits of testing an active KPI include:

- Avoid undetected outages

- Increase problem identification

- Diagnose and resolve problem identification in minutes instead of hours

- Lower operating costs

- Improve customer service levels

Unlike traditional system and network monitoring tools that only monitor the status of individual components of the call center, active QA programs monitor the customer experience by automatically placing test calls that emulate real-world customers, and measure KPIs affecting the customer experience, such as prompt integrity and host response time. The test calls can identify busy or out-of-order trunks, IVR port failures, prompt errors and slowdowns, database and host access issues, and other problems that can negatively impact customer service.

The active test system interacts with customer applications in exactly the same way a customer would—by dialing into the contact center, "listening" to IVR and other system prompts, determining if the right prompt is playing, and entering the appropriate touch-tone or spoken responses to step through a call flow (see Figure 13.4). Throughout a test call, the system takes timing measurements to check for possible outages and other problems. If at any point the system does not get the expected response from the contact center systems, including IVR, or the response time exceeds a pre-established limit, the test system can immediately page the appropriate technical manager to correct the problem. The page can indicate in which system the problem was encountered and where in the call flow it occurred.

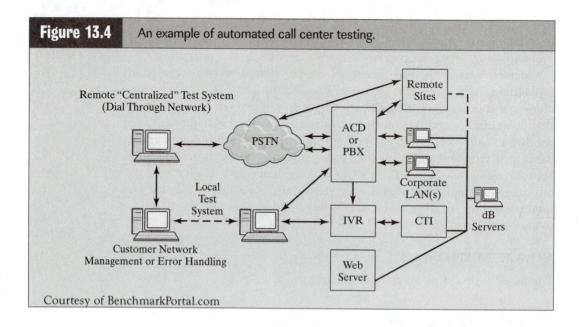

Figure 13.4   An example of automated call center testing.

Courtesy of BenchmarkPortal.com

Achieving Improved Call Center Reliability—The High Cost of Call Center Down Time

The benefits resulting from improved application software and system reliability in call centers can be significant. In a call center receiving 1,000 calls an hour (i.e., approximately 1,600,000 calls per year), a 30-minute outage can potentially mean 500 customers that are negatively impacted (see Figure 13.5). If a Web site is down or overloaded and difficult to reach, it could be negatively impacting similar numbers of customers, and it most probably will not be known to be down. Even a brief outage can translate into hundreds

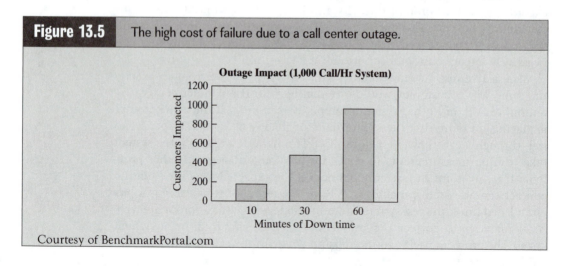

Figure 13.5   The high cost of failure due to a call center outage.

Courtesy of BenchmarkPortal.com

of thousands of dollars in lost revenue for an airline reservation center or brokerage firm.

In addition to measuring the cost of lost customer transactions, one may also need to consider the cost of losing a customer. What is the expected revenue value of a lost customer to your business? How much does it cost to find a new customer to replace one that has been lost? We know from our research that the impact of customer dissatisfaction can be costly.

DISASTER RECOVERY PLANNING

Most organizations have business continuity or disaster recovery plans that address contact center accessibility in mission-critical operations. However, these same organizations may not have adequate controls to monitor accessibility and quickly identify slow or failed applications and systems. Traditional systems and network monitoring tools used in network operations centers cannot find many of the problems that can potentially impact today's contact center. For example, systems and network monitoring tools cannot identify busy trunks. They cannot identify if the wrong prompts are playing or if calls are being disconnected. They have trouble finding application slowdowns, or response time problems that negatively impact customer service levels.

In addition, contact center systems are increasingly distributed across different geographical regions. Without appropriate monitoring controls, it may take hours to recognize and isolate IVR or other system and application failures resulting in thousands of lost calls.

END-TO-END PERFORMANCE STRATEGY

Many organizations monitor each system, network connection, or application independently without consideration for monitoring the total end-to-end performance of a customer call. A performance degradation of any one system or network link could impact the performance of the entire customer transaction but may not be sufficient, in itself, to trigger an alarm with traditional system and network monitoring tools. For example, organizations that purchase extra trunk capacity for an investor hotline in anticipation of a spike in call volume, but run a CTI application on an aging computer with 32 terabytes of memory, will have serious customer service problems. As enterprises add additional services by implementing new telephony systems and applications, the risk of creating additional points of failure increases geometrically.

IMPLEMENTATION ISSUES

Inefficient, inadequate, or nonexistent testing of CRM, e-business, and CTI/IVR applications is the root cause of most implementation issues. For example, many companies implement IVR changes without comprehensively testing call routing features. When testing is performed, companies typically perform inadequate manual tests. In a manual test, only a few people are employed to interact with the IVR and identify programming errors or network routing issues based on the voice-prompt responses. Since these manual tests do not check all possible call flows, or simulate real world conditions, applications and systems may fail from incorrect configurations or inadequate engineering.

OUTSOURCING ISSUES

Some companies outsource either part or all of their contact center operations to control costs, manage seasonal variances in call volume, or focus on core competencies. Although service level agreements typically include key performance indicators and remedies, they may not provide senior executives with assurance that the metrics reported by the teleservices provider truly reflect the customer's actual service experience.

AVAILABILITY OF AUTOMATIC TECHNOLOGY TESTING SOLUTIONS

To minimize business risks, senior executives should embed comprehensive risk processes into their contact center business activities and drive risk management responsibilities down to all organizational layers. A risk assessment program will help align the objectives, risks, and control processes within the organization with life-cycle testing (see Figure 13.6). A review of many of the possible automatic testing solutions options are provided in this chapter, although not all of them were tested. Questions to ask when setting up a risk assessment program include:

- What are the business objectives?

- How do contact center technology initiatives support these objectives?

- What are the risks that could influence the achievement of these objectives?

- What current controls exist to monitor and mitigate these risks?

By aligning risks with business objectives and identifying appropriate control processes, senior executives take a proactive approach to risk management instead of reacting to unmanaged risk when it becomes a problem. An example of a reactive approach is when organizations, without further review, automatically increase trunk capacity after hearing customer complaints about busy signals. This may or may not solve the issue.

Organizations that embrace a proactive approach build controls and risk management processes into their activities. For example, a travel agency's objective is to reduce the amount of time agents spend on the phone and save money on network and agent costs. The company develops a new application that automatically retrieves a business customer's travel profile based on the originating telephone number, shaving approximately 15 seconds from each call. A key risk to increasing agent productivity is that the agents do not understand how to use the new application, or the application does not work correctly. The controls would be to test the appli-

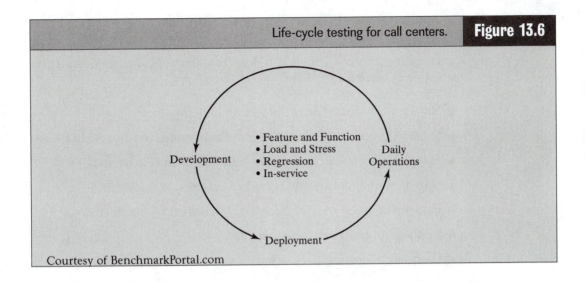

Life-cycle testing for call centers.   **Figure 13.6**

Development

- Feature and Function
- Load and Stress
- Regression
- In-service

Daily Operations

Deployment

Courtesy of BenchmarkPortal.com

cation prior to deployment, monitor the end-to-end network performance, and implement a training program for all agents.

AUTOMATED PERFORMANCE TESTING AND MONITORING TECHNOLOGY BENEFITS

The benefits of automated performance testing and monitoring include:

- Avoiding call center application failures and call center downtime
- Pinpointing and isolating problems quickly
- Tests that are systematic and repeatable
- Automated testing that saves time and money
- Avoiding customer frustration, loss, and lower revenue
- Ensuring optimal telecommunications system and network performance
- Reducing costs
- Improving service

A comprehensive quality assurance program proactively mitigates financial and operational risks associated with automated self-service applications. A typical program involves customer satisfaction surveys, proactive, real-time monitoring controls, and customer contact center testing. Customer satisfaction surveys would allow a customer to exit out of an automated call flow to provide direct feedback on the call to an agent. Monitoring controls assures senior executives that the systems, applications, and the network are functional and meeting the customer's quality of service expectations.

CUSTOMER CONTACT CENTER TESTING TECHNOLOGY

The weakest area for many companies in implementing a QA program is customer contact center testing technology. Examples of customer contact center testing need to assure that:

- Software is tested to detect programming errors
- Software is tested to ensure it operates as intended in a live environment
- Modifications made subsequent to initial testing are retested
- Systems and applications are backed up prior to installation
- Implementations are authorized and signed-off by management
- Application features are documented
- Users are trained on the software

Many applications, such as IVRs, are not tested before they are implemented. Other applications are tested manually by a few employees, which does not provide assurance that the application will function properly when processing thousands of calls or that the tests are performed consistently. The solution to customer contact center testing weaknesses is to use automated testing tools. Automated testing using automated call generators and other sophisticated tools allows complex call flows to be completely tested in a simulated production environment prior to actual deployment in the contact center.

EARLY ALERTS OF DEGRADING CALL CENTER APPLICATIONS THROUGH TESTING

Early alerts include the measurement of active KPIs that provide executives with a proactive ability to quickly solve call center issues. For call center operations managers and business managers who want to deploy new or updated CTI, IVR, and ACD installations with absolute certainty that they will work under real world conditions, using an automated test solution for load testing call center applications and systems can verify performance under real-world call traffic conditions prior to deployment.

TECHNOLOGY APPLICATION TESTS

Customer contact center testing should involve the following application tests using automated test technology tools:

- Functional testing of new applications
- Load and stress testing of call center components
- Regression testing of software before implementation into a production environment

Functional tests ensure the features and functions of a new application are working as designed. Load and stress tests determine the specific conditions where the software will fail and identifies system, network, and application bottlenecks. Automated testing tools provide features for varying the load on the application. An application that supports 48 simultaneous calls may not scale up to support 96 simultaneous calls. Regression tests need to occur prior to deployment and ensure that recent software changes do not contain any bugs.

AUTOMATED TECHNOLOGY TESTING

An automated technology test tool (that is connected to telephone lines) calls an inbound contact center, or connects to a Web server, and interacts with the contact center like a real customer. The test tool can be programmed to run every fifteen minutes on a 24/7 schedule. It provides vital information on call handling or transaction errors such as network and system delays, call mis-routing, and dropped calls. In the case of a system or network failure, in-service testing can quickly pinpoint the source of the failure.

Experience shows that manual testing uncovers only a portion of the hidden problems in call center systems. That's because manual testing cannot come close to duplicating real-world conditions. Automated load testing gives call centers a powerful new tool for ensuring that their systems have been properly engineered to meet current and future performance requirements. Automatic call center telephony testing systems can detect and measure:

- Configuration errors
- Resource problems
- Busy or out-of-service trunks
- IVR and ACD prompt errors
- Performance bottlenecks
- Prompt timing problems
- IVR/Host response times
- Database response times

AUTOMATED TEST CALLS

With a call center telephony testing system, one can quickly and easily generate thousands of automated test calls. Unlike bulk call generators, an automated test call system can precisely duplicate realistic customer calling conditions. Just like actual customers, the system can dial into the systems under test, entering account numbers and PIN numbers, listening to ensure that the right prompt responses are being played, and measuring system and network response times throughout each test call. If response times exceed pre-established thresholds, or if any other problem is found, the system logs the error and its location in the call flow to a database as well as displaying test results in real-time. The system can even be set to immediately page a technical support resource for problem correction. Every aspect of a call flow can be controlled with this system including the entry of variable information using touch-tones, and playing an unlimited number of voice files, for testing speech recognition-based systems. This type of prompt recognition capability even allows one to automatically verify that the correct prompts are being played in IVR and ACD/PBX systems.

LOAD TESTING TECHNOLOGY

Many call center system and application failures will only show up under load. Load and stress testing allows call center developers to know where, when, and how call center systems and Web sites will fail. Load and stress testing needs to be performed on the integrated call center and Web site systems. Even though individual component systems may pass tests successfully, this provides no assurance that the systems will work properly when they are integrated.

Ideally, a test plan duplicates actual expected calling and Web site usage conditions and patterns. Automated testing is capable of generating thousands of test calls or Web hits. Test systems should be capable of also duplicating the variable actions of real callers or Web site users, including the ability to step through IVR call paths, determine if the correct prompts are playing, and measure timings. The test plan should identify stress bottlenecks in the systems and develop a load service curve that can be used for capacity planning purposes. Under life-cycle testing, regression tests are run on all new software releases and bug fixes prior to deployment on live systems. Regression tests are used to determine that nothing new has broken and that the application and system performance characteristics haven't been adversely affected. Once automated call center system and application tests have been created, regression tests are fast and easy to run.

IN-SERVICE TESTING TECHNOLOGY

If quality is being measured only by the monitoring of agent interactions or measuring service statistics like wait time, one may be missing significant potential sources of customer dissatisfaction. It is possible that customer calls or contact attempts may not even be reaching the point where they show up as a statistic in a call center. This is why in-service testing is a vital component of a life-cycle testing program. In-service testing generates periodic test calls that duplicate the actions of real callers that use the public telephone system to call contact center systems, just the way actual callers would.

With the increasing complexity and number of contact center applications, manual testing performed on individual systems may not identify critical problems that would surface in a production environment. In-service testing or monitoring creates an effective monitoring control by simulating the customer's experience with an automated self-service application. It tests the end-to-end call flow by placing test calls that duplicate the real-world actions of customers.

ONGOING MONITORING TECHNOLOGY

There are systems that automate continuous quality monitoring of IVR applications. These monitoring systems can be scheduled to dial into a call center's IVR systems and applications on a regular basis and verify that everything is working properly. Just like a customer, the monitoring system can dial out from a central location and place calls to a company's call center. On placing a test call, the monitoring system listens to verify that it is able to get through to the call center and whether or not the IVR answers the call. Its users can establish preset answering thresholds. If the IVR answering time exceeds the threshold or the system encounters a busy signal or other telephone line problem, the monitoring system can be set to immediately page a technical support person to correct the problem or log the problem to a database for later resolution. Once the IVR system answers, the monitoring system uses speech recognition technology to verify that the correct prompt is being played by the IVR.

If the correct prompt is playing, the monitoring system then starts stepping through the IVR menu choices just the way an actual customer would. The system can enter touch-tones, or play a voice file in response to any IVR prompt. It then listens for the right response from the IVR system and measures how long it takes for the IVR system to respond. Based on where a failure or error condition occurs in an IVR call flow, the test system can deduce the probable source of the problem. For example, if there is an excessive delay in system response at the IVR prompt which performs a mainframe database lookup, it could be deduced that there is either a mainframe problem or a network problem. It can then perform further tests to isolate the most likely cause. This can mean significant time savings in finding and correcting the source of the problem and getting IVR applications back in service. If the system finds an error that is not serious enough to warrant immediate attention, the monitoring system can simply log the problem to its built-in unresolved-issue database.

To further illustrate how this testing works, in response to an IVR prompt, the monitoring system can be set up to enter a customer account number either using touch-tone or playing a recorded voice file (if the IVR is set up to use speech recognition). The monitoring system then measures how long it takes for the IVR system to respond. If the IVR's response time exceeds a pre-established threshold it most likely would indicate that there is either a problem with the mainframe database used for account number lookups or there is a network problem. The monitoring system could then check if the network is working by "pinging" a network server. If the network responds, the monitoring system can deduce that the problem lies in the mainframe and immediately page the appropriate technical person. This automated narrowing of possible trouble areas to pinpoint the source of a problem can save significant time in restoring an IVR application to service and thereby reduce call center transaction costs.

AUTOMATIC MONITORING CASE STUDIES

One Bank's Experience

Prior to installing a monitoring system, one major bank in the United States was experiencing, on average, three or more problems each week across an IVR network of over 100 systems. Most of these IVR problems were the result of back-end system failures or slowdowns in the firm's local area and wide area networks, mainframes, and CTI. The impact of IVR outages on the bank's call centers was significant. It was estimated that, on average, a single 20-minute IVR outage resulted in nearly four hours of call center overload. The costs of these IVR outages included extra staffing expense in the call center, extra lines required because of repeated customer calls during IVR outages, and extra toll expenses due to increase wait times. Most significantly, $7.25 in additional expense was incurred for each call handled by a CSR that would previously have been handled by one of the bank's IVR systems.

After initially trying manual in-service testing of their IVR systems, the bank learned about automated IVR test solutions and decided to purchase a system. The benefits from continuous testing of the bank's IVRs were immediate. The bank's IVR support group no longer had to wait for customers to call and complain. Instead, the support group knew almost immediately about any failures or problems in the IVR systems. With continuous monitoring the IVR support group was able to identify and fix the IVR problems more quickly. Monitoring systems helped reduce the bank's average IVR outage time from four hours to just 12 minutes.

A Teleservices Company

This company had at least 50 separate tools to monitor and measure performance. When the customer picked up the phone and attempted to connect to the IVR platform, the call passed through numerous PSTN systems outside of their control. They wanted to be able to quantify the entire customer experience, not just the IVR system. What they found was that the best network management tools available only report on how they were handling those calls they already answered—it didn't tell them that customers couldn't get to them or they were not answering the phone. In this company, before using a testing system that could measure active KPIs, it could take as long as an hour to find and resolve a problem with one of the IVR systems. With a pro-active testing system, a problem was resolved in about five minutes. They found that being able to quantify their face to the outside world was invaluable for customer retention.

Before using the systems for proactive testing, it was customers who reported an issue. Those calls were virtually eliminated in the first week after the system was installed. This type of testing is utilized as their first line of attack for quickly finding and resolving any performance degradations in the network or IVR systems. Twenty-four hours a day, seven days a week, the test systems are proactively placing periodic test calls, ensuring that the customers receive the most reliable service possible.

When they were first introducing the idea of adding active KPI testing to the passive KPI testing, it was a tough sell in terms of the investment to be made. But within a week or two, the significant gain in overall quality helped management see the value it brought to the business in terms of improved quality of service that easily translated into profit and revenue. The automated testing paid for itself because the monitoring of the call center systems saved money by:

- Increasing the percentage of calls terminating in the IVR and not going to a TSR

- Reducing toll charges by keeping more calls in IVR systems

- Reducing the number of calls lost due to trunk outages and IVR problems

- Reducing the time it takes to find and solve IVR problems from hours down to minutes

An increasing number of customer interactions with the contact center are now automated by self-service applications, including Web site sessions and IVR transactions. Companies may be exposed to operational and financial risks because of the complexity of innovative contact center technologies, the growing number of potential failure points, and the reduced number of agent interactions that previously provided some level of assurance over the customer's experience.

To mitigate these business risks, senior executives should embed comprehensive risk management processes into their contact center business activities and identify appropriate controls. Critical to this is a comprehensive quality assurance technology program that leverages automated testing tools to provide strong controls over change management, and monitoring of contact center systems and applications; in particular, customer self-service systems and applications.

In short, proactive monitoring and testing combined with continuous benchmarking can not only improve the caller's experience, but add substantial cost savings to the complete customer contact center operations.

References

Alder, Paul S. 1997. *Perspectives on work.* Center For Human Resources at the Wharton School and Institute for Work and Employment Research 1:61.

Anton, J. 1994. Internal research report. (May) West Lafayette, IN: Purdue University Center for Custom-Driven Quality.

Anton, J., R. Bennett, and R. Widdows. 1994. *Call-Center Design and Implementation.* Houston, TX: Dame Publications.

Anton, J., and J.C. de Ruyter. 1991. Van Klachten naar Managementinformatie. *Harvard Holland Review* 27 (Fall).

Barker, Joel. 1993. *Paradigms: The Business of Discovering the Future.* New York: Harper and Row.

Berry, L. L. 1988. Delivering excellent service in retailing. Arthur Andersen Retailing Issues Letter (April).

Berry, L. L., and A. Parasuraman. 1991. *Marketing Services.* New York: The Free Press.

Betts, M. 1993. Real IS payoff lies in business benefits. *Computerworld* 56 (March).

Buckingham, Marcus, and Curt Coffman. 1999. *First Break All The Rules.* New York: Simon & Schuster.

Clark, T. 1993. Marketing key to HP's battle plan. *Business Marketing* 15 (July).

Clemmer, J. 1993. Making change work: Integrating focus, effort, and direction. *Canadian Business Review* 30 (Winter).

Covey, Stephen. 1990. *Seven Habits of Highly Effective People.* New York: Simon & Schuster.

Cronin, J. J., and S. A. Taylor. 1992. Measuring service quality. *Journal of Marketing* 56 (July).

Davidow, W. H. and B. Uttal. 1989. *Total Customer Service.* New York: Harper and Row.

Davis, T. R. V. 1992. Satisfying internal customers: The link to external customer satisfaction. *Planning Review* 35 (January/February).

de Bono, Edward. 1999. *Six Thinking Hat Processes.* New York: Little Brown and Company.

Drucker, P. F. 1979 *Adventures of a Bystander.* New York: Harper & Row.

Dutka, A. 1993. *AMA Handbook for Customer Satisfaction.* Lincolnwood, IL: NTC Publishing Group.

Ernst & Young Survey. 1990. Biggest challenge for next five years. *Electronic Business Magazine* 33 (March).

Feinberg, R., and R. Widdows. (n.d). The critical incident technique. *Mobious* 8.2, 8.

The Financial Accounting Standards Board. 1999. Measuring the invisibles. *Business Spirit Journal* (March/April): 1. Also see *www.bizspirit.com.*

Fournies, Ferdinand. 1999. *Why Employees Don't Do What They're Supposed to Do and What to Do About It.* New York: McGraw-Hill.

Freedman, D. H. 1993. A model worth copying. *CIO Magazine* 42 (August).

Gale, B.T. 1992. Relative perceived quality. *Planning Review* 7 (July/August).

"Gallup Organization: New Research Links Emotional Intelligence With Profitability." 1998. *The Inner Edge Journal* (December): 5. Also see *www.gallup.com.*

Goleman, Daniel. 1995, 1998. *Emotional Intelligence and Working With Emotional Intelligence.* New York: Bantam Books.

Hamilton-Smith, K., and T. Morris. 1993. Market-driven quality. *CMA Magazine* 24 (May).

Harris, A.S. 1991. The customer's always right. *Black Enterprises* 234 (June).

Heskett, J., W. E. Sasser, and L. Schlesinger. 1997 *The Service Profit Chain.* New York: The Free Press.

Hughes, D.H. 1992. We can't get there from here. *CMA Magazine* 12 (November).

Huselid, Mark A. 2000. McKinsey and Co. study "War of Talent" in the impact of human resources management practices on turnover, productivity, and corporate financial performance, *AMA Journal* 63 (3).

The INC/Gallup Survey. *INC Magazine* 1996, 1997, 1998, 1999, and 2000.

Kanigel, Robert. 1997. *The One Best Way: Frederick Winslow Taylor and the Enigma of Efficiency.* New York: Viking Penguin.

Knauer, V. 1992. *Increasing Customer Satisfaction.* Pueblo, CO: United States Office of Consumer Affairs.

Kotter, John. 1995. Leading change: Why transformations efforts fail. *Harvard Business Review* (January).

Lawton, L. 1991. Creating a customer-centered culture in service industries. *Quality Process* 71 (September).

Learning, Motivation, and Results. *www.imrassociates.com*.

Lian, T. 1994. Helping hands. *Bank Marketing* 25 (February).

Mackay, H. 1993. *Swim with the Sharks without being eaten alive*. New York: William Morrow & Company.

Mather, H. F. 1993. Do more than just satisfy your customers—profitably delight them. *Industrial Marketing* 11 (March/April).

McGarvey, R. 1995. The big thrill. *Entrepreneur* 86 (July).

Oakley, Ed. 1991. *Enlightened Leadership*. New York: Simon and Schuster.

Panepinto, J. 1994. Going out on a wireless. *Computerworld* 99 (February).

Peters, Tom. 1988. *Thriving on Chaos*. New York: Harper and Row.

Plotkin, Harris. 1997. *Building a Winning Team*. New York: Griffin.

Plymire, J. 1991. Complaints as opportunities. *Business Horizons* 80. (March/April).

Reichheld, F. F. 1996. *The Loyalty Effect: The Hidden Force Behind Growth, Profits, and Lasting Value*. Boston: Harvard Business School Press.

Reichheld, F. F., and W. E. Sasser Jr. 1990. Zero defects: Quality comes to services. *Harvard Business Review* 106 (September/October).

Rosener, Judy. 1997. *America's Competitive Secret: Women Managers*. Oxford: Oxford University Press.

Rosener, Judy. 1990. Ways women lead. *Harvard Business Review* (November/December).

Rosener, Judy. 1991. *Workforce America! Managing Employee Diversity as a Vital Resource*. New York: Business One Irwin.

Rust, R. T., A. J. Zahorik, and T. L Keiningham. 1994. *Return on Quality*. Chicago: Probus Publishing Company.

Sager, I. 1994. The few, the true, the blue. *Business Week* 124 (May 30).

Senge, Peter. 1994. *The Fifth Discipline: The Art and Practice of the Learning Organization*. New York: Doubleday.

Shetty, Y. K. 1993. The quest for quality excellence: Lessons from the Malcolm Baldrige Quality Award. *Advanced Management Journal* 37 (Spring).

Shrednick, H. R. 1995. A decade of improvements. *Information Week* 112 (January 30).

Shycon, H. N. 1992. Improving customer service: Measuring the payoff. *Journal of Business Strategy* 15 (January/February).

Spector, P.E. (n.d.). Summated rating scale construction: An introduction paper series on quantitative applications in the social services. Series Number 07–082. Newbury Park, CA: Sage University.

Tanaka, J. 1991. Going for the glory. *Business Week* 60 (October).

Taylor, Frederick W. 1911. *The Principles of Scientific Management*. Reprint, New York: Dover, 1998.

Tehrani, N. 1993. Customer service & inbound telemarketing . . . The new powerful way to expand market share. *Telemarketing* 76 (March).

Tschohl, J. 1993. For service that sells, you need service strategy. *Chain Store Age Executive* 60 (June).

Ulrich, Dave. 1999. *Delivering Results.* Boston: Harvard Business Review Press.

Wheatley, Margaret J. 1994. *Leadership and the New Science: Learning about Organization from An Orderly Universe.* San Francisco: Berrett-Koehler.

Whyte, David. 1996. *The Heart Aroused: Poetry and the Preservation of the Soul in Corporate America.* Chicago: Doubleday.

Whyte, William H. Jr. 1956. *The Organization Man.* New York: Doubleday.

Williamson, M. 1993. Golden handcuffs. *CIO Magazine* 48, 49.

Zeithaml, V., A. Parasuraman, L. L. Berry 1990. *Delivering Quality Service.* New York: The Free Press.

Index

DATE DUE

07/13/05